A DREAMSPEAKER CRUISING GU

Desolation Sound &
The Discovery Islands

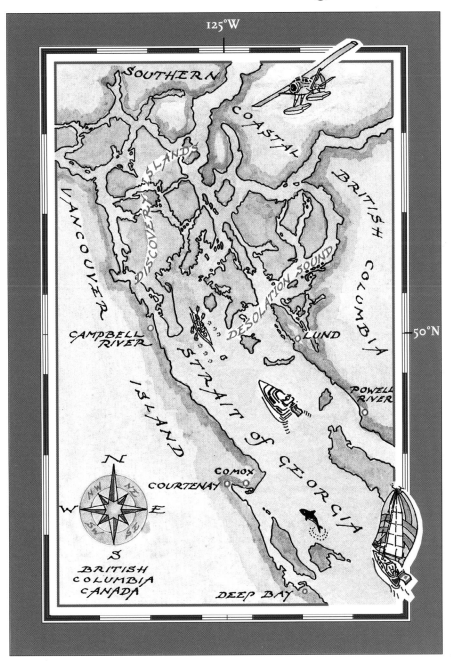

A N N E   &   L A U R E N C E   Y E A D O N - J O N E S

RAINCOAST BOOKS

Vancouver

FEATURED DESTINATIONS

TABLE OF CONTENTS

WE WOULD LIKE TO HEAR FROM YOU!

We hope you enjoyed using Volume 2 of *A Dreamspeaker Cruising Guide*. We welcome your comments, suggestions, corrections and any ideas about what you would like to see in future editions of the guide. Please drop us a line at our address above (c/o Dreamspeaker), or send an E-mail to:

dreamspeaker@raincoast.com

Text copyright © 2000 by Anne and Laurence Yeadon-Jones
Photographs & illustrations copyright © 2000 by Laurence Yeadon-Jones except where otherwise noted

All rights reserved. No part of this publication may be reproduced or transmitted in any form or by any means, electronic or mechanical, including photocopying, recording or by any information storage and retrieval system, now known or to be invented, without permission in writing from the publisher.

First published in 2000 by
Raincoast Books
8680 Cambie Street
Vancouver, B.C.
V6P 6M9
www.raincoast.com

1 2 3 4 5 6 7 8 9 10

CANADIAN CATALOGUING IN PUBLICATION DATA

Yeadon-Jones, Anne
A Dreamspeaker cruising guide
Contents: Vol. II, Desolation Sound & the Discovery Islands
Includes bibliographical reference and index.

ISBN 1-55192-272-x

1. Desolation Sound (B.C.) – Guidebooks. 2. Discovery Islands (B.C.) – Guidebooks. 3. Boats and boating – British Columbia – Desolation Sound – Guidebooks. 4. Boats and boating – British Columbia – Discovery Islands – Guidebooks. 5. Dreamspeaker (Yacht) I. Yeadon-Jones, Laurence. II Title.

FC3845.D47Y42 2000   797.1'09711'31   C99-910409-8
F1089.D47Y42 2000

ISSN 1481-1359

Chart data of Canadian waters are reproduced under License Agreement 19970004 with the Canadian Hydrographic Service. Reproduction of information from Canadian Hydrographic Service charts is for illustrative purposes only. Such reproductions do not meet the requirements of the Canadian Charts and Nautical Publications Regulations and are not to be used for navigation. The appropriate charts, corrected up-to-date, and the relevant complementary publications required under the Charts and Nautical Publications Regulations of the Canada Shipping Act must be used for navigation.

Nautical Data International, Inc. (NDI) is Canada's sole supplier of official Digital Hydrographic Data Products on behalf of the Canadian Hydrographic Service (CHS). NDI is a private company incorporated in mid-1993 to establish a public/private sector partnership with the CHS, the Canadian Federal Government agency responsible for the production and distribution of Nautical Charts and Publications for Canadian territorial waters. The partnership, in the form of a multi-year Agreement between CHS and NDI, establishes the joint production, marketing and distribution of electronic charts and other digital nautical data products. For more information, please visit NDI's website: www.ndi.nf.ca or contact NDI at:
P.O. Box 127, Station C, St. John's NF A1C 5H5
Telephone: (709) 576-0634 or (800) 563-0634
Fax: (709) 576-0636
Email: info@ndi.nf.ca

Caution: This book is meant to provide experienced boaters with cruising information about the waters covered. The suggestions offered are not all-inclusive and, due to the possibility of differences of interpretation, oversights and factual errors, none of the information contained in this book is warranted to be accurate or appropriate for any purpose other than the pursuit of great adventuring and memorable voyages. A Dreamspeaker Cruising Guide should be viewed as a guide only and not as a substitute for official government charts, tide and current tables, coast pilots, sailing directions and local notices to boaters. Excerpts from CHS charts are for passage planning only and are not to be used for navigation. Shoreline plans are not to scale and are not to be used for navigation. The publisher and authors cannot accept any responsibility for misadventure resulting from the use of this guide and can accept no liability for damages incurred.

PRINTED IN ITALY.

Raincoast Books gratefully acknowledges the support of the Government of Canada, through the Book Publishing Industry Development Program, the Canada Council for the Arts and the Department of Canadian Heritage. We also acknowledge the assistance of the Province of British Columbia, through the British Columbia Arts Council.

FOREWORD

The sheer magnificence of the geography of the Desolation Sound and Discovery Islands area cannot be truly appreciated without exploring it first-hand. Canadian Hydrographic Service (CHS) field surveyors, frequently wearied with years of experience in remote, scenic locations, and many others earning their livelihood on or near the water, never fail to be moved by travels in this region.

In any voyage by sea, preparation and planning is key to a successful outcome. From a navigation standpoint, official CHS charts and other nautical publications are required to safely reach one's desired destination. In addition to these official publications, many enthusiastic explorers, boaters and kayakers will seek further knowledge of their destinations through other literature. *Desolation Sound & The Discovery Islands, A Dreamspeaker Cruising Guide*, Volume 2, is the perfect follow-up to the first informative and successful book in the series *(Gulf Islands & Vancouver Island, Sooke to Nanaimo)* and is an excellent source of additional, vital information on this beautiful cruising ground.

Through hand-drawn shoreline plans, photographs and written descriptions of this exceptionally beautiful and abundant region, Anne and Laurence Yeadon-Jones once again pass on their extensive boating knowledge and experience in an easy and effective style. This colourful, sturdy book is a well-organized and handy reference that provides a full suite of pertinent information, from the charts required to get you to your destination, to safe anchorages, to the restaurants and shops to explore once you've arrived. Local knowledge, insights and tips contained within this cruising guide can all play a crucial role in making any journey both safe and enjoyable.

This second volume of *A Dreamspeaker Cruising Guide* complements the official CHS charts and publications and will undoubtedly have a reassuring presence near the helm for all cruisers and coastal explorers travelling in the area.

George Eaton
Director, Hydrography
Canadian Hydrographic Service, Pacific Region

Mike and trusty Beaver floatplane.

SPECIAL THANKS TO:

Captain Mike Ferrel and *Air Rainbow* for the aerial perspective.
Jim MacDonald and *C Tow* for the swift and efficient assistance.

GRATEFUL APPRECIATION TO OUR SPONSORS AND THEIR SUPPORT:

Canadian Hydrographic Services, charts, nautical publications and technical editing.
Nautical Data International, *St John's, Newfoundland, Electronic Navigation Charts.*
Nobeltec, *Issaquah, Washington, Navigational Software.*
Kodak Canada Ltd., *Toronto, Ontario. Kodak Professional Film.*
Custom Color, *Vancouver, B.C., professional film processing.*
Canon Canada Ltd., *Mississauga, Ontario, camera and lenses.*
Mustang Survival Ltd., *Vancouver, B.C., personal flotation devices.*
C Tow, *Vancouver, B.C., Marine Assistance Network.*
Force 10 Marine, *Richmond, B.C., galley equipment.*

ACKNOWLEDGEMENTS:

Extra special thanks to George Eaton, Ardene Philp, Bodo R. de Lange Boom, David Fisher, Brian Watt and Ron Bell, Canadian Hydrographic Service, Pacific Region.
We would also like to thank Tony O'Connor and Roberto Doria, Canadian Hydrographic Service, Ottawa; Brenda and Ken at M.Y. Office and Maluca Van den Bergh, word processor extraordinaire, for their great support and service; Lynn Ove Mortensen for her photographic contributions; Ted Kramer and Vicki Haberi, BC Provincial Parks and Alison Mewett, Comox-Strathcona Regional District Parks; Duart Snow, Pacific Yachting; Bob and Lois Stevenson, Desolation Sound Yacht Charters; Lisa Piercey, Nautical Data International (NDI); Al Wood, Lund Water Taxi; all the coastal people who generously gave us their time; the publishing gang at Raincoast Books, Carol Watterson, Brian Scrivener, Rachelle Kanefsky, Les Smith, Ruth Linka, Tessa Vanderkop and Derek Fairbridge; and finally, our family and friends, for their patience and enthusiastic support.

To Jim, Ruby, Tilly and Vera, for inspiring us.

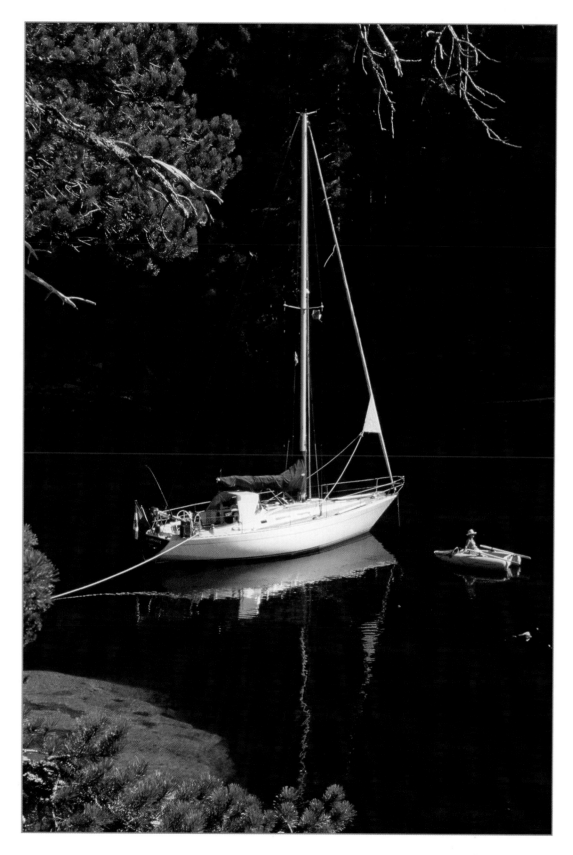

And to *Dreamspeaker*, for getting us there.

Chapter 1

DESOLATION SOUND & THE DISCOVERY ISLANDS

"The mountains grew higher and higher, and gossiped together across our heads. And somewhere down at their feet, on that narrow ribbon of water, our boat with the white sails flew swiftly along, completely dwarfed by its surroundings."

—*Muriel Wylie Blanchet*, The Curve of Time

DESOLATION SOUND & THE DISCOVERY ISLANDS

CUSTOMS

The ports of entry covered by this guide for recreational boaters entering Canadian waters are located in Powell River, at the public wharf, and in Campbell River, at the Coast Marina. Contact Canada Customs toll free at 1-888-226-7277. The following are the main ports of entry in waters South of this guide: Victoria, Sidney, Bedwell Harbour, Nanaimo, White Rock, Steveston and Vancouver.

NO-SEWAGE-DISCHARGE SITES

Current sites where the use of holding tanks is mandatory: Baynes Sound, Prideaux Haven, Roscoe Bay, Cortes Bay, Squirrel Cove, Mansons Landing Marine Park, Gorge Harbour, Pendrell Sound and Carrington Bay. All craft are required to use holding tanks. Pump-out stations are currently available in Campbell River and at Brown Bay Marina. NOTE: Check annually for further designations.

Quadra/Cortes Inter Island Ferry.

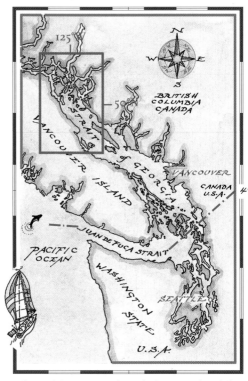

The cruising waters of Desolation Sound and the Discovery Islands.

In Volume 2 of *A Dreamspeaker Cruising Guide*, we focus on the cruising waters of Desolation Sound and the Discovery Islands. This seductive maze of interconnecting waterways also encompasses large tracts of accessible wilderness, and although the more adventurous boater and kayaker will be challenged by hazardous tidal rapids, the reward will be a rare opportunity to observe wildlife at close quarters. We introduce you to a wealth of protected anchorages, hideaway picnic stops, tranquil marine parks, well-maintained marinas and convenient public wharfs; we also show you where to hike, beachcomb, dig clams at leisure or indulge in some warm-water swimming and freshwater bathing. Provisioning stops are numerous and range from large urban centres to charming island stores. Those willing to venture off the beaten track may be rewarded with majestic fjords, cascading waterfalls, snow-capped mountains and, best of all, a moment to enjoy the quiet and solitude.

Although sport fishing was once the mainstay of this area, yacht charters and eco-tourism are fast becoming major attractions, and traditional fishing lodges now welcome boaters to enjoy their cosy facilities and hearty home cooking. The warmer, more popular cruising months are July and August, although weather from mid-May to June and during September is often idyllic, with the lack of crowds making up for a drop in temperatures.

The cruising waters in the Northern Strait of Georgia are bordered by four very accessible urban, rendezvous centres that provide easy connections by land, sea and air to Vancouver, Victoria and Seattle. The bustling towns of Powell River on the mainland, Courtenay, Comox and Campbell River on Vancouver Island's eastern shoreline serve as convenient gateways to all island destinations.

To help protect and preserve the sensitive ecosystems of these shorelines and islands, we encourage boaters to keep unnecessary wake and noise to a minimum, pack out all garbage and be aware of the official "no-sewage-discharge sites". Private-property boundaries are often unfenced and should be respected at all times. The summer season is short, and local enterprises really appreciate the patronage of visiting boaters, who will be rewarded with friendly service, local knowledge and an insight into island life.

The threat of our peaceful waterways becoming noisy highways in the busy summer months is very real, and the delicate balance of these unspoiled cruising grounds lies in the hands of every boater or kayaker who comes to enjoy the rugged beauty of British Columbia's coastal waters.

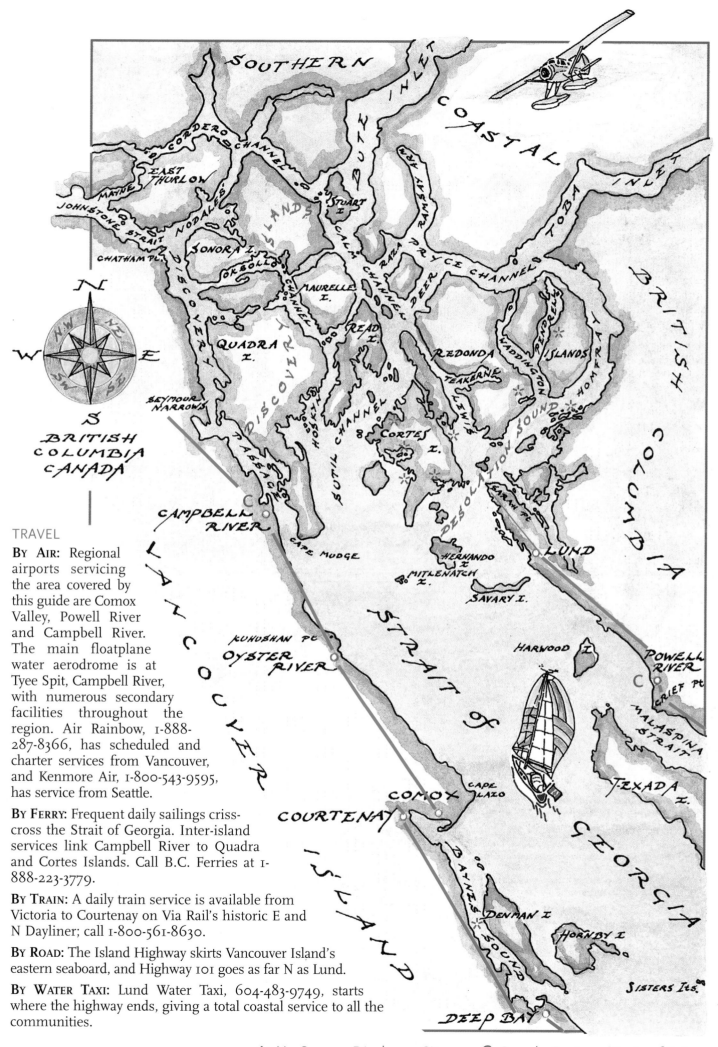

TRAVEL

BY AIR: Regional airports servicing the area covered by this guide are Comox Valley, Powell River and Campbell River. The main floatplane water aerodrome is at Tyee Spit, Campbell River, with numerous secondary facilities throughout the region. Air Rainbow, 1-888-287-8366, has scheduled and charter services from Vancouver, and Kenmore Air, 1-800-543-9595, has service from Seattle.

BY FERRY: Frequent daily sailings criss-cross the Strait of Georgia. Inter-island services link Campbell River to Quadra and Cortes Islands. Call B.C. Ferries at 1-888-223-3779.

BY TRAIN: A daily train service is available from Victoria to Courtenay on Via Rail's historic E and N Dayliner; call 1-800-561-8630.

BY ROAD: The Island Highway skirts Vancouver Island's eastern seaboard, and Highway 101 goes as far N as Lund.

BY WATER TAXI: Lund Water Taxi, 604-483-9749, starts where the highway ends, giving a total coastal service to all the communities.

✳ No Sewage Discharge Sites   **C** Canada Customs Ports of Entry

WEATHER & WIND

Small craft warning, Strait of Georgia. Winds 20 – 33 knots.

WEATHER A well-trained and experienced weather eye is a great asset, but a diligent weather ear regularly tuned to the marine forecasts will keep you well informed.

MARINE FORECASTS and warnings are available as continuous marine broadcasts on the following VHF channels and frequencies: WX1: 162.55; WX2: 162.40; WX3: 162.475; and 21B: 161.65. Alternatively phone the following continuous marine weather recordings:

VANCOUVER:	604-666-3655
COMOX:	250-339-5044
CAMPBELL RIVER:	250-286-3575

For further information on weather products and services, contact Environment Canada at 604-664-9080 or visit its Web site at www.weatheroffice.com.

ENVIRONMENT CANADA WEST COAST WEATHER PUBLICATIONS

Mariner's Guide: West Coast Marine Weather Services.

Marine Weather Hazards Manual— West Coast: A Guide to Local Forecasts and Conditions.

The Wind Came All Ways, by Owen Lange.

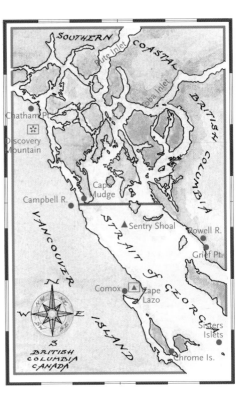

- ● Marine Weather Reporting Station
- ▲ Marine Weather Buoy
- ⌘ 21B 161.65 MHz
- ▣ WX1 162.55 MHz

WEATHER in the summer months, from mid-June to mid-September is influenced by the arrival of the Pacific high pressure systems. As the pressure builds and anchors itself over the coast, sunshine and light winds are often the norm. Summer mean maximum temperatures vary from 19° C (66° F) in the north to 22° C (72° F) in Desolation Sound. The prevailing summer winds are westerlies, being strongest as the high-pressure ridge approaches. As the land warms, afternoon southerly or southwesterly sea breezes develop and penetrate into the channels of Desolation Sound and become inflow / up-inlet winds. As the land cools, overnight outflow / down-inlet winds often rattle the rigging of boats at anchor in the early morning hours. The forecast for southeasterly winds generally means the return to unsettled, rainy weather. The coast has a few idiosyncratic "local weather hazards," which we describe at the beginning of each chapter.

However, from November to April, the "raincoast," as the region is known, is very cold, wet and windy, weather not at all conducive to the pleasantries of messing about in boats.

SUMMER WINDS: Courtesy of Environment Canada Weather Information Brochure 1996.

JOHNSTONE STRAIT: Westerly winds that begin as a 15 - 20 knot sea breeze in Queen Charlotte Strait during the afternoon gradually increase as they move into Johnstone Strait. These winds often reach 25 - 30 knots off Chatham Point by late evening. Even stronger winds may occur just to the west of Chatham Point. The westerly winds usually become light during the early morning hours.

STRAIT OF GEORGIA "NORTH": Northwesterly winds of 10 - 15 knots (occasionally 20 knots) spread down the strait during the early morning hours. Beginning near Campbell River at a little after midnight, these winds usually stop near Nanaimo but occasionally reach all the way down to the Vancouver area. The northwesterlies generally become light during the early afternoon.

MARINE FORECAST ISSUE TIMES: 0400. 1030. 1600 & 2130. Issue times remain the same throughout the year.

WAVES, TIDES & CURRENTS

TIDE AND CURRENT TABLES provide essential navigational information and must be acquired prior to venturing into these waters. A working knowledge of tides and currents, and their interplay with the wind, is especially important in this region.

Each chapter begins with Volume 5 or 6 of the *Canadian Tide and Current Tables* referenced. Tides (reference port and secondary ports) and currents (reference station and sec-ondary stations) are followed by a note describing any local tidal peculiarities or currents that may occur within the boundaries covered by the chapter.

OFFICIAL PUBLICATIONS

Refer to *Canadian Tide and Current Tables, Volume 5: Juan de Fuca Strait and Strait of Georgia* and *Volume 6: Discovery Passage and the West Coast of Vancouver Island.*

Hazardous tidal rapids cleary visible in Seymour Narrows.

WAVES: Hazardous wave action in this region develops as a result of the wind interacting with the tidal current. In general, conditions can be very dangerous when the wind opposes the current. It's best to travel when the winds are in the same direction as the current. The "small-craft warning" means just that: winds forecast at between 20 and 30 knots can be hazardous to small craft. The seas that subsequently develop can become treacherous in a wind-against-current situation.

TIDES (the vertical movement of water): Due to the meeting of the two flooding streams, the tidal range (rise and fall of the water) is large, with a maximum range of over 5.5 m (18 ft) in Prideaux Haven. The boundary between the two volumes is a line drawn through the southeastern end of the Discovery Islands to the mainland. The line is just north of the convergence of the northerly flowing flood tide, Volume 5, and the southerly flowing flood tide, Volume 6. The actual convergence is more complex, shifting due to weather, wind and freshwater-runoff conditions.

CURRENTS (the horizontal movement of water): The tidal rise and fall results in currents flooding into and ebbing out of the Strait of Georgia. The currents in the Northern Strait of Georgia rarely exceed 2 knots, but they can increase wave height dramatically in a wind-against-current situation. Currents in the Desolation Sound region are minimal, allowing the surface water temperature to rise substantially. Stronger currents exist in the channels, passages and narrows that make up the waterways between the Discovery Islands and Vancouver Island. Where the channels narrow, the currents accelerate to produce exceedingly hazardous tidal rapids, which should only be negotiated at times of slack water.

CAUTIONARY NOTES: Times of slack water (turns) at the rapids may differ significantly from the times of shore-side high and low water. It's of paramount importance to be able to read and interpolate the tide and current tables accurately.

Tides	•	Reference Port
Currents	■	Reference Station
Direction	➤	Flood Tide

CHARTS & NAUTICAL PUBLICATIONS

We have carefully designed this cruising guide to work in conjunction with Canadian Hydrographic Service (CHS) charts and nautical publications. Above each destination, we reference the appropriate charts in the following order:

- Individual chart number.
- Chart 3312 (*Jervis Inlet & Desolation Sound*) with page number.
- In Chapters 2, 4, 5 and 6 strip charts and Chart 3311 are also cross-referenced.

Individual charts are the primary tools of the professional mariner. However, their size is often a problem on a small craft. The CHS has specifically designed the cruising atlas (Chart 3312, *Jervis Inlet & Desolation Sound*) for the recreational boater. Chart 3312 is also a navigational resource with extensive supplementary information, extracts from the *Sailing Directions* (see Nautical Publications below) and approach photographs to certain anchorages and passes. We strongly recommend Chart 3312 for its size, comprehensive coverage and excellent value. The package of five strip charts (Chart 3311) is a handy addition if voyaging from Vancouver to Desolation Sound via the southern coastal mainland, known locally as the "Sunshine Coast." All charts referenced are metric editions.

ELECTRONIC CHARTS

Electronic charts are raster scans of CHS individual charts, produced under license by Nautical Data International (NDI), 709-576-0634. They may be viewed independently on your computer or with the appropriate navigational software as an onboard aid to navigation. We recommend the following navigational software (compatible with NDI charts): Nobeltec Inc. Visual Navigation Suite, 1-800-495-6279.

APPROACH WAYPOINTS *

Approach waypoints are latitude and longitude positions based on NAD 83 and are shown in degrees, minutes and decimals of a minute. They are located in deep water from a position where the feature as illustrated will in daylight be readily descernable.

PUBLICATIONS

We recommend the following publications to accompany your copy of Volume 2 of *A Dreamspeaker Cruising Guide*. For further reading, consult the Selected Reading list at the back of this book.

NAUTICAL PUBLICATIONS, CHS

Canadian Tide and Current Tables, Volume 5: Juan de Fuca Strait and Strait of Georgia.
Canadian Tide and Current Tables, Volume 6: Discovery Passage and the West Coast of Vancouver Island.
Catalogue of Nautical Charts and Related Publications: Pacific Coast 2. (Also includes a full list of nautical publications available.)
Sailing Directions: British Columbia Coast (South Portion).
Symbols and Abbreviations Used on Canadian Charts: Chart 1.

WEATHER PUBLICATIONS, ENVIRONMENT CANADA

Marine Weather Hazards Manual— West Coast: A Guide to Local Forecasts and Conditions.
Mariner's Guide: West Coast Marine Weather Services.

BOATING SAFETY PUBLICATIONS, CANADIAN COAST GUARD

The Canadian Aids to Navigation System: Marine Navigation Services Directorate.
List of Lights, Buoys and Fog Signals: Pacific Coast.
Protecting British Columbia's Aquatic Environment: A Boater's Guide.

EMERGENCY PROCEDURES & HOW TO USE THIS BOOK

THE CANADIAN COAST GUARD is a multitask organization whose primary role of search and rescue is supported by the following roles: maintaining the Aids to Navigation, operating the Office of Safe Boating, and, in association with Environment Canada, the Marine Weather Forecast. For a copy of the Safe Boating Guide, call 1-800-267-6687. For search and rescue, call

TELEPHONE   1-800-567-5111
CELLULAR   *311
VHF CHANNEL   16

EMERGENCY RADIO PROCEDURES

MAYDAY: For *immediate danger* to life or vessel.

PAN-PAN: For *urgency* but no immediate danger to life or vessel.

For MAYDAY or PAN-PAN, transmit the following on VHF channel 16 or 2182 KHZ.

1. MAYDAY, MAYDAY, MAYDAY (or PAN-PAN, PAN-PAN, PAN-PAN), this is [vessel name and radio call sign].

2. State your position and the nature of the distress.

3. State the number of people onboard and describe the vessel [length, make / type, colour, power, registration number].

NOTE: If the distress is not life-threatening, the Coast Guard will put out a general call to boaters in your area for assistance. A tow at sea by a commercial operator can be expensive, however, C.Tow, 1-800-747-8877, operates a marine-assistance network in B.C. waters and for an annual fee, will rapidly assist members in a non-life threatening situation.

HOW TO USE THIS BOOK

This sample layout identifies the various features of this cruising guide that will help you to reach your destination safely and well informed.

Chapter & featured destination reference
Chapter legend
Destination locator
* Approach Waypoint Latitude & longitude
Tips on best approach & anchorages
Cautionary note

Depth contour (approximate position). Depths reduced to lowest normal tide (zero tide)
Solid black line indicates high water mark
Green area indicates land above high water mark
Sepia area indicates shoreline that covers & uncovers with the tide
Blue area indicates shallower water
White area indicates deeper water that is safe for navigation
* Asterix indicates approximate position of approach waypoint
Boats at anchor
Red broken line indicates a safe approach course
Aerial approach or ambient photograph

HW: high water
LW: low water

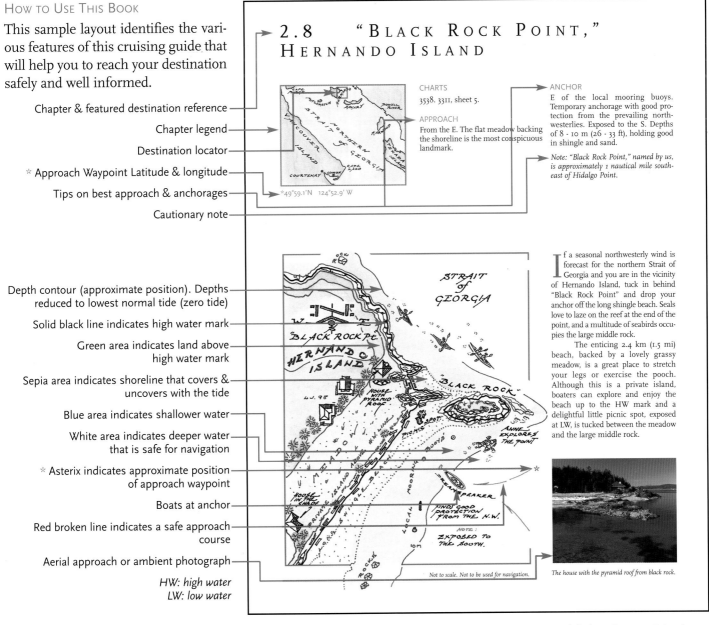

2.8   "BLACK ROCK POINT," HERNANDO ISLAND

CHARTS
3538. 3311, sheet 5.

APPROACH
From the E. The flat meadow backing the shoreline is the most conspicuous landmark.

*49°59.1'N   124°52.9' W

ANCHOR
E of the local mooring buoys. Temporary anchorage with good protection from the prevailing north-westerlies. Exposed to the S. Depths of 8 - 10 m (26 - 33 ft), holding good in shingle and sand.

Note: "Black Rock Point," named by us, is approximately 1 nautical mile southeast of Hidalgo Point.

If a seasonal northwesterly wind is forecast for the northern Strait of Georgia and you are in the vicinity of Hernando Island, tuck in behind "Black Rock Point" and drop your anchor off the long shingle beach. Seals love to laze on the reef at the end of the point, and a multitude of seabirds occupies the large middle rock.

The enticing 2.4 km (1.5 mi) beach, backed by a lovely grassy meadow, is a great place to stretch your legs or exercise the pooch. Although this is a private island, boaters can explore and enjoy the beach up to the HW mark and a delightful little picnic spot, exposed at LW, is tucked between the meadow and the large middle rock.

Not to scale. Not to be used for navigation.

The house with the pyramid roof from black rock.

PASSAGES NORTH

MAJOR MARINE CENTRES & ANCHORAGES

Prior to the forthcoming publication of *Vol. III: Vancouver, Howe Sound and the Sunshine Coast*, Passages North describes the major marine centres and anchorages the cruising boater will find between *Vol. I: The Gulf Islands & Vancouver Island* and this volume (*II*).

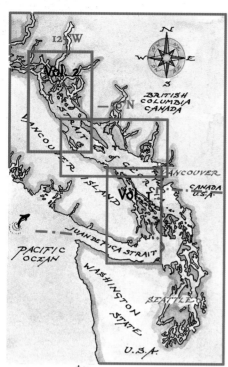

SUNSHINE COAST: Departing Vancouver

1. Snug Cove: moorage, fuel
2. Gibsons: moorage, fuel
3. Plumper Cove Marine Park: anchorage
4. Smuggler Cove Marine Park: anchorage
5. Secret Cove: moorage, fuel, anchorage
6. Pender Harbour: moorage, fuel, anchorage
7. Hardy Island Marine Park: anchorage
8. Powell River, Chapter 4.
   Westview 4.1: moorage, fuel
   Beach Gardens 4.3: moorage, fuel

Passages North – – – – – – – –
Ferry Routes – – – – – – – –
Road Links ————

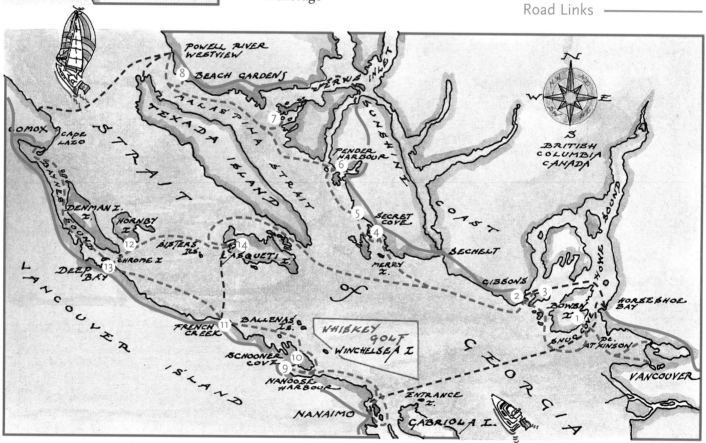

VANCOUVER ISLAND: Departing Nanaimo (Volume 1 of A Dreamspeaker Cruising Guide)

9. Nanoose Harbour: moorage, fuel, anchorage
10. Schooner Cove: moorage, fuel
11. French Creek: moorage, fuel
12. Baynes Sound, Chapter 3.
    Ford Cove 3.4: moorage, fuel, anchorage
    Deep Bay 3.1: moorage, anchorage

13. Northern Strait of Georgia, Chapter 2. Comox 2.2: moorage, fuel, anchorage
14. As a midway crossing stopover, Lasqueti Island has good anchorage in False Bay and fuel and limited moorage in Mud Bay

Area "Whiskey Golf" is a Torpedo Testing Range; when active, it's a no-go zone for all craft. Listen for notice to shipping as part of the continuous marine weather forecast or call Winchelsea Control at 1-888-221-1011 or contact them on VHF channel 10 or 16 (for information on safe transit).

Chapter 2
Northern
Strait
of Georgia

View from Savary Island towards Desolation Sound.

The Artisans Courtyard, downtown cosmopolitan Courtenay.

Chapter 2
NORTHERN STRAIT OF GEORGIA

TIDES

Canadian Tide and Current Tables, Volume 5
Reference Port: Point Atkinson
Secondary Ports: Comox, Mitlenatch Island
Note: Travelling N to the Discovery Islands, you will also require Volume 6 of the Canadian Tide and Current Tables.

CURRENTS

No specific reference or secondary stations cover this chapter.

WEATHER

Area: Strait of Georgia (northern half)
Reporting Stations: Comox, Cape Lazo, Cape Mudge, Sentry Shoal (S of Mitlenatch)
Northwesterly winds prevail in the summer, and winds of 10 - 15 knots are common. They spread down the strait during the early morning hours, beginning near Cape Mudge a little after midnight. Occasionally, strong southeasterly winds may also be encountered.

CAUTIONARY NOTES:

Take caution regarding the current and sea conditions under SE winds near Cape Mudge. Listen for and take heed of the small-craft warning. This stretch of sea is no kids' playground. These warnings are issued beginning in April and continuing until November 11. Warnings are broadcast when winds are expected to rise to 20-30 knots, creating potentially dangerous conditions for small craft.

On your journey north to Desolation Sound and the Discovery Islands, you will have to cross the 40 kilometres (25 miles) of open water that lie north of Cape Lazo. If the forecast is for anything stronger than a moderate wind, then it would be advisable to break your journey and spend a day or two relaxing in sheltered Comox Harbour.

Take the opportunity to venture inland and discover the beautiful Comox Valley – gateway to Strathcona Park, British Columbia's oldest provincial park. Here hiking trails link Forbidden Plateau with Comox Glacier and the Mount Washington Resort, where a chair lift will transport you to spectacular panoramic views. This fertile valley also grows an abundance of organic produce, sold at local farm stands or weekly farmers' markets.

Comox is also conveniently situated for visitors wishing to charter a boat or meet up with family and friends before the big hop north. Easy connections can be made by air, floatplane, train or road from Vancouver, Victoria and Seattle (see page 3). The Powell River/Comox ferry terminal is also located nearby.

The charming "old town" of Courtenay is a delight to explore and offers an eclectic mix of shops, art galleries and restaurants, while the Courtenay River estuary affords a fascinating variety of bird life, easily viewed by kayak or canoe.

After rounding Cape Lazo, you might wonder if a convenient stopping-off point is available on the long coastal stretch north. The well-managed marina and resort at Oyster River comes as a pleasant surprise and provides sheltered moorage, hot showers and a small sandy beach.

In settled weather, don't miss the opportunity to visit some of the lovely islands lying in the northern strait. Grassy Mitlenatch Island, a provincial nature park, is far more accessible than it first appears, offering relatively sheltered day anchorage and a chance to observe its protected seabird colonies and abundant wildflowers.

Savary Island is perfect for an energetic fun day out. Pack a picnic lunch and hike, bike or explore the beautiful white sandy beaches. You can anchor off in settled weather or just hop onto the water taxi in Lund.

Finally, laze with the seals at "Black Rock Point" on Hernando Island, where a long shingle beach beckons you to stretch those sea-weary legs.

FEATURED DESTINATIONS

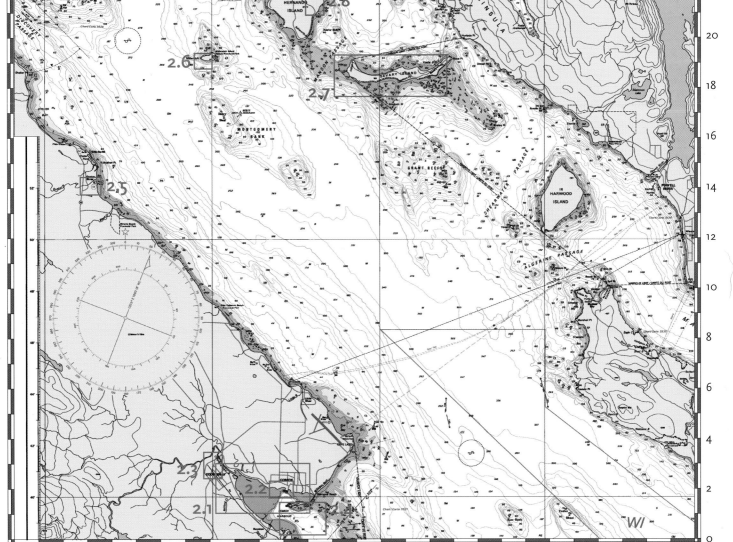

Not to be used for navigation.

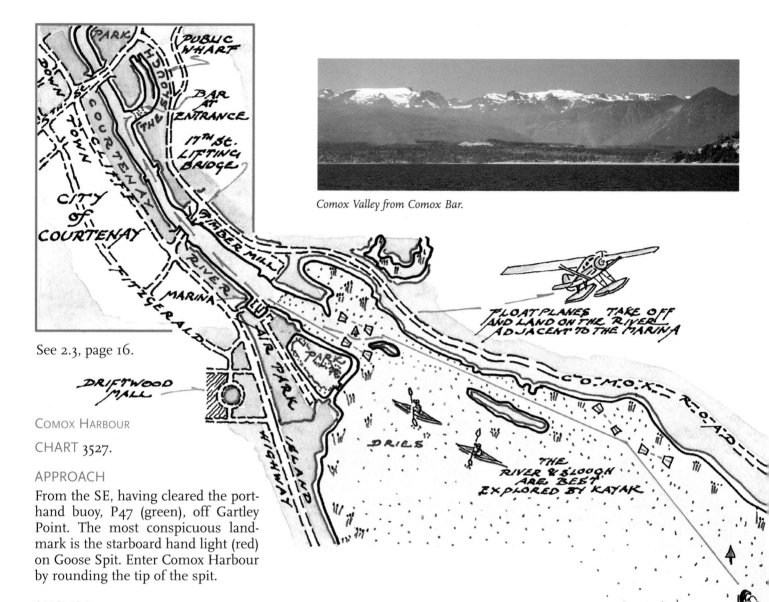

See 2.3, page 16.

Comox Valley from Comox Bar.

COMOX HARBOUR

CHART 3527.

APPROACH

From the SE, having cleared the port-hand buoy, P47 (green), off Gartley Point. The most conspicuous landmark is the starboard hand light (red) on Goose Spit. Enter Comox Harbour by rounding the tip of the spit.

ANCHOR

Good all-weather protection can be found behind Goose Spit W of the boats on mooring buoys (see note) or off and to the W of the breakwaters in depths of 10 - 15 m (33 - 49 ft). Holding good in sand and mud.

Note: Anchoring between HMCS Quadra and boats on mooring buoys is not recommended because you can foul your anchor with old log-booming debris.

The "Lagoon" (local name) is a shoal draft-boat anchorage not recommended for the visitor because the channel is very shallow and requires local guidance. A great place, however, for dinghy-sailing or windsurfing.

PUBLIC WHARF, MARINAS, BOAT LAUNCH & FUEL

See 2.2, page 14.

Comox Harbour, nestled below the majestic Comox Glacier on Vancouver Island's eastern coast, offers sheltered anchorage, a public wharf and expanded marina facilities. It is a key provisioning stop and a convenient base for boaters wishing to explore the delights of downtown Courtenay or the beauty of Comox Valley. (For Comox town and marinas, see page 14.)

Goose Spit, on the harbour's eastern side, provides protected anchorage and serves as the HMCS *QUADRA* CADET TRAINING CAMP. The clean and lovely sandy beaches surrounding the spit are for public day use. Fires are prohibited.

The Courtenay River offers access to downtown Courtenay, with moorage at the public wharf at the slough although this is not a straightforward undertaking for the recreational boater (see page 16). A fun alternative is to explore the river and slough by kayak or canoe and observe the fascinating variety of bird life and waterfowl. Proposed park plans for the year 2000 will improve the slough's present outlook and help to regain its former charm. These plans include a river walk and viewpoint, an interpretive route, native gardens and a park pavilion. For kayak and canoe rentals, call TREE ISLAND KAYAKING at 250-339-0580 or COMOX VALLEY KAYAKS at 250-334-2628. (For downtown Courtenay, see page 16.)

Courtenay River & Slough Vancouver Island

Courtenay River & Slough

Chart 3527.

Although Courtenay River is navigable from Comox Harbour to the public wharf at Courtenay Slough (max. 1.8 m, 6 ft, at LW), it is more than just a casual undertaking for the recreational boater and entails (1) crossing the river's drying mud flats on a suitable tide via a channel marked by day beacons and ranges and (2) timing your passage into the slough as close to high tide as possible, because sufficient depth is needed to clear the bar just inside the entrance.

Note: **!** *Light*

Range lights are in position atop the daymarks leading to the Courtenay River.

Local advice and guidance are highly recommended as conditions within the marked channel and on the river vary annually. Prior to your trip, contact the harbour manager at Comox Valley Harbour Authority, 250-339-6041, to secure moorage and to arrange the lifting of the 17th Street Bridge and the lowering of the seal fence. Note that the marina North of the Courtenay Airpark has a boat launch but no visitor moorage. A float for temporary moorage is available for boats waiting for the 17th Street Bridge to be lifted.

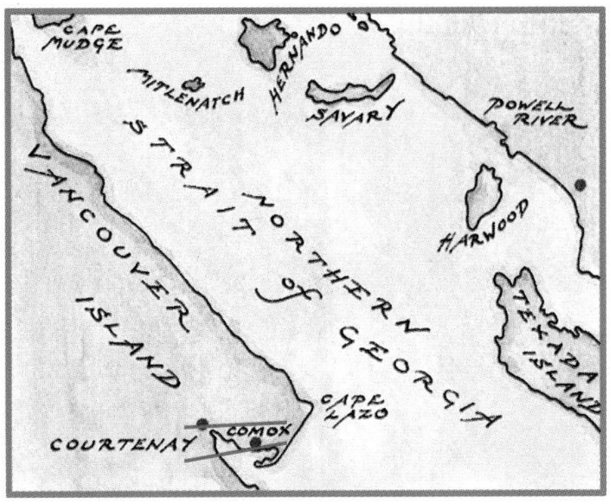

✲ 49°39.6' N 124° 55.8' W

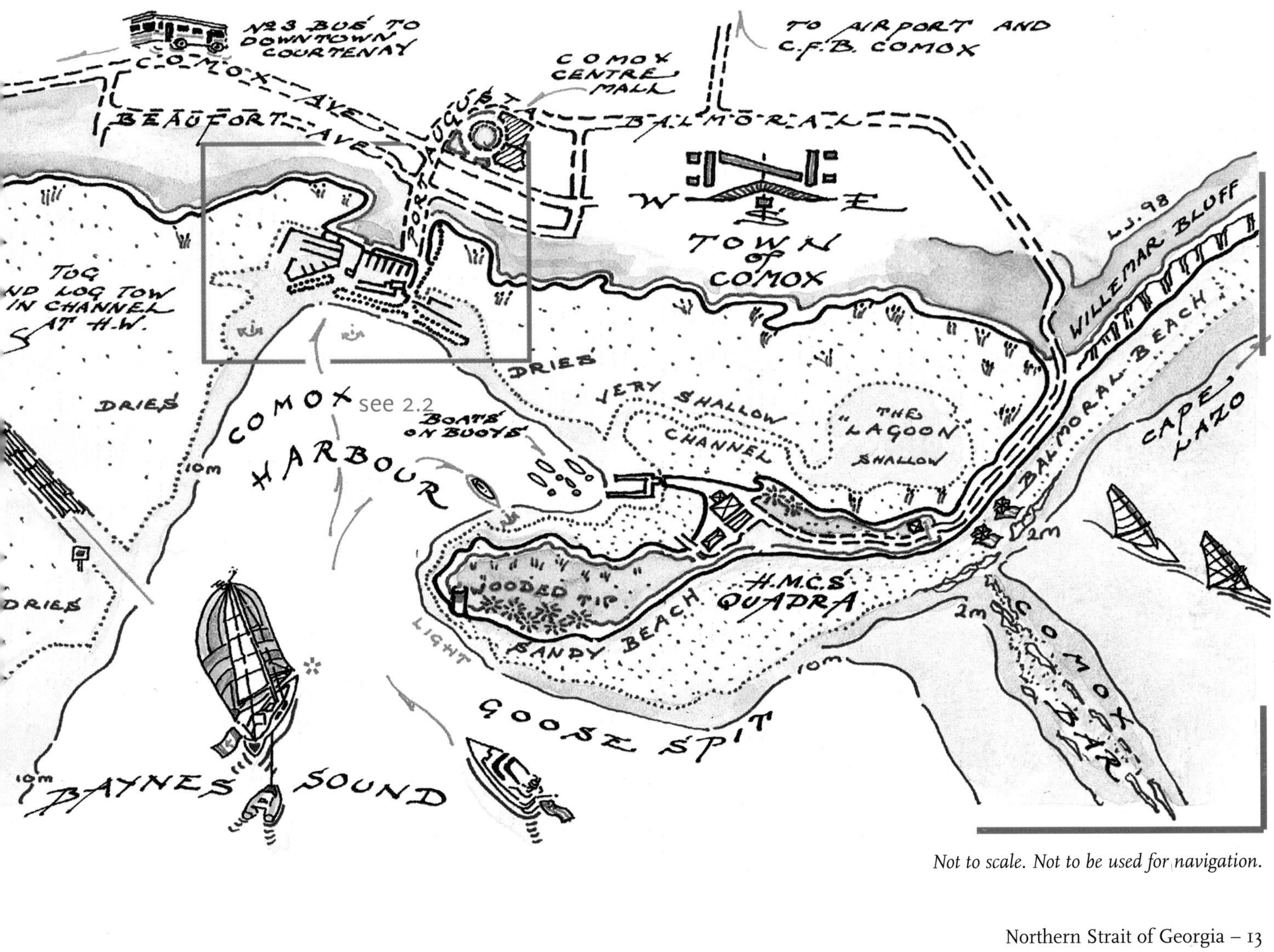

Not to scale. Not to be used for navigation.

2.2   TOWN OF COMOX, VANCOUVER ISLAND

✳ 49°40.1'N   124°55.8'W

Approaching the Comox breakwater, the entrance is to the left.

The colourful public wharf from the lookout pavilion.

The historic town of Comox provides a welcome haven and excellent provisioning facilities.

The COMOX CENTRE MALL, a short walk from the public wharf and marinas, is open 7 days a week and houses a large variety of shops, including a bank, supermarket (delivery to marinas), pharmacy and visitor information booth. Car hire can also be arranged from here. Pick up a *Comox Valley Visitors Guide* and *Where* magazine for the best information on local events. The number 3 bus to Courtenay also stops in front of the mall. For more information, call COMOX VALLEY VISITOR INFORMATION CENTRE, 250-334-3234.

You can spend a few pleasant hours shopping along Comox Avenue and browsing in BLUE HERON BOOKS, and the CROWSNEST MARINE CHANDLERY. For the largest breakfast-menu selection, visit SMITTY'S. The family-run PORTSIDE RESTAURANT specializes in great home-cooked Latin American dishes and offers a kids' menu.

A B.C. LIQUOR STORE is located on the corner of Church Street and Comox Avenue, and the LORNE HOTEL & PUB has a beer and wine store. Reputed to be the oldest licensed hotel in British Columbia, it has been offering a homely refuge to visitors since 1879.

The lovely shoreside trail above the marina complex takes you past the EDGEWATER PUB & GRILL – a great place to relax and view the Beaufort Mountain Range – to the boardwalk and view pavilions built above the long stone breakwater. Freshly caught fish and shrimp can be bought directly from local fish boats tied up at the public wharf, and SPANKY'S EXPRESSO EH! offers a shady retreat as you enjoy an iced latté or milkshake. Public shower and laundry facilities are located under the BLACK FIN PUB. Sample their tasty salmon pizza and local beer while your clothes tumble dry.

DESOLATION SOUND YACHT CHARTERS, 250-339-7222, offers an excellent selection of boats, both sail and power.

The nearby FILBERG LODGE & PARK, 250-339-2715, with its extensive gardens, hosts the annual Filberg Festival on the B.C. Day long weekend, featuring the province's finest artisans and craftspeople. The popular "Strawberry Tea," held on the first Saturday in July, offers traditional afternoon tea served on the sweeping lodge lawns.

CHART 3527.

APPROACH

From the S, having cleared the tip of Goose Spit. The stone breakwater with the silhouette of the town of Comox behind it is the most conspicuous landmark.

ANCHOR

Good all-weather protection can be found behind Goose Spit W of the boats on mooring buoys or off and to the W of the breakwaters in depths of 10 - 15m (33 - 49 ft). Holding good in sand and mud.

PUBLIC WHARF

The Comox Valley Harbour Authority, 250-339-6041, VHF 68, has extensive visitor moorage both E and W of the causeway.

MARINAS

Blackfin Marina, 250-339-4664, operates the fuel float and has two berths for visitors. Comox Bay Marina, 250-339-2930, VHF 68, has designated visitor moorage to the W of the fuel float. The municipal town marina is for local resident craft.

BOAT LAUNCH

At the foot of Wilcox Road.

Note: The public wharf and marina complex, with its mix of pleasure and commercial craft, makes for a busy place in the summer months.

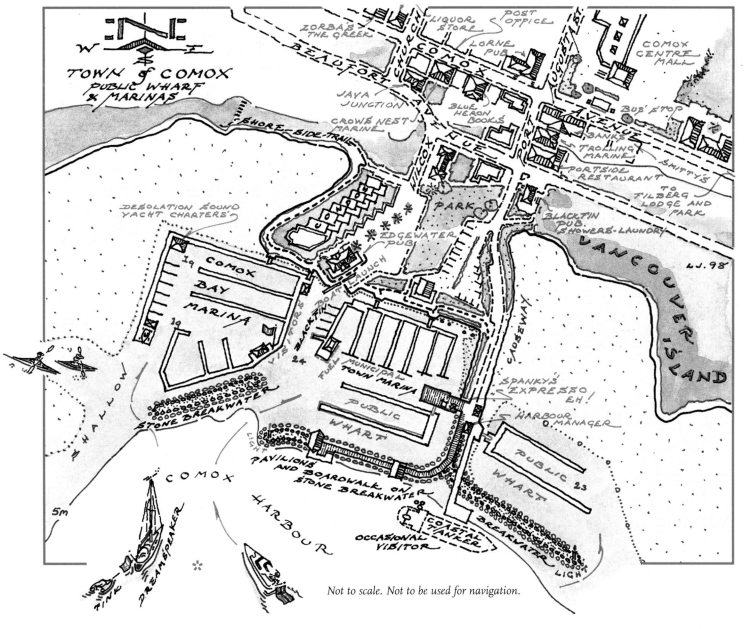

Not to scale. Not to be used for navigation.

2.3 Downtown Courtenay, Vancouver Island

✲ 49°41.2'N 124°59.4'W

CHART 3527.

APPROACH

Once you have cleared the lifting bridge and seal fence by prior arrangement, you will reach Courtenay Slough, located a short way upstream of the river on the northeast bank. Just inside the entrance lies a bar that dries 2.4 m (7.8 ft) at local chart datum, and inside the bar there is a minimum depth of 1.8 m (5.9 ft). The public wharf consists of 210 m (689 ft) of float space that extends from the head of the slough. Both power and water are available. (See 2.1, page 12, for navigation details.)

The Courtenay Slough, a downtown backwater just waiting to be discovered.

The City of Courtenay developed during the late 1800s along the banks of virtually the only navigable river on Vancouver Island. The river is still navigable by recreational craft if you plan carefully. However, the easiest way to visit the charming "old town" is to hop on the number 3 bus outside the Comox Centre Mall and enjoy the scenic route to Cliff Avenue and 5th Street – the hub of downtown Courtenay. Here you will find hanging baskets bursting with flowers and a wonderful variety of shops, bookstores, art galleries and restaurants to explore. Discover the city's Elasmosaur (12 m [39.4 ft] long) at the Courtenay Museum, or visit the Comox Valley Art Gallery, 250-338-6211, whose gallery shop contains a wonderful selection of handcrafted works. Take yourself on an enlightening Valley of the Arts tour by picking up a brochure at the Visitor Information Centre or by calling the art gallery.

A collective of local artists and potters shares the old Christy Building on the corner of Cliff Avenue and 5th Street, and their bright retail space is well worth a visit. The shaded old brick courtyard is also a peaceful spot to relax with a welcome pot of tea and freshly made sandwiches from the friendly Rose Tea Room. The Bar None Café, across from the museum, features local artists and serves vegetarian food and organic coffee, and the garden patio is a nonsmoking area. The Edible Island Wholefood Market is a great place to stock up on specialty foods or to pick up a picnic lunch.

Downtown Courtenay also hosts the popular Farmers Market every Wednesday (June - October) from 9 a.m. - 12 p.m. Available are local seasonal fruits and vegetables, preserves, honey and home-baked goods. The annual Market Day, in late July, is a festive and colourful family affair, not to be missed. A short walk across the bridge will take you to Lewis Park, Courtenay Slough, the old Courtenay Hotel and the highly acclaimed La Cremaillere, which serves excellent French cuisine. Call 250-338-8131 for reservations.

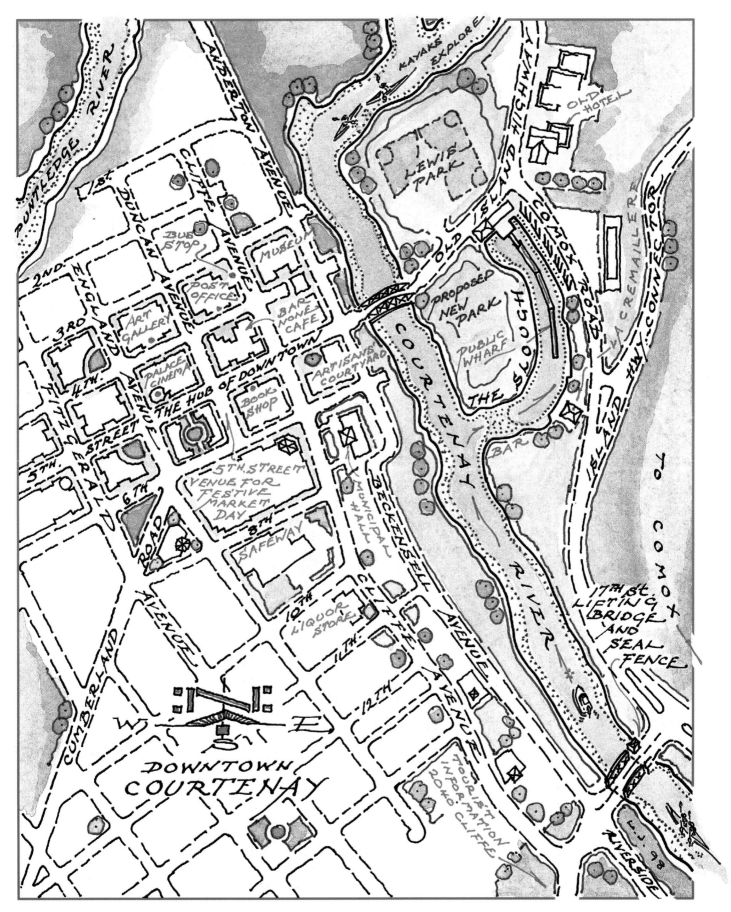

Not to scale. Not to be used for navigation.

2.4   COMOX BAR

❖ 1) 49°39.7'N   124°51.3'W   Strait of
    Georgia

❖ 2) 49°38.6'N   124°52.8'W   Baynes
    Sound

CHART 3527.

APPROACH

FROM THE STRAIT OF GEORGIA: The
outer starboard-hand buoy (red), P54,
has a bell, light and radar reflector.
The transit bearing of 222° true indicates the track across the bar in line
with the onshore ranges (leading
marks). A course made good of 200°
magnetic should carry you to the next
buoys and hence across the bar.

APPROACH

FROM BAYNES SOUND: The outer star-
board-hand buoy (red) P50 is unlit
and conical. The ranges (leading
marks) are obscured by houses and
trees until you are virtually on the
transit bearing of 222° true on the
stern. A course made good of 020°
magnetic should carry you to the next
buoy and hence across the bar.

Comox Bar is not a destination
but a gateway to many destinations. Although the passage
through the well-marked channel
seems to be straightforward, many
boats still run aground while attempting to negotiate the bar. Remember
that the ranges (leading marks) in daylight require powerful binoculars to be
seen clearly, the flood and ebb cross-
current can run up to 4 knots and that
a wind-against-current situation can
produce steep and occasionally break-
ing seas. The simplest way to cross the
bar in either direction is to locate the
outer buoy and point the bow at the
next buoy, leaving all buoys just to the S.

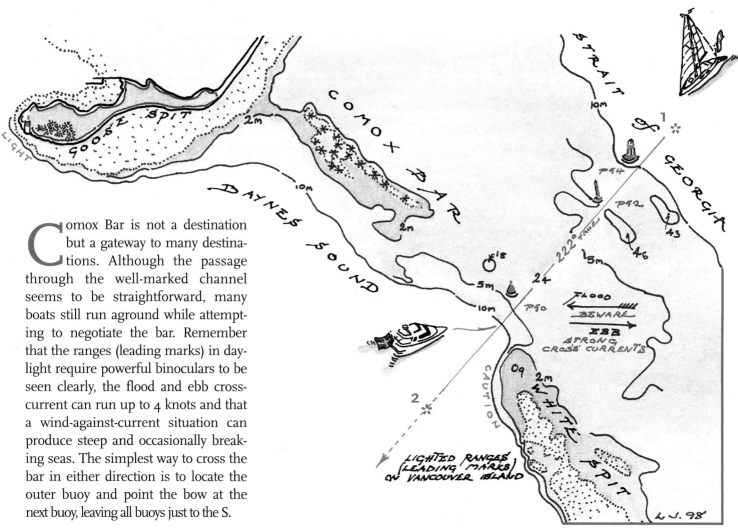

Not to scale. Not to be used for navigation.

CHART 3513.

APPROACH

Having lined up the pilings well out to sea, approach with extreme caution. From the E the channel to the marina is dredged to 1.2 m (4 ft) and lies just to the S of the river mouth, which has a bank of shingle extending 0.3 nautical miles from the shoreline. The channel is approximately 450 m (1,476 ft) long, very narrow and not entirely straight. It is best to negotiate the channel prior to HW, when the banks are still visible. The seaward end of the channel is marked by 2 piles. Enter between them and follow the remaining pilings in, on a 1.8m (6 ft) plus tide.

Note: The northern outer pile was not in place (1999)

MARINA

The PACIFIC PLAYGROUNDS MARINA AND RESORT, 250-337-5600, offers visitor moorage for boats up to 11m (36ft) long. Fuel is available, and there is a boat launch and tide grid.

✴ 49° 52.2'N 125° 6.2W

If you need to break your journey while voyaging N, pop into Oyster River Pacific Playgrounds Marina, on Vancouver Island's eastern coast, and tie up in the sheltered boat basin. Primarily a fishing and family resort, it also offers moorage for boats up to 11m (36 ft) long. Power, water, showers and laundry facilities are provided, and kids have their own fishing dock. The convenience store stocks ice, basic groceries, books, charts, fishing licenses, tackle and hardware and has an on-site freezing facility. A clean sandy beach, heated swimming pool and tennis courts are also available at this pleasant stopover.

Approach to Pacific Playgrounds Marina.

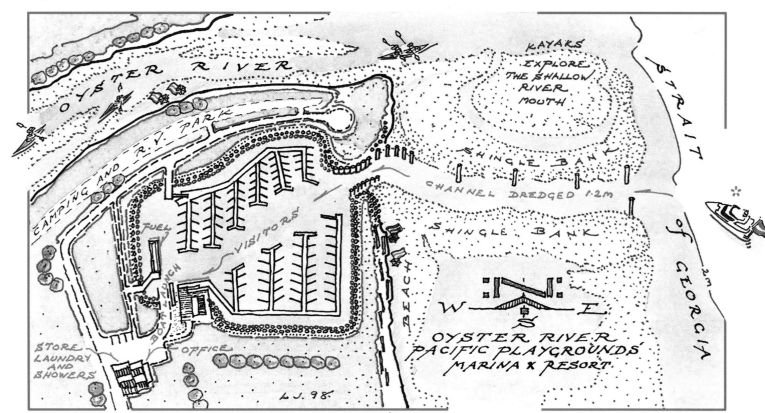

Not to scale. Not to be used for navigation.

2.6 MITLENATCH ISLAND PROVINCIAL NATURE PARK

✽ 49°56.8'N 124°59.6'W

Camp Bay, Mitlenatch Island, a unique setting.

"Northwest Bay" and a tranquil Strait of Georgia.

A Pelagic Cormorant nests on steep cliffs in loose colonies.

Low-lying and isolated Mitlenatch Island, at the southern entrance of Desolation Sound, is far more accessible than it first appears. Recreational boaters are welcome to visit the protected seabird colony as long as pets are kept on board, park rules are observed and nesting birds are not disturbed. The park boundary extends 300 m (1,000 ft) out from the shore, and all sedentary marine life – including abalones, oysters, scallops and sea cucumbers – are fully protected within this zone. Collecting is not permitted at Mitlenatch Island.

Anchorages on both the E and W sides of the island offer relatively sheltered protection from either NW or SE winds. If you are anchoring in Camp Bay, be sure to visit the friendly warden's cabin, where a volunteer naturalist will be happy to answer any questions. An informative brochure on the island's history and its protected seabirds and marine life is available from the information shelters.

"NORTHWEST BAY" has a beautiful shingle beach with easy access to the island's designated trails and wooden observation blind on East Hill. From here, the patient observer can view the glaucous-winged gull's family life, including its fascinating feeding ritual.

Spring and summer flowers abound on Mitlenatch Island from late April onward, and, because it is home to the largest seabird colony in the Strait of Georgia, be prepared for a high level of noise.

One of 3,000 pairs of Glaucous-winged Gulls that choose to nest on Mitlenatch Island.

CHARTS
3538.

APPROACH
Camp Bay: From the SE at LW with caution. The passage to the inner anchorage is fringed to the N with rocks and a reef.

ANCHOR
Camp Bay: Temporary anchorage giving protection from prevailing north-westerlies. For 3 small boats in depths of 1.8 - 3 m (6 - 10 ft), over mixed bottom of mud, sand, shell and grass with moderate holding.

Note: Alternative anchorage may be found off Northwest Bay in settled conditions or when seeking protection from a southeasterly.

Mitlenatch is also home to 12 species of starfish.

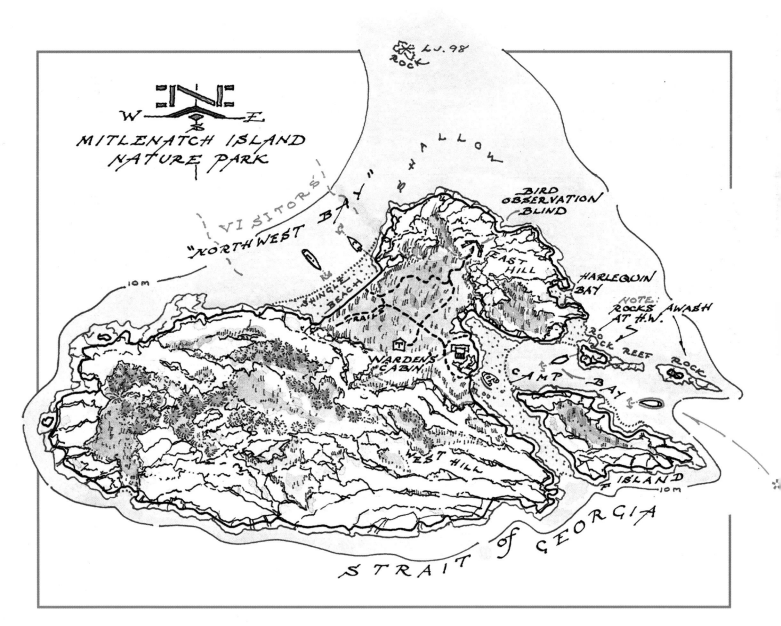

Not to scale. Not to be used for navigation.

2.7 SAVARY ISLAND

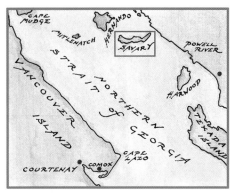

❀ 49°57.1'N 124°46.7'W Keefer Bay

Savary Island's sandstone cliffs are visible from Cape Lazo.

When viewed from the air, it seems that Savary Island and its beautiful white sandy beaches were towed from an archipelago in the South Pacific – perhaps by an old sea captain homesick for his West Coast roots.

Even though the island lacks an all-weather anchorage, good temporary holding is available E of the public wharf, where wooden boardwalks protect the fragile beaches from further erosion. The island is a great place to visit for a fun day out and can easily be accessed by water taxi from Lund. Al and Gina Wood can also arrange a land taxi for you on Savary; call LUND WATER TAXI 604-483-9749. There are wooded trails for hiking, unpaved roads for biking and a wonderful expanse of beach to be explored. Bike rentals are available at the SAVARY ISLAND GENERAL STORE & MARKET CAFÉ; call 604-483-2210. The store's entrepreneurial owners also operate RIGGERS, a fully licensed restaurant open 8am till late and an on-site bakery producing fresh bread, pies, cakes and picnic lunches-to-go, daily. The well stocked general store keeps fresh produce and frozen meat at competitive prices and a B.C. LIQUOR STORE outlet is proposed for 2000. A rigging/rope splicing service is also available. Kayakers can bring their craft over from Lund on the water taxi to explore the delights of Stradiotti and Mystery Reefs. Bed-and-breakfast accommodation is available on the island, and the low-key MINT B & B offers an alternative rustic cabin in the woods.

APPROACH

KEEFER BAY: From the NE, the jetty connecting the public wharf to the shore is the most conspicuous landmark.

ANCHOR

Temporary anchorage to the E of the public wharf in settled weather. Alternatively, if a northwesterly is blowing, tuck into the south of Mace Point. In depths of 4 - 8 m (13 - 26 ft), holding good in sand.

PUBLIC WHARF

Water taxi and local boat facility only. Best to row your dinghy ashore.

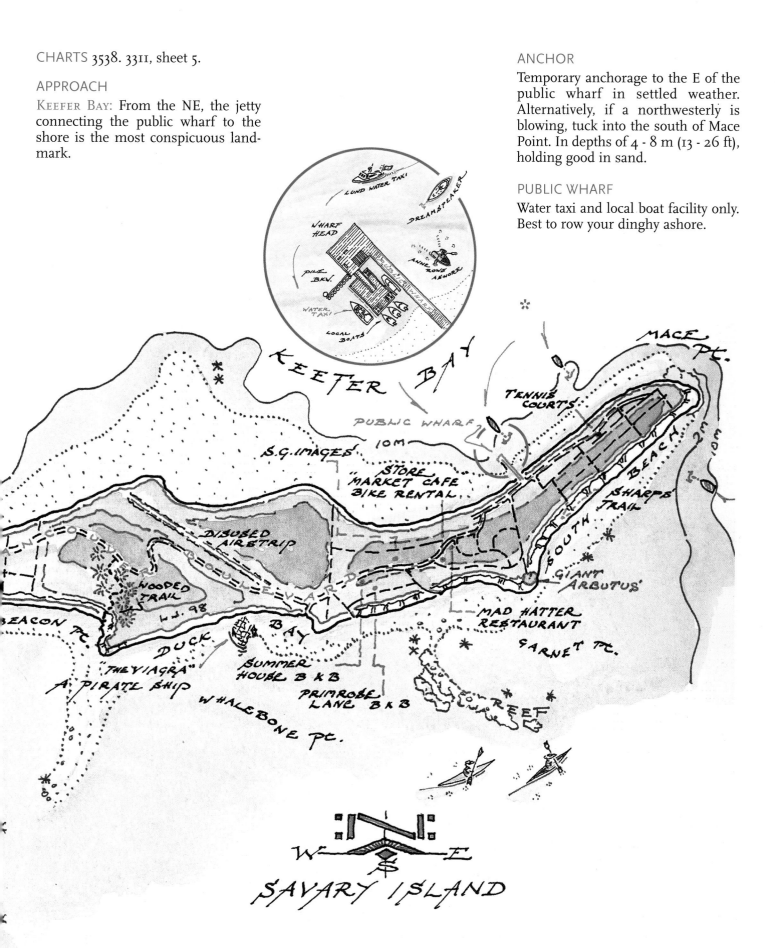

Not to scale. Not to be used for navigation.

2.8 "BLACK ROCK POINT," HERNANDO ISLAND

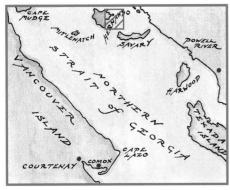

✻ 49°59.1'N 124°52.9' W

CHARTS

3538. 3311, sheet 5.

APPROACH

From the E. The flat meadow backing the shoreline is the most conspicuous landmark.

ANCHOR

E of the local mooring buoys. Temporary anchorage with good protection from the prevailing north-westerlies. Exposed to the S. Depths of 8 - 10 m (26 - 33 ft), holding good in shingle and sand.

Note: "Black Rock Point," named by us, is approximately 1 nautical mile southeast of Hidalgo Point.

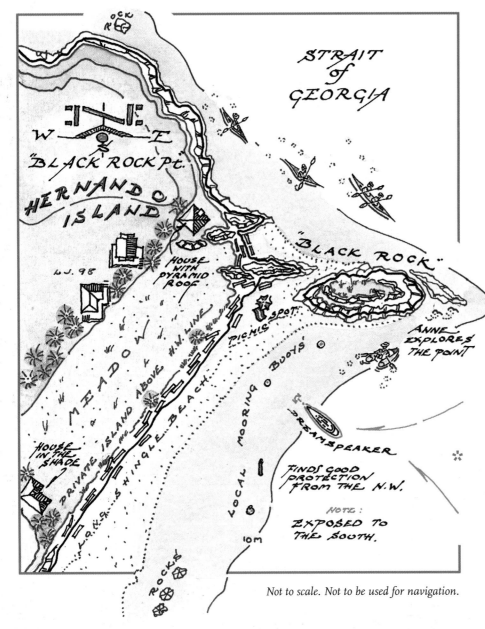

Not to scale. Not to be used for navigation.

If a seasonal northwesterly wind is forecast for the northern Strait of Georgia and you are in the vicinity of Hernando Island, tuck in behind "Black Rock Point" and drop your anchor off the long shingle beach. Seals love to laze on the reef at the end of the point, and a multitude of seabirds occupies the large middle rock.

The enticing 2.4 km (1.5 mi) beach, backed by a lovely grassy meadow, is a great place to stretch your legs or exercise the pooch. Although this is a private island, boaters can explore and enjoy the beach up to the HW mark and a delightful little picnic spot, exposed at LW, is tucked between the meadow and the large middle rock.

The house with the pyramid roof from black rock.

Chapter 3
BAYNES SOUND

The Chrome Island lighthouse stands guard at the southern entrance to Baynes Sound.

A calm evening off Tribune Bay.

Chapter 3
BAYNES SOUND

TIDES

Canadian Tide and Current Tables, Volume 5

Reference Port: Point Atkinson

Secondary Ports: Hornby Island, Denman Island

CURRENTS

Note: Although there is no reference station, tidal currents attain 2 - 3 knots out of the southern entrance to Baynes Sound.

WEATHER

Area: Strait of Georgia (northern half)

Reporting Stations: Sisters Island, Chrome Island

Strong southwesterly winds, known locally as "Qualicums," can build to 30 - 40 knots on summer afternoons. These strong winds extend from Qualicum Beach on Vancouver Island to the northern tip of Lasqueti Island and affect the southern shores of Hornby Island.

CAUTIONARY NOTES

At the southern entrance to Baynes Sound, an ebb tide creates rough seas when a strong southeasterly wind is blowing.
Strong southwesterly winds, known locally as "Qualicums," can build to 30 - 40 knots on summer afternoons. These strong winds extend from Qualicum Beach on Vancouver Island to the northern tip of Lasqueti Island and affect the southern shores of Hornby Island.
Both conditions present potentially hazardous conditions for small craft navigating on these waters.

Baynes Sound, the sheltered neck of water sandwiched between the shores of Vancouver and Denman Islands, is a welcome sight to the weary boater battling north from Nanaimo against prevailing summer northwesterlies. Also included in this chapter are breezy Lambert Channel and the rocky shores of Denman and Hornby Islands.

The colourful Chrome Island light, at the southeast end of Denman Island, welcomes you into Baynes Sound. Be sure to keep well clear of the sand-and-mud spit off Mapleguard Point. Once you've cleared the point, it's safe to tuck into peaceful Deep Bay for the night. This often uncrowded spot offers hot showers, a well-stocked general store, licensed café, walks along the sandy spit and spectacular views up Baynes Sound.

The waters of Baynes Sound are well reputed for their variety of quality oysters, which can be sampled at local restaurants or bought fresh along the way. Treat yourself to a platter of Fanny Bay oysters aboard the SS *Brico*, ashore on the shingle beach. This is also a good spot to stop if you plan to explore nearby Denman Island, as the old public wharf in Denman Village was removed in 1998, leaving the cruising boater with little or no access to the island. A five-minute taxi ride will take you from Fanny Bay to the Denman-Hornby ferry terminal at Buckley Bay, with an hourly service to Denman Village. Pop into the general store (a five-minute walk from the ferry), rent a bike or scooter, buy a picnic lunch and set off for the delights of Fillongley Park, Chicadee Lake or Boyle Point Provincial Park, where the social antics of sea lions can be experienced firsthand. Local artists and home businesses en route welcome visitors to their gardens, studios and workshops.

Sandy Island Marine Park and its beautiful clean beaches are located at the northern tip of Denman Island, and at low water you can beachcomb for four kilometres (two and a half miles), from the northern tip of White Spit S to Longbeak Point.

Hornby Island has an all-weather protected anchorage in Ford Cove and is famous for its mile-long stretch of fine white sand at Tribune Bay, where you can spend a few blissful days lazing on the beach and enjoying the warm water. There are also grassy bluffs to be hiked, winding roads to be biked and rocky islets to be explored. Hornby is a friendly island filled with an eclectic mix of talented artisans who welcome visitors to their workshops and galleries, and local farms will often sell fresh organic produce from their roadside stands.

FEATURED DESTINATIONS

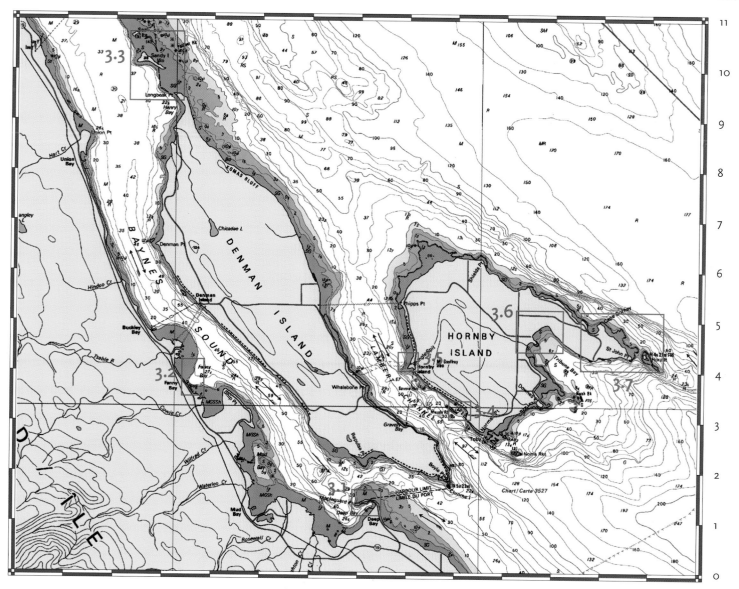

nautical miles

Not to be used for navigation.

3.1   DEEP BAY, VANCOUVER ISLAND

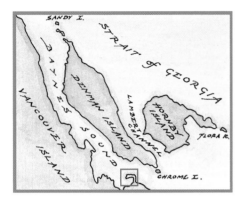

✥ 49° 28.0' N   124° 44.3' W

The approach to Deep Bay.

Baynes Sound sunset from Deep Bay.

If you get caught out by the sudden onset of a southerly or "Qualicum" wind, pop into cosy Deep Bay, the safest natural anchorage between Nanaimo and Comox. This peaceful and friendly bay also offers spectacular views up Baynes Sound.

Moorage at the public wharf is plentiful but popular with local boats, so be prepared to raft up if necessary. Power and water are available, and shower and laundry facilities are located at SHIP & SHORE MARINE, 250-757-8399. Here you will also find a well-stocked general store, a licensed café, a campground with RV and tenting spots and a nontidal boat ramp. As of 1998, this industrious establishment is run by new and energetic owners. The café serves breakfast, lunch and dinner, and patio picnic tables enable you to enjoy their delicious burgers along with the view. This is also the perfect spot for kayakers to set up camp while exploring southern Baynes Sound, and sites even come equipped with pot-bellied stoves for outdoor cooking. When the local fish boats come home with their catch, don't miss the opportunity to purchase freshly caught shrimp.

The private marina, run by the MAPLEGUARD RESORT, welcomes visitors but has limited transient moorage. The boat-weary traveller can, however, book into one of the convenient motel rooms for the night. The marina is also home to the DEEP BAY YACHT CLUB.

SEASIDE, located on the northern shores of the spit, offers bed-and-breakfast accommodation as well as kayak and canoe rentals and wildlife and fishing tours. Call 1-888-878-2200 or 250-757-2000.

A fingerlike natural spit protects Deep Bay from virtually all winds, and although most of the spit is private there is public access to the lovely sandy beach along Mapleguard Point – the best place to stretch your legs with a leisurely sunset walk.

CHARTS 3527 & 3513.

APPROACH

From the NW; the most conspicuous landmark is the Deep Bay light amid the white sands and bush of Mapleguard Point.

Note: Extensive sand flats extend northward from Mapleguard Point; leave both port-hand (green) buoys, P39 and P41, to the S if approaching Baynes Sound from the E.

ANCHOR

Good protection from southeasterly winds may be found SW of the break-water in variable depths of 4 - 10 m (13 - 33 ft), holding good in mud. Alternative all-weather protection in deeper water N of the marina. Depths, holding and bottom condition unrecorded.

PUBLIC WHARF

The wharf has extensive moorage, and visitors can usually find space, though rafting is the norm. Power and water on the floats.

MARINA

A marina, essentially for local boats, is operated by the MAPLEGUARD RESORT, 250-757-9211. Visitor or reciprocal moorage if available.

BOAT LAUNCH

Private, operated by SHIP & SHORE MARINE.

FUEL

No fuel float.

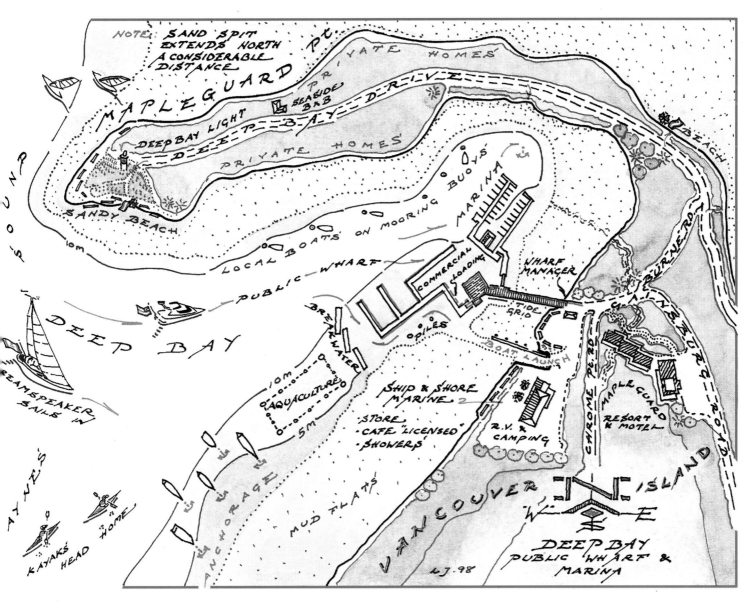

Not to scale. Not to be used for navigation.

CHART 3527.

APPROACH

From the NE, the red hull of the SS *Brico* and a white water tower are conspicuous landmarks.

ANCHOR

Temporary anchorage may be found E of the wharfhead. Depth, holding and bottom condition unrecorded.

PUBLIC WHARF

Limited float space, home to local oyster and shrimp boats.

BOAT LAUNCH

Public, unpaved, mainly used by kayaks.

Note: Extensive drying mud flats fringe Fanny Bay to the SE and NW.

❉ 49°30.5'N   124°49.3'W

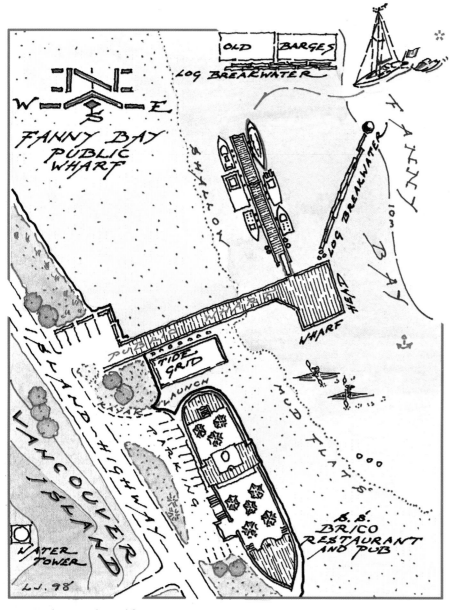

Not to scale. Not to be used for navigation.

Shellfish lovers should take the opportunity to indulge in a platter of delicious Fanny Bay oysters (*Crass ostrea gigas*) at the unique SS *BRICO* RESTAURANT & PUB. Commissioned for 32 years as the B.C. Tel cable ship, SS *Brico* was happily saved from the scrap yard by the McLellan family and is now well secured in the mud flats off Fanny Bay. If the public wharf is full, anchor E of the wharfhead, row ashore and settle yourself under one of the colourful deck umbrellas. You can purchase fresh oysters and shellfish at MAC'S OYSTERS, just a short walk from the public wharf. The Denman-Hornby ferry terminal is just a 5-minute taxi ride away in Buckley Bay.

The approach to Fanny Bay public wharf.

CHART 3527.

APPROACH

Sandy Island and Henry Bay lie at the northern tip of Denman Island. Approach from Baynes Sound with caution, because the sand bank drops off dramatically.

ANCHOR

Good protection can be found from northwesterly winds off Sandy Island, but this anchorage is open to southeasterly winds. Better all-weather protection is available in Henry Bay, SE of Longbeak Point. Depths of 6 - 12 m (19.5 - 39 ft), holding good in sand.

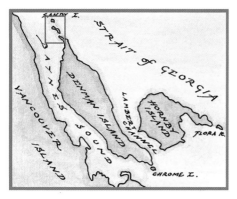

✣ 49°36.7' N   124°51.1' W

White Spit at L.W. from Baynes Sound.

Known locally as "Tree Island," this wonderful park also includes Seal Islets to the N and is often missed by the cruising boater. The islands are best explored at LW, and you can stretch your boat-weary legs beachcombing from the northern tip of White Spit to Longbeak Point on Denman Island. Henry Bay, just S of here, provides sheltered overnight anchorage when a southeasterly springs up.

The most popular day anchorage is on Sandy Island's southern shore. Its clean, inviting waters, white shell-and-sand beach and grassy uplands also make it a camper's paradise. Kayakers can pitch their tents right on the beach or under the shady canopy of trees behind it.

Not to scale. Not to be used for navigation.

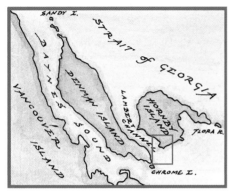

CHART 3527.

APPROACH

From the S. The stone breakwater and the community behind it form the most conspicuous landmarks. Enter E of the port-hand buoy, P37 (green).

ANCHOR

Good protection from southerly winds can be found NW of floating breakwater and E of Maude Reef. Depths are 3 - 5 m (10 - 16 ft). Good holding in sand and mud. Anchoring with stern line to the floating break-water is not recommended because the anchor can become entangled with the chains and anchors holding the breakwater.

PUBLIC WHARF

Extensive but usually crowded with local boats rafted 2 - 3 deep. Power, no water.

BOAT LAUNCH

Public.

FUEL

Float operated by FORD COVE MARINA, 250-335-2169.

Ford Cove, Hornby Island's only all-weather anchorage, provides more than just a bolt hole when the southeasterly and "Qualicum" winds make nearby Tribune Bay an uncomfortable and potentially danger-ous anchorage.

FORD COVE MARINA operates the wharf, fuel dock, RV/campsite, cabins and well-stocked store, where ice, fresh produce and fresh and frozen seafood are also available.

ARBUTUS ARTS, has weekly exhibi-tions showcasing excellent works by local artists. HORNBY ISLAND DIVING, offers guided dives to Flora Islet.

The lower bench trail, easily accessed from the cove, offers you a pleasant 45-minute walk along the cliffs to Shingle Spit.

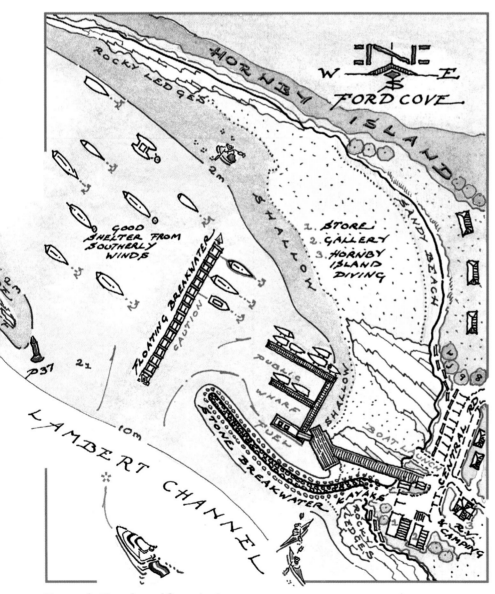

Not to scale. Not to be used for navigation.

Entrance to Ford Cove.

SHINGLE SPIT, HORNBY ISLAND

CHART 3527.

APPROACH

From the SW. The Denman-Hornby B.C. Ferries terminal is the most conspicuous landmark.

ANCHOR

The spit provides good protection from northwesterly winds but is exposed to southerly winds blowing up Lambert Channel. Depths are 2 - 4 m (6.5 - 13 ft), and holding is moderate over a shingle bottom.

MARINA

Pub float is for patrons and shoal draft boats only. Very shallow alongside at LW.

BOAT LAUNCH

Public.

✽ 49° 30.6' N   124° 42.4' W

Shingle Spit extends into Lambert Channel and provides good protection from prevailing northwesterly winds. It is a good spot for boaters wishing to anchor and stretch their legs, walk the pooch or indulge in a leisurely pub lunch. The Denman-Hornby ferry terminal is also located here. HORNBY ISLAND RESORT, 250-335-0136, located on the spit, includes the Thatch Pub, the Wheelhouse Restaurant and a campground with RV spots. Shower and laundry facilities are also available. MOUNT GEOFFREY REGIONAL NATURE PARK and its network of public hiking and biking trails are easily accessible from the resort.

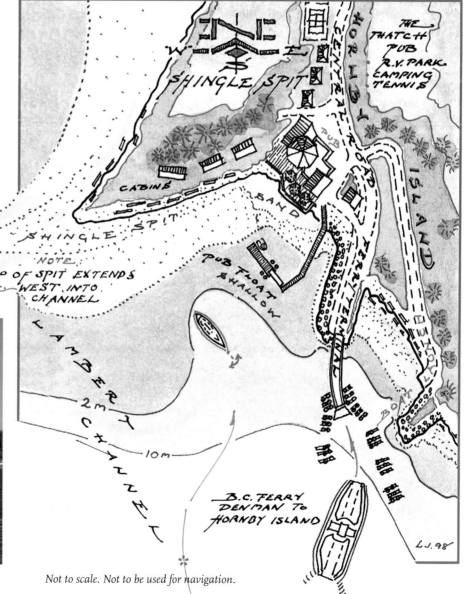

Approach to Shingle Spit.

Not to scale. Not to be used for navigation.

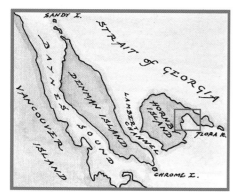

�֍ 49° 30.6' N   124° 36.3' W

The bluffs on Helliwell Park. Follow the cliffs into Tribune Bay.

A southerly wind can do more than just rock the boats at anchor in Tribune Bay.

Beautiful Tribune Bay is completely exposed to the S. Fortunately, the prevailing summer winds in the northern Strait of Georgia are from the NW, making safe anchorage possible for a good portion of the season. In settled weather, stay awhile and enjoy the bay's mile-long sweep of fine white sand and idyllic warm-water swimming.

This magnificent stretch of clean beach is backed by Tribune Bay Provincial Park, well used by locals and visitors alike. Overnight camping is not permitted, but a wooden gazebo, picnic tables and fire rings are provided for day use. Changing cabins, toilets and a hand pump for water are located near the parking area.

Kayakers wishing to explore the delights of Hornby Island can pitch their tents adjacent to the park in the TRIBUNE BAY CAMPSITE. It offers hot showers and beach access from "Little Tribune Bay" (local name), W of Spray Point; the bay is also a popular spot for sunbathing au naturel. For a fun sunrise or sunset kayak tour, call HORNBY OCEAN KAYAKS, 250-335-2726.

If you enjoy a good hike, visit HELLIWELL PARK and its scenic bluff trail (see page 36), easily accessed from St. John Point Road, N of the park. An alternative route for visitors without dogs or bikes is possible from the turnoff to High Salal. Continue along the private road until you reach lot 16-17. From there a trail leads through private land out to the cliffs.

The CO-OP GENERAL STORE & RINGSIDE MARKET, with its eclectic mix of shops, is a 5-minute walk from the western corner of Tribune Bay beach. The Co-op offers an excellent selection of bulk foods, fresh and organic produce, specialty items and hardware. It also houses the post office. The Ringside Market has an ambience all its own, with an emphasis on local arts, crafts and pottery, and is the perfect rendezvous spot for both islanders and visitors. Relax with a latté and a freshly baked muffin while planning your bike trip – the best way to discover both Hornby and Denman Islands. HORNBY ISLAND BICYCLES is located in the market and will provide you with rental bikes, an informative map and local knowledge. A visitors guide/map is also available by calling 250-335-2293.

The HORNBY ISLAND SUMMER FESTIVAL, a musical extravaganza, takes place in the first week of August. for other festivals and events, call the COMOX VALLEY VISITOR INFORMATION CENTRE, 250-334-3234.

CHART 3527.

APPROACH

From the SE. The bluffs on Helliwell Park are the most conspicuous landmark. Follow the cliffs into the bay.

ANCHOR

Although well protected from the NW, the anchorage must be regarded only as temporary, even in settled weather. Anchor in depths of 3 - 6 m (10 - 19.5 ft). Holding good in sand.

Note: If the forecast indicates "Qualicum" or southerly winds, Tribune Bay will become a lee shore. Substantial swells can develop and enter the bay in only moderate conditions. On entering or leaving Tribune Bay, clear the port-hand buoy, P35 (green), off Nash Rock by leaving it to the S.

The beach is a terrific playground.

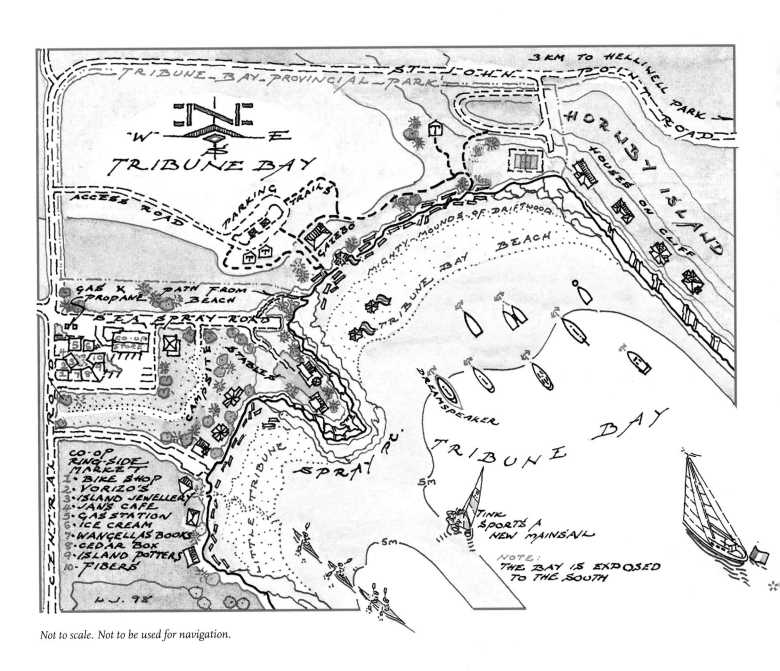

Not to scale. Not to be used for navigation.

3.7   HELLIWELL PROVINCIAL PARK & FLORA ISLET, HORNBY ISLAND

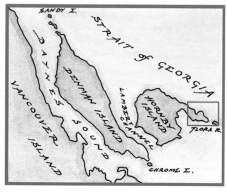

✳ 49° 30.8' N   124° 34.8' W

CHART 3527.

Note:

(1) Helliwell Provincial Park is best visited as a day hike while your boat is anchored at Tribune Bay (see page 34) or Ford Cove (see page 32). However, day anchorage is possible off the bluff in two small bights.

(2) Flora Islet is best visited by dinghy or kayak.

(3) The small-craft passage between St. John Point and Flora Islet should only be attempted at LW and in calm seas. Temporary anchorage is also possible here.

(4) Give the reef off the tip of Flora Islet a wide berth.

A leisurely hike in the cool of the evening to the grassy bluffs in Helliwell Provincial Park is quite an experience. The park is a must for visitors to the island, and the 5 km (3.1 mi) loop from the information shelter takes approximately 1.5 hours to complete. Alternatively, take a LW hop, skip and jump along the sandstone ledges from Whaling Station Bay to St. John Point and join the trail back to Helliwell Park Road. If you are exploring the bluffs by boat, two temporary anchorages are available. The sheer sandstone and conglomerate cliffs are home to an intriguing variety of bird life, including nesting murres and cormorants. Whaling Station Bay, en route to the park, has a wonderful expanse of compacted white sand beach, only visible at LW, and public access is possible from St. John Point Road.

Flora Islet, now a protected area, provides several buoys for visiting divers. It is not advisable to anchor along the reef, as damage to its delicate structure is often irreparable. The islet offers oysters in abundance and a profusion of wildflowers in the spring.

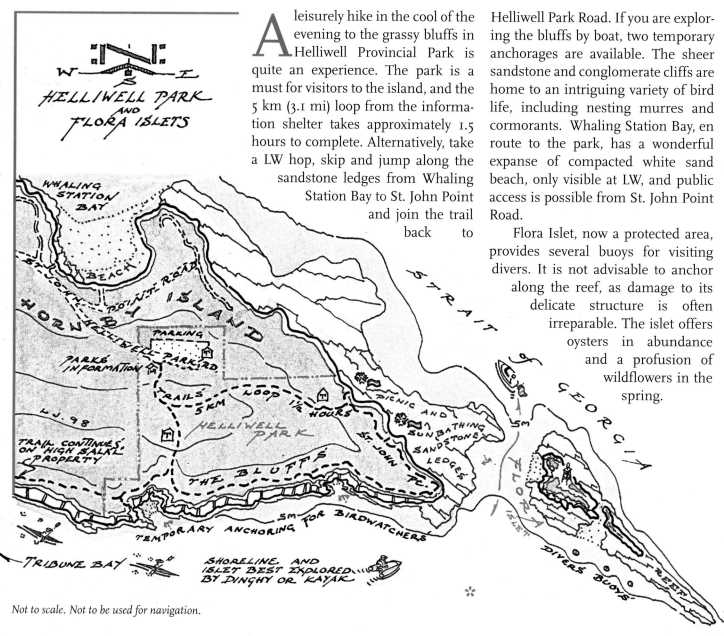

Not to scale. Not to be used for navigation.

Chapter 4
POWELL
RIVER

A tug passing Grief Point reminds us that these waters are also commercial arteries.

Chapter 4
POWELL RIVER

A welcome in Westview.

TIDES

Canadian Tide and Current Tables, Volume 5
Reference Port: Point Atkinson
Secondary Ports: Powell River, Blubber Bay

CURRENTS

Note: Although there is no reference station, tidal currents attain 1 - 2 knots in Malaspina Strait. Beware of the potential for a wind-against-current situation.

WEATHER

Area: Strait of Georgia (northern half)
Reporting Station: Grief Point

Note: Southeasterly winds accelerate around Grief Point, giving speeds 5 - 10 knots higher than the area forecast (listen for the weather report from Grief Point).

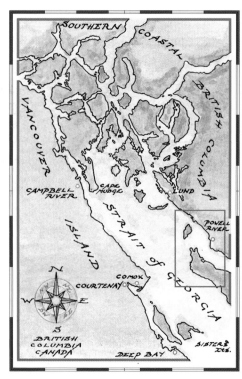

CAUTIONARY NOTES

The Malaspina Strait between Grief Point and Northern Texada Island is notorious for steep seas produced by a wind-against-current situation.

The above situation is potentially dangerous to small craft.

This compact but essential chapter encompasses Powell River on the mainland shore, the northern tip of Texada Island and the northern approaches to Malaspina Strait.

The cruising boater may be lulled into a false sense of security by the calm waters in the lee of Texada Island but should be aware that the area in the vicinity of Grief Point is renowned for its strong winds and ferocious seas – in fact, the weather proved so brutal in 1913 that it sank the union steamship *Cheslakee* off the wharf in Van Anda Cove on Texada Island.

If you do happen to be caught in the strait in unfavourable conditions, pop into BEACH GARDENS MARINA AND RESORT for the night and take advantage of the spa, gym and pool facilities. The marina also provides a convenient courtesy bus into Powell River. Sturt Bay and the community of Van Anda, on the northern tip of Texada Island, are steeped in history and offer sheltered anchorage, visitor moorage and an insight into its colourful past from the friendly, locally run enterprises. A water taxi to Powell River is also available.

On the mainland shore the town of Powell River is accessible by land and air, and provides the cruising boater with a convenient rendezvous and provisioning centre. The Westview public wharf offers well managed facilities and the only access to the district's lively downtown and the national heritage district of TOWNSITE, a wonderful example of town planning in the early 1900s. Extensive plans to develop recreational marine facilities along the waterfront are also underway.

A courtesy bus services the TOWN CENTRE MALL, which houses over forty stores and a walk along Marine and Willingdon Avenues is well worthwhile and offers a wide variety of excellent restaurants, cafés, bookstores and a real italian deli! From here you can also hike the spectacular SUNSHINE COAST TRAIL that hugs the Malaspina shoreline, skirts lakes and waterfalls and travels through old growth forest - an experience not to be missed.

FEATURED DESTINATIONS

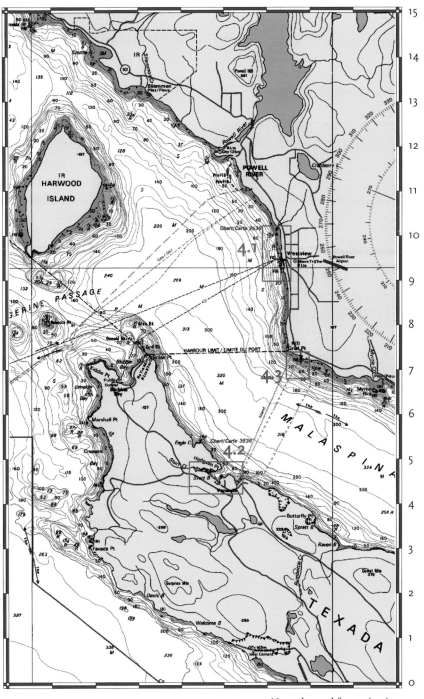

nautical
miles

Not to be used for navigation.

✲ 49° 50.0' N   124 31.9' W

Westview, the ferry terminal, and breakwater from the S.W.

Approach to the public wharf from the SW.

Westview, one of the 4 communities that make up Powell River, offers cruising boaters the only means of access to the district's lively downtown, although extensive plans to develop marine facilities on the waterfront have been proposed as of 1998.

The friendly and well-managed public wharf, adjacent to the ferry terminal serving Texada Island and Comox, offers extensive visitor and commercial moorage. It prides itself on having the cleanest shower facilities on the B.C. coast, and the wharf manager will be happy to pass on any local information you might need. Power and water are available on the docks, and laundry facilities can be found nearby.

The best way to enjoy a day at Westview is to take a leisurely walk N up Marine Avenue to WILLINGDON PARK & BEACH and to return via Willingdon Avenue. Here you will find a wide variety of restaurants, shops and services, including a bakery, marine store, two bookstores and a real Italian deli. THE CHOPPING BLOCK, a well-reputed butcher and fishmonger near the beach, also sells excellent fresh produce and tasty picnic fare.

A fast and efficient way to view the town is to hop onto a local transit bus, and maps are available at the INFORMATION BUREAU for a self-guided architectural tour of TOWNSITE – now a national heritage district. A courtesy bus will also transport you to the TOWN CENTRE MALL, which houses over 40 shops, including a B.C. LIQUOR STORE. Pickup from Westview Marina can also be arranged by calling the Town Centre Mall, 604-485-4681.

Powell River built the first pulp and paper mill in western Canada. Today PACIFIC PAPERS offers visitors fascinating tours; call 604-485-4701. BACK COUNTRY ADVENTURES specializes in tours of working B.C. forests, including heli-logging; call 604-485-4226 for pickup. The Parks & Wilderness Society has now completed (1999) the spectacular 180 km (112 mi) SUNSHINE COAST TRAIL, which winds from Sarah Point in the N to Saltery Bay in the S; call 604-485-4701 for a trail package, which includes cosy bed-and-breakfast stops along the way.

Some fun events and dates to note:
- SEA FAIR FESTIVAL, WILLINGDON BEACH, second week of August
- BLACKBERRY FESTIVAL (includes farmers market and vintners tasting), last week in August.

CHARTS 3536. 3311, sheet 5.

APPROACH

The public wharf at Westview from the W. The entrance lies to the S of the ferry terminal.

ANCHOR

Day/picnic anchorage in calm settled weather is possible off Willingdon Beach. Depths, holding and bottom condition unrecorded.

PUBLIC WHARF

A small boat basin lies behind a rock-mound breakwater, with extensive moorage facilities. Floats 1 & 2 strictly for commercial fishing boats, 3 - 6 for resident and visiting boats. Smaller boats, 20 - 30 ft, on 3 & 4. Larger boats, 40 - 50 ft, on 5 & 6. Power, water, plus excellent shower facilities.

MARINA

The municipal marina has no designated visitor moorage.

BOAT LAUNCH

Public, at the municipal marina. Kayaks can be launched from Willingdon Beach.

FUEL

A fuel float lies in the S of the small boat basin.

Note: Extreme caution should be exercised upon entering the small boat basin, because boats may be exiting, and manoeuvring is restricted.

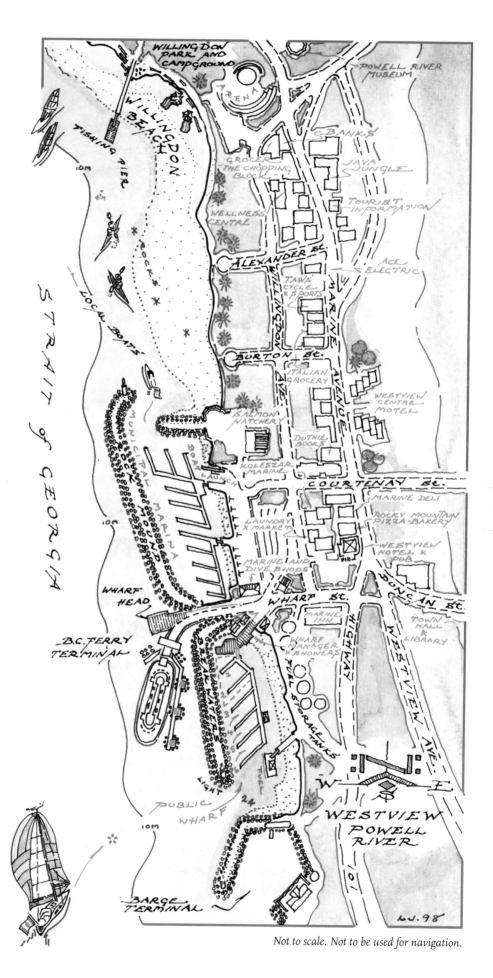

Not to scale. Not to be used for navigation.

4.2 Sturt Bay & Van Anda Cove, Northern Texada Island

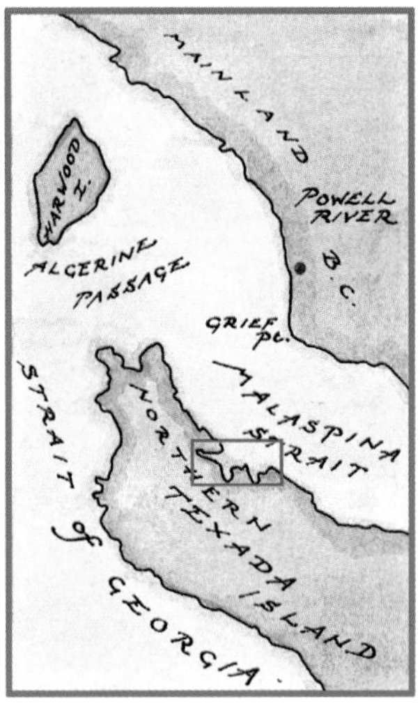

49° 45.8' N 124 33.4' W

CHARTS 3536. 3311, sheet 5.

APPROACH

To Sturt Bay. Enter between the starboard day mark (red) off Hodgson Point and between the porthand day mark (green) that marks the tip of the reef that extends out from Ursula Rock and the breakwater.

ANCHOR

Good temporary anchorage may be found in the western corner of Sturt Bay, with good protection from northwesterly winds. Depths 4 - 12 m (13 - 39 ft), holding good in mud and gravel. For alternative all-weather protection in deep water, anchor in Caesar Cove.

If you are up against a strong northwesterly wind or ferocious seas in Malaspina Strait, tuck into Sturt Bay (known locally as "Marble Bay"), where protected anchorage, visitor moorage and a taste of island history await you.

The Texada Island Boat Club owns and operates the marina below Marble Bluff Park and welcomes visiting boaters. Hot showers (and a fresh towel) are offered at the Texada Island Inn, 604-486-7711, on Gillies Bay Road, and the view across the strait from the shaded deck is spectacular. Laundry facilities are available at the gas station a little farther S, or call Sandra at Texada Laundry, 604-486-7747, for a 24-hour pickup and drop-off service from the dock – and relax!

The small, exposed public wharf in Van Anda Cove is used only for loading and unloading purposes. The union steamship *Cheslakee* met its fateful end in 1913 a short distance from this wharf.

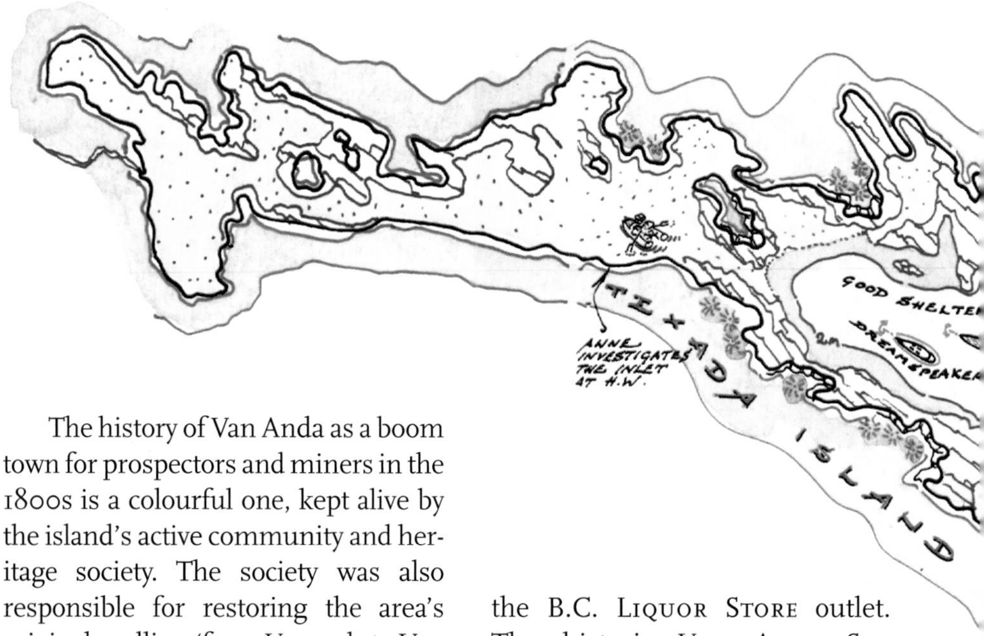

The history of Van Anda as a boom town for prospectors and miners in the 1800s is a colourful one, kept alive by the island's active community and heritage society. The society was also responsible for restoring the area's original spelling (from Vananda to Van Anda). Call the Van Anda Heritage Society, 604-486-7261, for an informative brochure.

To meet the locals and do some provisioning, you can take a pleasant half-hour stroll from the marina to the Texada Food Market, well stocked with fresh produce, basic provisions and cold beer and wine from the B.C. Liquor Store outlet. The historic Van Anda Store, owned by Joseph Kempe since 1947, is famed for its candies and is a great place to browse for knick-knacks. Mail a letter, send a fax or just relax with coffee at Abacus, the all-in-one store and bakery. A short walk down Van Anda Road will take you past the *Cheslakee* steamship memorial and on to Van Anda Point.

PUBLIC WHARF

In Van Anda Cove. Approach from the N. The wharf is exposed to northwesterly winds and offers little protection from the SE. It is operated by Transport Canada, essentially as a dock for its fuel barges. A small loading and unloading float for temporary moorage lies along the NE side. Depths alongside unrecorded.

MARINA

The TEXADA ISLAND BOAT CLUB encourages visitors to use its moorage. If the designated visitor float is full, the manager will try to find additional space.

BOAT LAUNCH

At end of breakwater.

Approaching the breakwater in Stuart Bay.

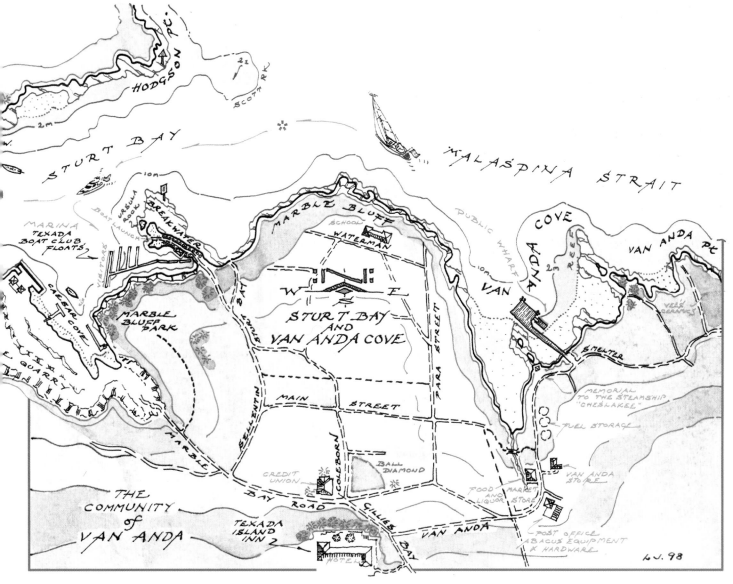

Not to scale. Not to be used for navigation.

4.3 BEACH GARDENS MARINA & RESORT, GRIEF POINT, POWELL RIVER

❈ 49° 47.9' N 124° 31.2' W

CHARTS

3513, sheet 5.

APPROACH

The marina breakwater lies approximately .5 nautical miles SE of Grief Point. Approach the entrance from the SW.

MARINA

The marina is operated by the BEACH GARDENS RESORT, 604-485-6267 or 1-800-663-7070, which welcomes visitors to use its moorage and resort facilities. In summer it is advisable to reserve a berth in advance.

BOAT LAUNCH

No paved launch, but kayaks may access the beaches on either side of the marina.

FUEL

Fuel float operated by the marina.

Boaters are given a warm welcome when they stop for the night at the Beach Gardens Marina. Power, water and garbage drop-off are available, and shower facilities come equipped with a spa, gym and pool! A guest laundry room and ice machine are also provided. The well-stocked cold beer and wine store is part of the complex, and the nearby THUNDER BAY STORE carries basic provisions. For a shopping spree into Powell River, hop onto the courtesy bus, which will transport you to the TOWN CENTRE MALL in Westview (see Westview, page 40).

Take advantage of the resort's glorious view across Malaspina Strait from the GARDEN BISTRO deck while enjoying a sumptuous seafood platter.

Not to scale. Not to be used for navigation.

Entrance to Beach Gardens Marina.

Chapter 5
DESOLATION SOUND

Laura Cove, the quintessential Desolation experience.

Chapter 5
DESOLATION SOUND

Ray Rock, kayakers in heaven.

TIDES

Canadian Tide and Current Tables, Volume 5
Reference Port: Point Atkinson
Secondary Ports: Lund, Okeover Inlet, Prideaux Haven

CURRENTS

Note: Although there are no reference and secondary current stations, tidal currents stream through the inlets at rates of 1-2 knots. Tidal streams attain 2-4 knots in the entrance of Malaspina Inlet.

WEATHER

Note: Although no specific reporting station covers this area, weather forecasting is a matter of extrapolation of weather forecasts for the Strait of Georgia (northern half) and Johnstone Strait.

CAUTIONARY NOTES

Desolation Sound enjoys prolonged periods of light or windless days. However, on a weather change, the leading edge of the approaching system will create strong winds that tend to swirl down and through the anchorages.

The featured destinations all have their fair share of rocks, reefs and ledges that annually seek out unwary skippers. Be aware of the many isolated rocks that dot these waters even in deep channels and keep a careful lookout for Sky Pilot Rock, north of Otter Island, which dries on a 1.2 m (4 ft) tide.

The alluring waters of Desolation Sound, named by a disenchanted Captain Vancouver in 1792, lie south of West Redonda Island. The sound's southern shore is dominated by the legendary Desolation Sound Marine Park, with its maze of deep, interconnecting inlets and cosy, hideaway anchorages. To date it is the largest marine park in British Columbia, and it is treasured by boaters and kayakers as one of the most accessible tracts of wilderness almost anywhere in the world.

The park's boundaries include Gifford Peninsula, Prideaux Haven, Tenedos Bay and Grace Harbour. This extensive chapter also encompasses the far reaches of Malaspina, Okeover, Lancelot and Theodosia Inlets.

Breathtaking vistas, an abundance of protected anchorages and the rare opportunity to observe wildlife at close quarters are not all that Desolation Sound Marine Park has to offer. Its geographical location also ensures mainly light summer breezes and blissfully warm water temperatures, which come as a surprise, because this stretch of water experiences one of the largest tidal ranges (5.5 m/18 ft) on the B.C. coast.

For some freshwater bathing, visit Unwin Lake, just a short hike from Tenedos Bay and blessed with a variety of hideaway "hot tubs," cascading falls and warm-water pools.

Those journeying by road to Desolation Sound with trailer boats or kayaks can use the boat launch in Lund. Situated at the end of Highway 101 and only a 20-minute drive from Powell River, this enterprising community offers moorage, marine facilities, boardwalk cafés and a reputable bakery. It is also the only fuelling and provisioning stop mentioned in this chapter – Refuge Cove, on West Redonda Island, being the other alternative (see Chapter 7.2).

Okeover Landing, on Malaspina Peninsula's eastern shore, is a popular and more convenient spot to launch kayaks and canoes because it is located only about five km (three mi) from the sheltered waters of Desolation Sound Marine Park. The barbecue-weary boater will also find the Laughing Oyster Restaurant a very pleasant surprise.

Finally those wishing to avoid the summer crowds and experience Desolation Sound in its undisturbed glory should consider visiting this coastal jewel during late spring or early fall.

FEATURED DESTINATIONS

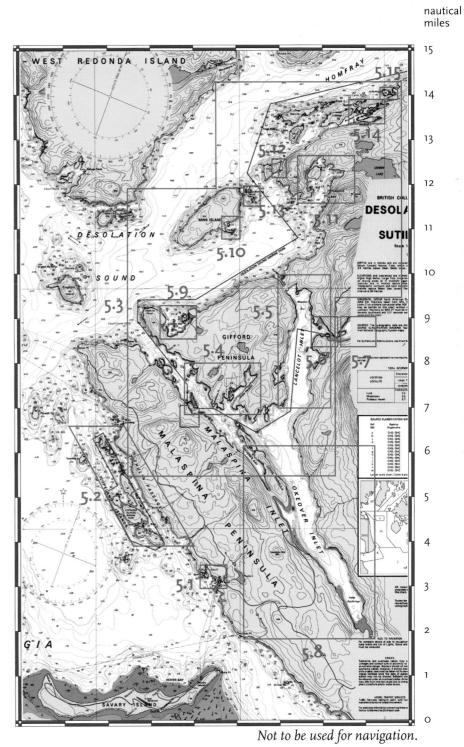

nautical miles

Not to be used for navigation.

5.1 Lund, Malaspina Peninsula

✲ 49° 58.9' N 124° 45.9' W

The historic Lund Hotel from the hotel floats.

A variety of freshly baked bread pastries at Nancy's Bakery.

Highway 101, originally known as the Pan-American, extends over 15,000 km (9,300 mi) from Puerto Montt, Chile, to Lund, British Columbia – the cruising boaters' gateway to Desolation Sound and beyond. Lund's colourful and enterprising community welcomes visitors arriving by road or sea as tourism is its livelihood and the summer season is short. As of 1999 the Lund Hotel is up for sale, and plans to enhance Lund's waterfront have also been proposed.

Moorage is offered at the public wharf, where both power and water are available, and overflow boats can tie up alongside one of the floating breakwaters. Showers and washrooms are available adjacent to the wharf manager's office open 7am-8pm in the summer months. The RV park and campground provide shower and laundry facilities and house the Lund Market, a convenience store well stocked with a variety of groceries, fresh and organic produce and a tempting selection of specialty ice cream. Diving & Kayaking, 604-483-3223, offers kayak rentals and tours.

Float plane connections are possible from Vancouver and Powell River (see page 40), and Lund Water Taxi provides a scheduled daily service to Savary Island (see page 22). Individual trips can also be arranged; call 604-483-9749.

Nancy's Bakery, famed for its oversized, melt-in-the-mouth cinnamon buns, also produces a variety of freshly baked pastries and excellent bread. Its cappuccino bar offers specialty coffees, which can be enjoyed on the deck or picnic lawn. Fish and shellfish that come straight off the boats can be purchased at the Seafood Shop.

It is well worth taking a stroll along the path and boardwalk to the Starboard Café. Seat yourself on the shaded deck and enjoy your choice of excellent specials and a selection of local wines. The Portside Grill located N of Hoeger Yachting, is reputed for its hearty breakfasts as well as its excellent burgers and steaks; call 604-483-9002.

Lund is one of the last "urban" stops as you head N, and marine services are provided by both Lund Auto & Outboard, 604-483-4612, and Hoeger Yachting, 604-483-9002.

CHARTS 3538. 3311, sheet 5.

APPROACH

From the W, the most conspicuous landmark being the black-and-white structure of the Lund Hotel, which lies back from the wharfhead.

PUBLIC WHARF

Enter close to the ends of the floating breakwater. The northern float is designated for recreational craft, and visitors are encouraged to raft up or use the inside of the floating breakwater. Harbour Office Tel. 604-483-4711. Summer Hours: 7am- - 8pm.

MARINA

As of 1999 the Lund Hotel & Marina are up for sale. The floats are exposed to westerly swell and the wakes of passing boats.

FUEL

The fuel float is located N of the public wharf.

BOAT LAUNCH

Public.

Note: Finn Cove, just N of Lund, will provide emergency shelter. Although anchoring is discouraged, the locals confirm that the holding is good. Finn Cove also has a public wharf used mainly by resident boats.

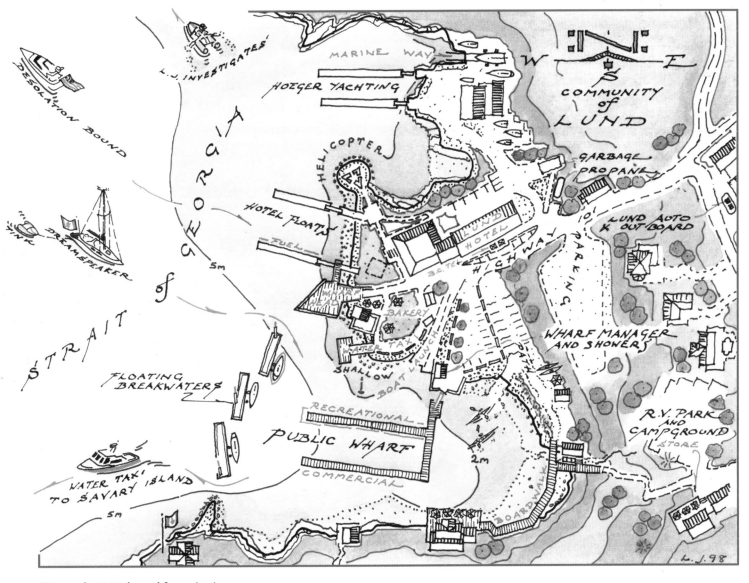

Not to scale. Not to be used for navigation.

5.2 Copeland Islands Marine Park, Thulin Passage

✲ 50° 0.7′ N 124° 48.5′ W

"Midway Cove" from Thulin Passage looking NW.

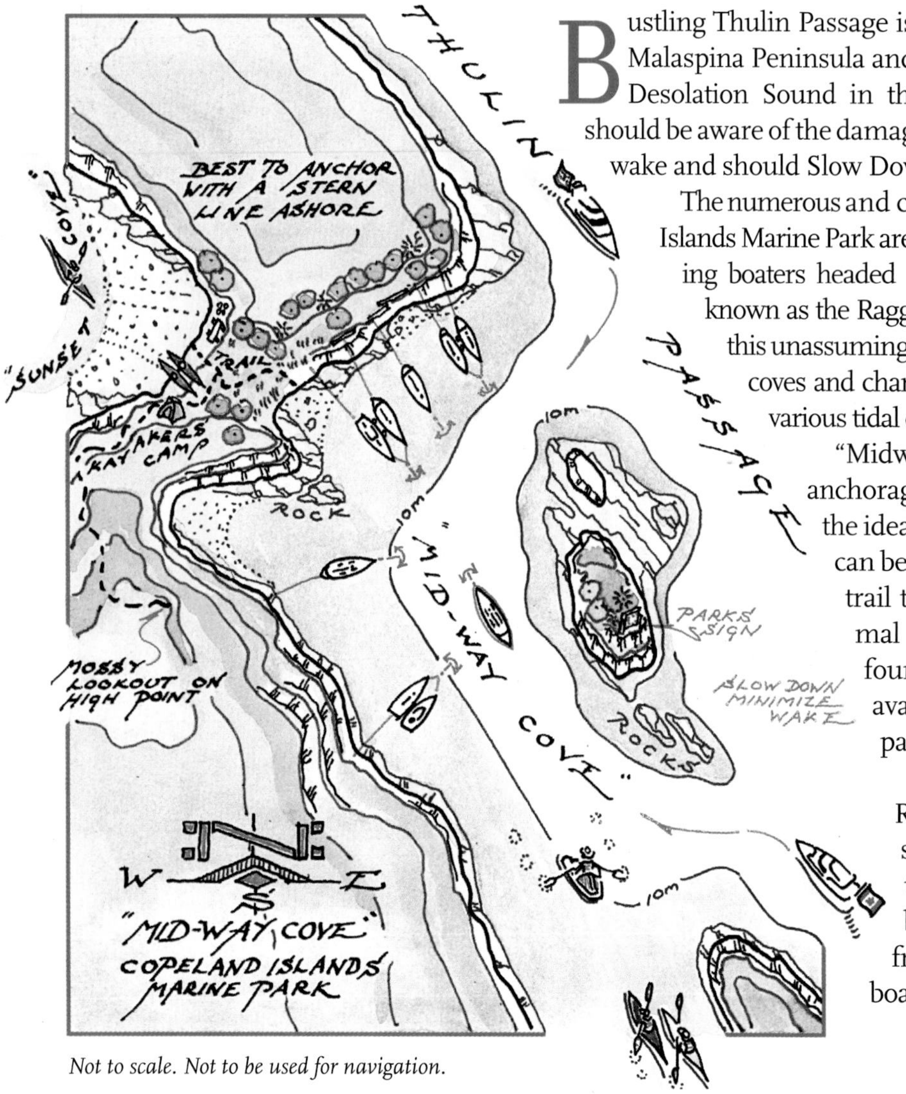

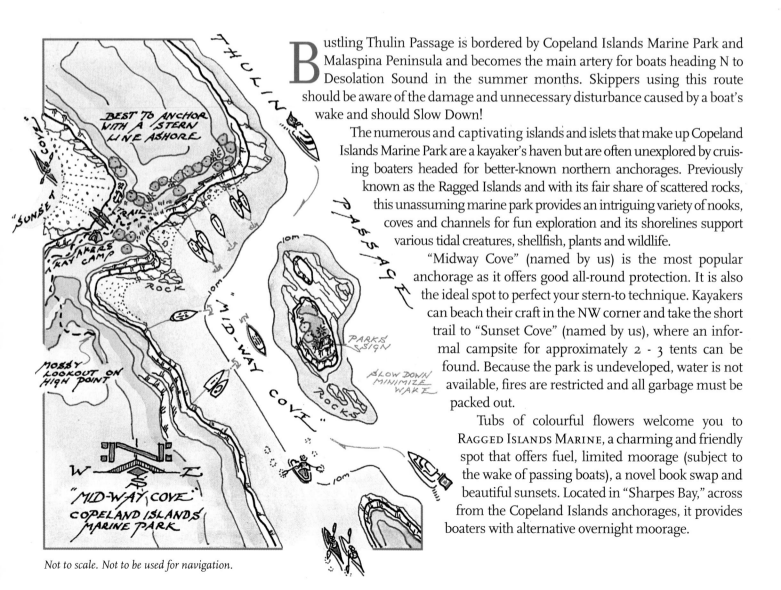

Not to scale. Not to be used for navigation.

Bustling Thulin Passage is bordered by Copeland Islands Marine Park and Malaspina Peninsula and becomes the main artery for boats heading N to Desolation Sound in the summer months. Skippers using this route should be aware of the damage and unnecessary disturbance caused by a boat's wake and should Slow Down!

The numerous and captivating islands and islets that make up Copeland Islands Marine Park are a kayaker's haven but are often unexplored by cruising boaters headed for better-known northern anchorages. Previously known as the Ragged Islands and with its fair share of scattered rocks, this unassuming marine park provides an intriguing variety of nooks, coves and channels for fun exploration and its shorelines support various tidal creatures, shellfish, plants and wildlife.

"Midway Cove" (named by us) is the most popular anchorage as it offers good all-round protection. It is also the ideal spot to perfect your stern-to technique. Kayakers can beach their craft in the NW corner and take the short trail to "Sunset Cove" (named by us), where an informal campsite for approximately 2 - 3 tents can be found. Because the park is undeveloped, water is not available, fires are restricted and all garbage must be packed out.

Tubs of colourful flowers welcome you to Ragged Islands Marine, a charming and friendly spot that offers fuel, limited moorage (subject to the wake of passing boats), a novel book swap and beautiful sunsets. Located in "Sharpes Bay," across from the Copeland Islands anchorages, it provides boaters with alternative overnight moorage.

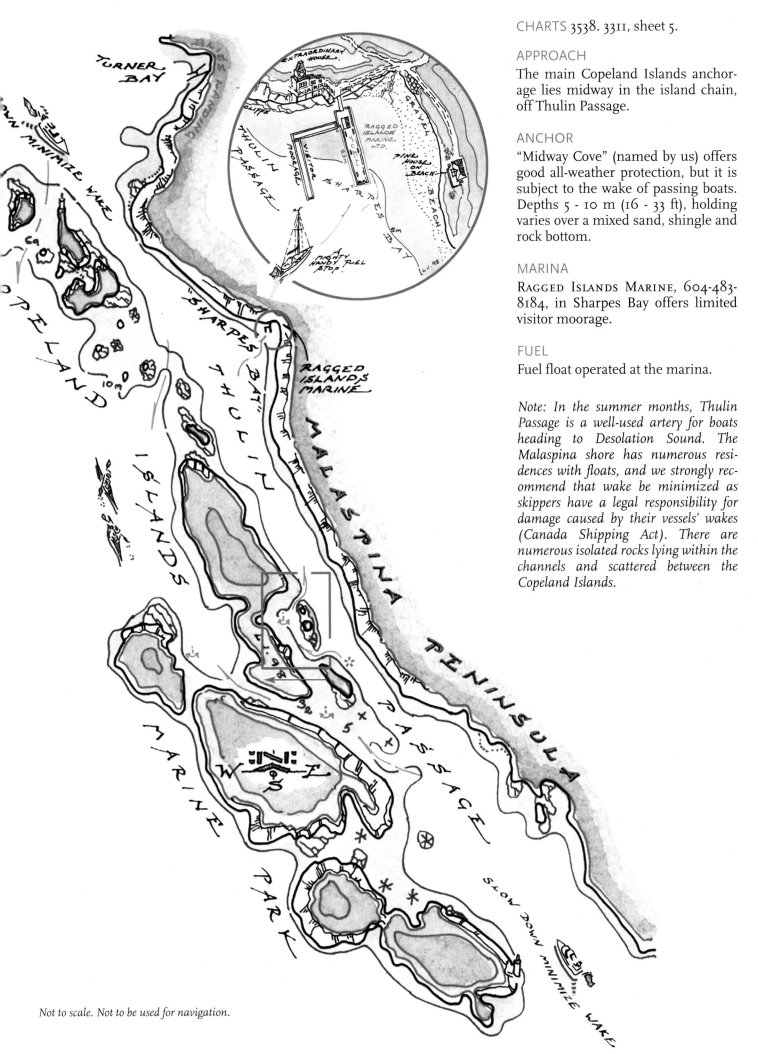

CHARTS 3538. 3311, sheet 5.

APPROACH

The main Copeland Islands anchorage lies midway in the island chain, off Thulin Passage.

ANCHOR

"Midway Cove" (named by us) offers good all-weather protection, but it is subject to the wake of passing boats. Depths 5 - 10 m (16 - 33 ft), holding varies over a mixed sand, shingle and rock bottom.

MARINA

RAGGED ISLANDS MARINE, 604-483-8184, in Sharpes Bay offers limited visitor moorage.

FUEL

Fuel float operated at the marina.

Note: In the summer months, Thulin Passage is a well-used artery for boats heading to Desolation Sound. The Malaspina shore has numerous residences with floats, and we strongly recommend that wake be minimized as skippers have a legal responsibility for damage caused by their vessels' wakes (Canada Shipping Act). There are numerous isolated rocks lying within the channels and scattered between the Copeland Islands.

Not to scale. Not to be used for navigation.

5.3 DESOLATION SOUND MARINE PARK

✣ 50° 5.0′ N   124° 48.7′ W

On rounding Sarah Point, the full majesty of Desolation Sound comes into view.

Dreamspeaker in Prideaux Haven. (5.14)

British Columbia's largest marine park encompasses one of the most beautiful cruising areas in the world. Desolation Sound Marine Park is blessed with remarkably warm waters, a variety of safe anchorages and spectacular scenery, and it is only accessible by water-craft. The park is also protected by a "minimal development policy" to ensure that its 60 km (37.3 mi) of wilderness are preserved for future generations.

Desolation Sound Marine Park's popularity as the "ultimate destination" for local and visiting boaters and kayakers leads to overcrowding in the major anchorages during the busy summer months of July and August. However, boaters willing to venture into the more than 30 lesser known coves will often be rewarded with total solitude.

In this chapter we cover the 5 all-time favourite anchorages in the park: Grace Harbour (see page 54), Tenedos Bay (see page 64) and Prideaux Haven and Melanie and Laura Coves (see page 68). We also include 11 delightful alternative anchorages.

It should be noted that 4 parcels of private land still remain within the park and due respect should be paid to their boundaries.

Note: The local road goes from Lund (see page 48) to the tip of Malaspina Peninsula, where small craft can be launched. Alternatively, use the launch at Okeover Arm (see page 60).

Bald Eagles inhabit the park.

FEATURED ANCHORAGES

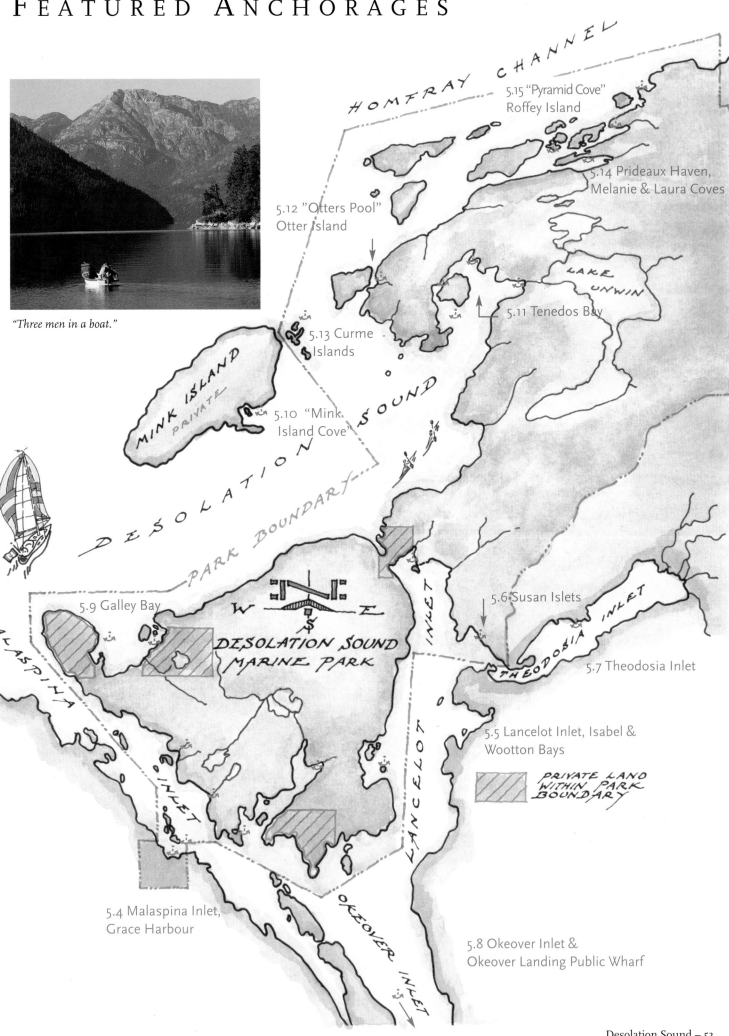

"Three men in a boat."

HOMFRAY CHANNEL

5.15 "Pyramid Cove" Roffey Island

5.14 Prideaux Haven, Melanie & Laura Coves

5.12 "Otters Pool" Otter Island

LAKE UNWIN

5.11 Tenedos Bay

5.13 Curme Islands

MINK ISLAND *PRIVATE*

DESOLATION SOUND

5.10 "Mink Island Cove"

PARK BOUNDARY

N
W · E
S

DESOLATION SOUND MARINE PARK

5.9 Galley Bay

5.6 Susan Islets

THEODOSIA INLET

5.7 Theodosia Inlet

LANCELOT INLET

5.5 Lancelot Inlet, Isabel & Wootton Bays

PRIVATE LAND WITHIN PARK BOUNDARY

MALASPINA INLET

5.4 Malaspina Inlet, Grace Harbour

OKEOVER INLET

5.8 Okeover Inlet & Okeover Landing Public Wharf

✻ 50° 3.1' N   124° 46.9' W

CHARTS 3559. 3312, pages 12 & 13.

APPROACH: MALASPINA INLET

The Malaspina Inlet's featured anchorages by leaving Rosetta Rock to the N.

ANCHOR

Temporary anchorage can be found along the inlet's NE shore and to the SW of the Cochrane Islands. Depths 4 - 10 m (13 - 33 ft). Holding varies in a mix of rock, sand and mud.

Evening row in Grace Harbour.

The hidden charms of Malaspina Inlet, well known to kayakers, are often missed by boaters en route to Grace Harbour or Lancelot, Theodosia and Okeover Inlets. Protected from most prevailing summer winds, these hideaway anchorages often can accommodate only 1 or 2 boats, but they provide the perfect opportunity to take a break from the crowds, explore tidal pools teeming with life and pick fresh oysters.

    Although careful navigation is required to avoid the numerous unmarked rocks in the inlet, there are 4 cosy spots to choose from before you reach Scott Point.
1. After giving Rosetta Rock off Cross Islet a wide berth, tuck into the nook behind "Eagles Island" (named by us), take a stern line ashore and watch the world pass by from the comfort of your cockpit.
2. The snug bight behind Neville Islet is backed by a small rocky beach and fed by a freshwater stream – a truly delightful spot to watch the sun go down.
3. The peaceful one-boat cove between Kakaekae & Scott Points requires a bit of tricky manoeuvring and a stern line ashore, but it is well worth the effort for the solitude that it provides.
4. The oyster-covered reefs and tidal pools between N & S Cochrane Islands are wonderful to explore at LW as the warm waters and tidal currents of Malaspina Inlet encourage a large variety of intertidal life to develop. Protected anchorage can be found between the islands and Malaspina Peninsula.

Evening light over the Gifford Peninsula.

GRACE HARBOUR, DESOLATION SOUND MARINE PARK

Grace Harbour, one of Desolation Sound Marine Park's most protected and popular all-weather anchorages, also wins hands down for attracting the largest quantity of nonstinging jellyfish to its warm, sheltered waters (generators beware!). "Sunset Boulevard" (named by us), at the head of the basin, retains light the longest, providing the most idyllic spot to relax and sip a long, cool sun downer. "Cabin Cove" (also named by us), behind Jean Island, offers alternative anchorage for boaters in a less sociable mood. Kayakers can set up camp in the northern arm of the harbour, where wooden camping platforms and pit toilets are provided. A pleasant half-mile trail leads from there to a freshwater lake with inviting swimming rocks – and not a jellyfish in sight!

Note: Stock up on your favourite brand of mosquito repellent to ensure a peaceful night's sleep at anchor or while camping.

APPROACH: GRACE HARBOUR

Grace Harbour between Scott and Moss Points; enter by leaving Jean Island to the N.

ANCHOR

Good all-weather protection can be found throughout the harbour. Depths 2 - 8 m (6.5 - 26 ft). Holding good in dense mud.

Note: The anchorage is well used in the summer. Stern lines are recommended.

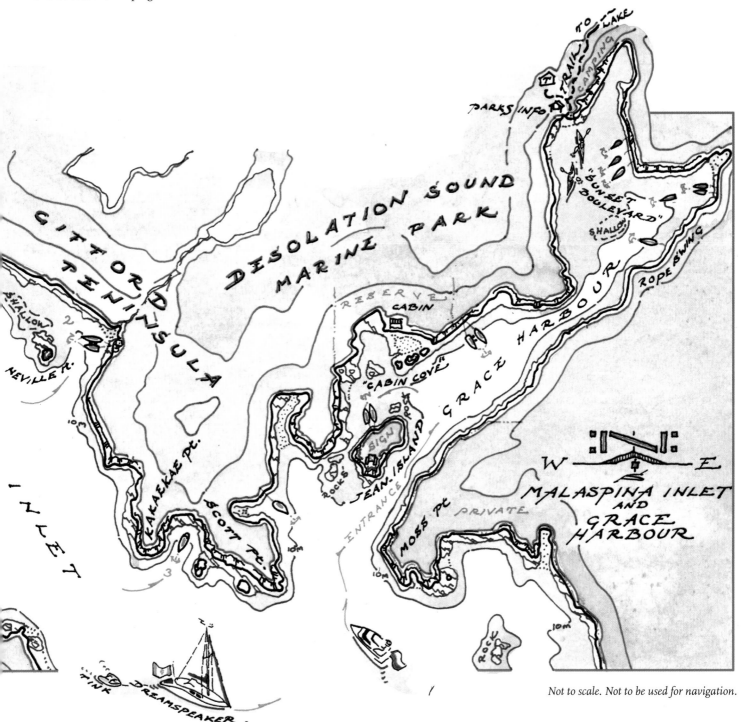

Not to scale. Not to be used for navigation.

✳ 50° 2.3' N   124° 43.5' W

CHARTS 3559. 3312, pages 13 - 15.

APPROACH: LANCELOT INLET

Lancelot Inlet branches N from the junction of Malaspina and Okeover Inlets.

Steep-sided Lancelot Inlet, sandwiched between Gifford Peninsula and the mainland, penetrates deep into Desolation Sound Marine Park and affords numerous anchorages just waiting to be discovered. Two parcels of private land still exist within the park – one at the northwestern end of Wootton Bay, the other S of the entrance to Theodosia Inlet.

Ancient navigational symbol!

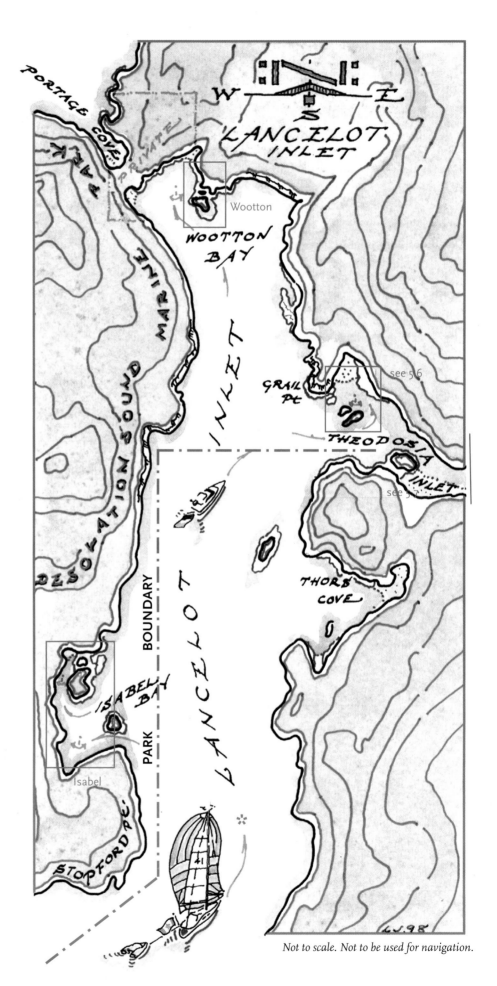

Not to scale. Not to be used for navigation.

ISABEL & WOOTTON BAYS, DESOLATION SOUND MARINE PARK

ANCHOR: ISABEL BAY

Good all-weather protection can be found NW of Madge Island. Take a stern line ashore as there is little room to swing. Alternative anchorage in the SW corner, which affords good protection from the SE. Depths, holding and bottom conditions vary.

Note: Passage is possible S of Polly Island, but favour the Polly Island shore. If entering or exiting between Polly and Madge Islands, watch out for a rock that lies N of Polly Island.

Lovely Isabel Bay offers protected, though limited, anchorage tucked behind Polly and Madge Islands, but be prepared to find an alternative spot in the busy summer months. If you're one of the lucky ones, be sure to take a stern line ashore; then hop into your dinghy or kayak and set out to discover the "sights," including a suspended outhouse and a skinny-dipping hideaway.

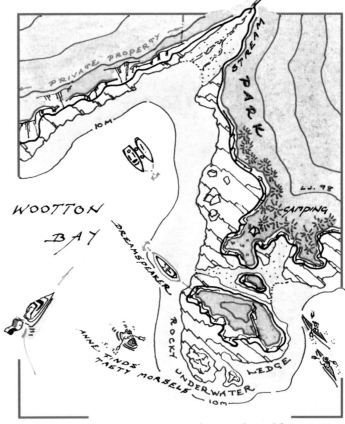

Not to scale. Not to be used for navigation.

ANCHOR: WOOTTON BAY

Although it seems rather open, the NE corner affords reasonable protection from outflow and southeasterly winds. Depths 8 - 12 m (26 - 39 ft), holding fair over a sand and rock bottom.

Note: Give a wide berth to the rocky underwater ledges that extend a deceptively long way S of the islet.

Wootton Bay is a pleasant alternative to Isabel Bay and is reasonably protected from prevailing summer winds. Flat, mossy camping ledges and a bountiful supply of fresh shellfish have made the bay a kayaker's haven.

Note: There is no public access to Portage Cove from Wootton Bay because the land is privately owned.

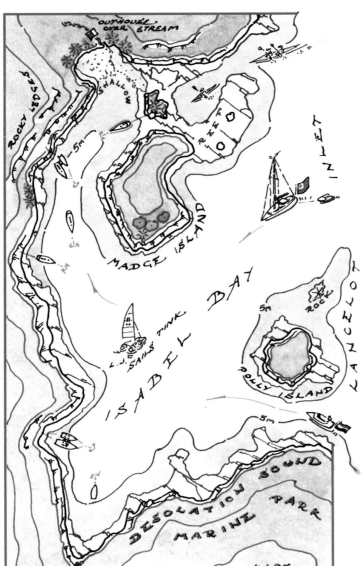

Not to scale. Not to be used for navigation.

Dreamspeaker seeks shelter in Isabel Bay.

5.6 SUSAN ISLETS, DESOLATION SOUND MARINE PARK

✽ 50° 4.1' N 124° 42.1' W

CHARTS 3559. 3312, page 15.

APPROACH
From the W out of Lancelot Inlet, turning N to enter the anchorage between Susan Islets and the mainland.

ANCHOR
N of the islets and E of the rocks. Depths 4 - 8 m (13 - 26 ft). Holding good in mud.

Note: It is possible to pass between the smaller northern islet and the rocks to the S of Grail Point.

A quiet little anchorage can be found just N of the narrow entrance to Theodosia Inlet, tucked behind wooded Susan Islets. This is a wonderful spot to observe wildlife from the comfort of your cockpit, although the conical rock on the smaller Islet has become a favourite with local birds, which often stop to view the antics of cruising boaters at anchor! This intimate bay also provides lovely views down Lancelot Inlet and great sunsets.

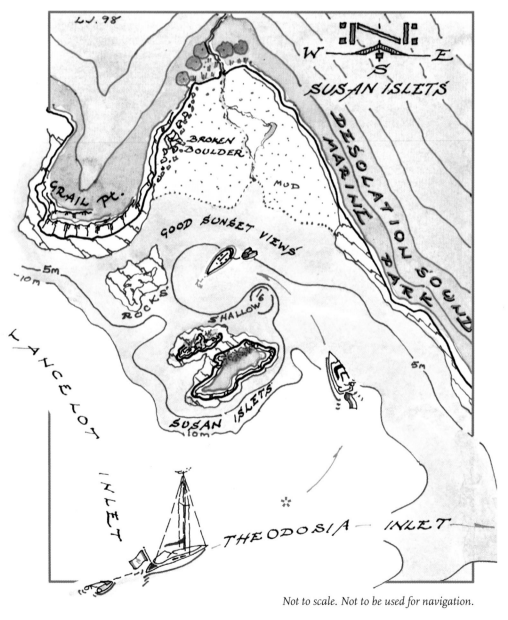

Not to scale. Not to be used for navigation.

An intimate bay, a place to commune with nature.

THEODOSIA INLET 5.7

CHARTS 3559. 3312, page 15.

APPROACH

From the W, to the S of Susan Islets. The channel to Theodosia Inlet has a minimum charted depth of 2.4 m (nearly 8 ft). Stay in the centre of the channel and watch for rocks just visible at HW off the northern shore.

ANCHOR

Generally a good anchorage with fair protection, although the winds do whistle down off the surrounding mountains. Depths 4 - 6 m (13 - 19.5 ft). Holding good in mud.

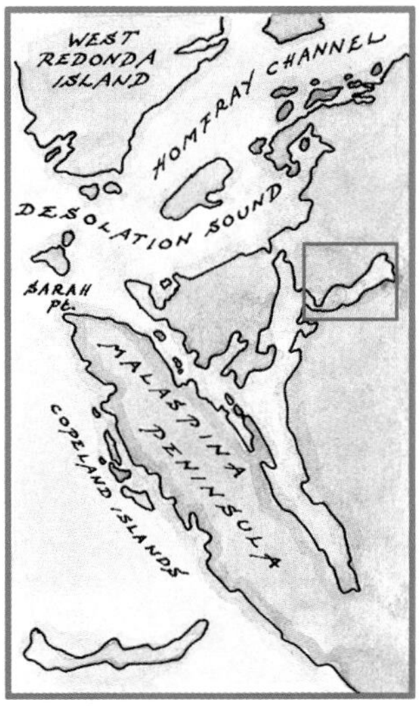

50° 4.1' N 124° 42.1' W

Navigating Theodosia Inlet's entrance and narrow, snake-like channel is straightforward if you anticipate the currents, stay in the centre and keep a careful lookout for wayward boulders just visible at HW off the northern shore. The narrows suddenly open up to reveal a beautiful, lakelike anchorage with the rarely seen coastal mountain range creating a stunning backdrop. The inlet itself is fairly well protected, but boats can also tuck in behind the northern islet or between the rock bluff and the grassy isthmus further E. Even though logging operations are ongoing (as of 1998), a water taxi transports loggers out of the inlet by 4:30 p.m., leaving you alone to enjoy the tranquil surroundings. The logging road can also be used for hiking after hours, and the expansive mud flats are fun to explore by dinghy or kayak at HW.

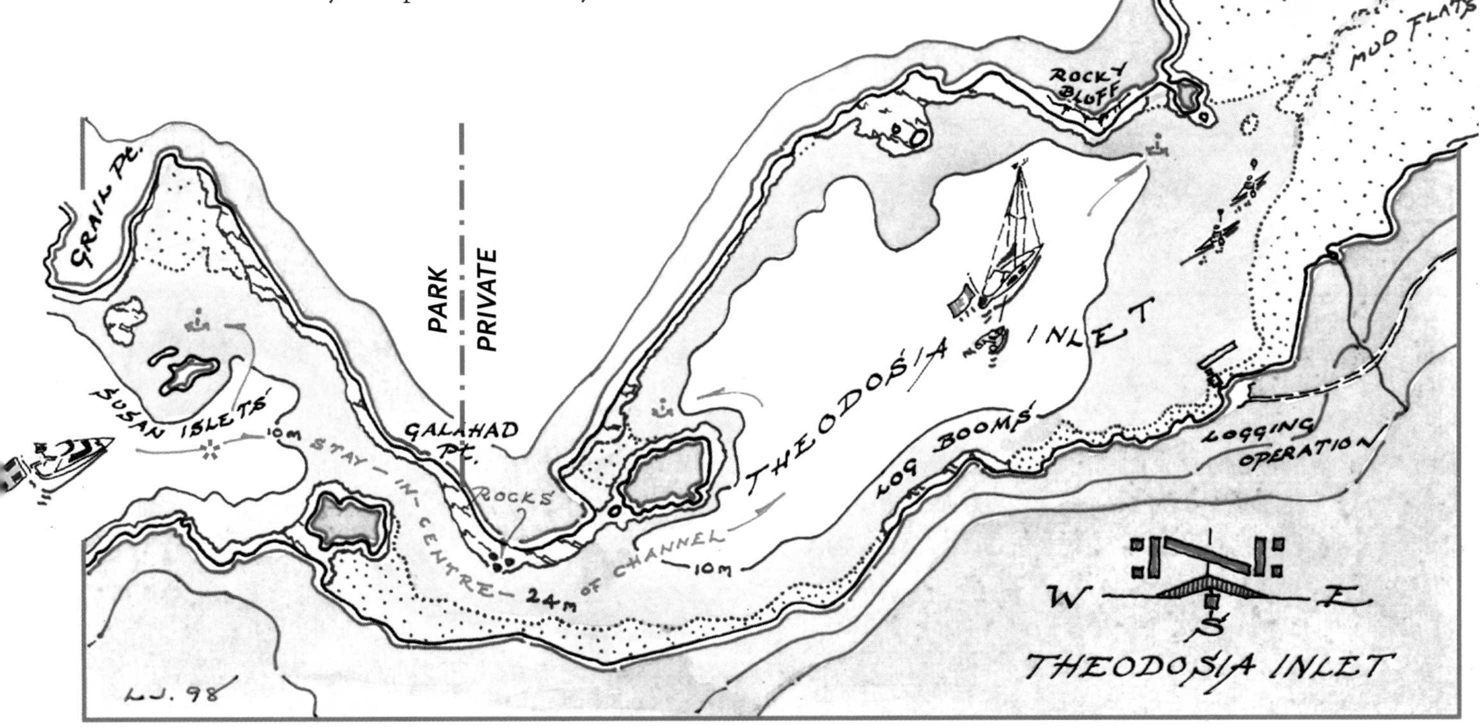

Not to scale. Not to be used for navigation.

5.8   OKEOVER INLET & OKEOVER LANDING PUBLIC WHARF

✤ 50° 1.5' N   124° 43.5' W

CHARTS 3559. 3312, page 14.

APPROACH

Okeover Inlet is deep with few navigational obstructions. Approach Okeover Landing from the NE. The building housing the restaurant on the hillside above the wharf is the most conspicuous landmark.

Note: Leave Boundary Rock, off the southern tip of Coode Peninsula, to the N.

ANCHOR

Due to the steep-to shoreline, there are limited anchoring possibilities.

PENROSE BAY

Well protected from the NW but open to southeasterlies. Depths 4 - 10 m (13 - 33 ft), holding good in sand.

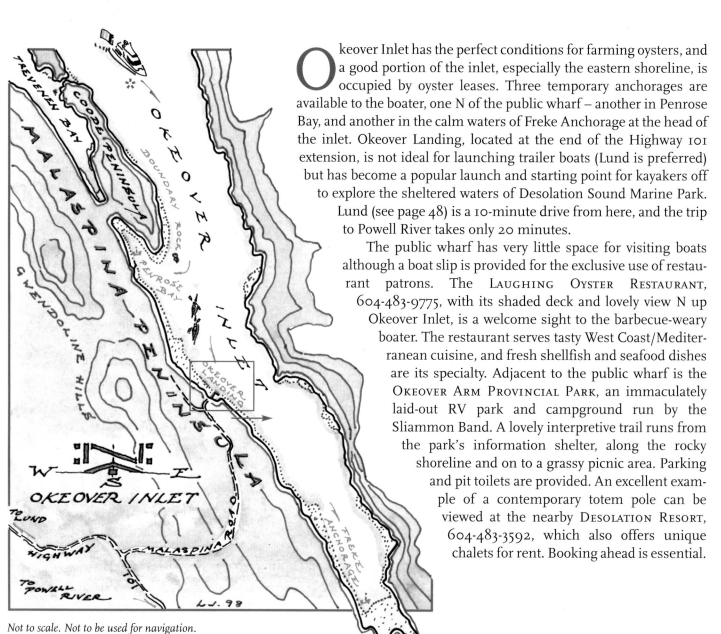

Okeover Inlet has the perfect conditions for farming oysters, and a good portion of the inlet, especially the eastern shoreline, is occupied by oyster leases. Three temporary anchorages are available to the boater, one N of the public wharf – another in Penrose Bay, and another in the calm waters of Freke Anchorage at the head of the inlet. Okeover Landing, located at the end of the Highway 101 extension, is not ideal for launching trailer boats (Lund is preferred) but has become a popular launch and starting point for kayakers off to explore the sheltered waters of Desolation Sound Marine Park. Lund (see page 48) is a 10-minute drive from here, and the trip to Powell River takes only 20 minutes.

The public wharf has very little space for visiting boats although a boat slip is provided for the exclusive use of restaurant patrons. The LAUGHING OYSTER RESTAURANT, 604-483-9775, with its shaded deck and lovely view N up Okeover Inlet, is a welcome sight to the barbecue-weary boater. The restaurant serves tasty West Coast/Mediterranean cuisine, and fresh shellfish and seafood dishes are its specialty. Adjacent to the public wharf is the OKEOVER ARM PROVINCIAL PARK, an immaculately laid-out RV park and campground run by the Sliammon Band. A lovely interpretive trail runs from the park's information shelter, along the rocky shoreline and on to a grassy picnic area. Parking and pit toilets are provided. An excellent example of a contemporary totem pole can be viewed at the nearby DESOLATION RESORT, 604-483-3592, which also offers unique chalets for rent. Booking ahead is essential.

Not to scale. Not to be used for navigation.

OKEOVER LANDING

N of public wharf and submarine cable. Very temporary. Depths 4 - 10 m (13 - 33 ft). Holding dependent on getting anchor to set in hard-packed shingle.

FREKE ANCHORAGE

N of the mud flats. Good shelter from the SE, exposed to the N. Depths, holding and bottom condition unrecorded.

PUBLIC WHARF

The L-shaped float is well used by local boats, leaving limited float space for visitors. However, management of the Laughing Oyster Restaurant have added a designated float for patrons.

BOAT LAUNCH

Public.

Note: Breakwater is awash at HW.

A modern day Totem Pole at Desolation Resort.

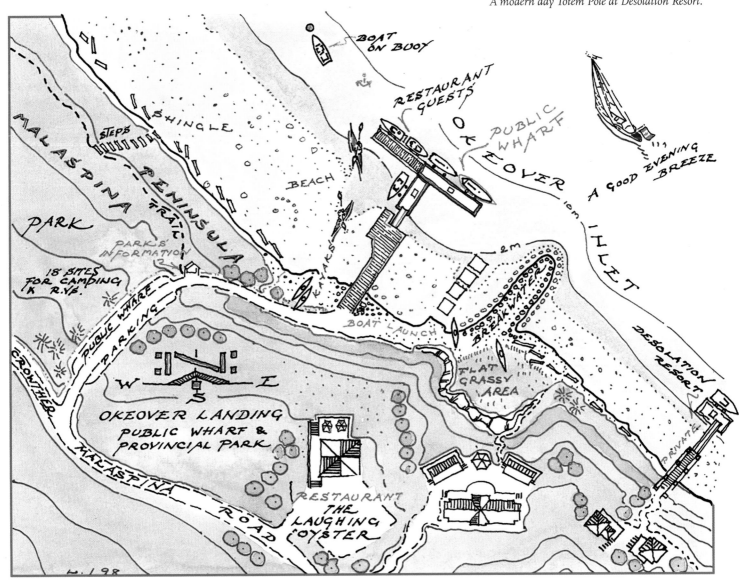

Not to scale. Not to be used for navigation.

5.9 GALLEY BAY, DESOLATION SOUND MARINE PARK

✢ 50° 4.4' N 124° 47.2' W

CHARTS 3559. 3312, page 12.

APPROACH

From the N.

Note: There are rocks in the centre of the bay and to the N of the little peninsula that forms "Buff Cove" (named by us).

ANCHOR

SE of "Maiden Island" (named by us), with good protection from prevailing winds. Depths 4 - 10 m (13 - 33 ft), moderate holding over a sand and gravel bottom. Alternatively in "Buff Cove," which is often subject to overnight outflow winds and chop from Desolation Sound. Depths, holding and bottom condition unrecorded.

Galley Bay, tucked behind Zephine Head, is the first major anchorage available to the cruising boater after rounding Sarah Point and entering Desolation Sound.

Two parcels of land within the park are privately owned, and their boundaries should be respected. "Buff Cove" (named by us), the westernmost anchorage, once housed an alternative, back-to-basics community in the '6os and '7os, and, although its reputation lives on, the rustic cabins have been replaced with well-appointed private homes. The cove provides fairly sheltered protection and easy access to the park on its eastern shoreline. A second, more protected anchorage behind "Maiden Island" (named by us) is also backed by private homes and is a lovely spot to explore at LW.

Not to scale. Not to be used for navigation.

CHARTS 3538. 3312, page 9.

APPROACH

From the E. Beware of the rocky ledges that fringe the anchorage.

ANCHOR

In the NW corner for the best protection or to the S of "Goat Islet" (named by us) with stern anchor or line ashore. Depths, holding and bottom condition unrecorded.

❊ 50° 6.3' N   124° 45.1' W

Mink Island is privately owned, with large signs displayed along the shoreline requesting 'no fires at anytime - PLEASE.'

Good protection, warm water and an unobstructed view up Homfray Channel to the snow-capped mountains beyond make "Mink Island Cove" (local name) a good temporary anchorage in the summer months, and boaters should be aware that floatplanes frequent the private dock. The rocky ledges surrounding "Goat Islet" (named by us) are fun to explore by dinghy at LW, and the small lagoon behind provides delightful warm-water swimming.

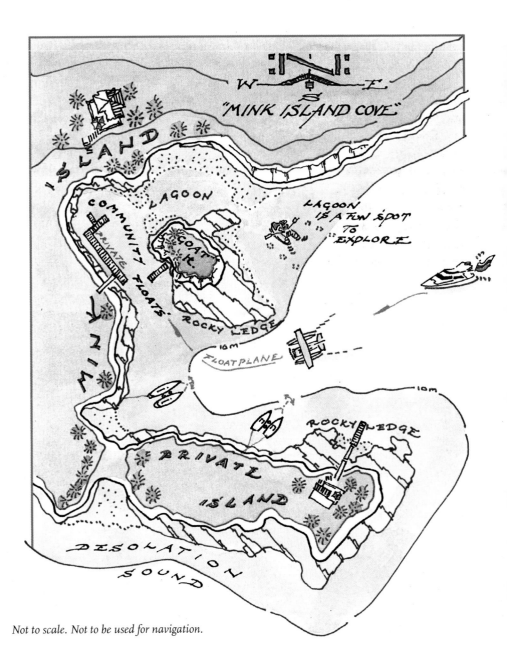

Rowing a longboat past Mink Island.

Not to scale. Not to be used for navigation.

5.11 TENEDOS BAY, DESOLATION SOUND MARINE PARK

✣ 50° 6.8' N 124° 42.3' W

Approaching the entrance to Tenedos Bay.

Weighing anchor in the NW cove.

Nestled between Bold Head and Mount Spooner, the clear but extremely deep waters of Tenedos Bay are still able to provide the visiting boater with four delightful spots suitable for anchoring. Keep a careful lookout for prominent rocks often hidden just below the surface and lying in wait for the distracted skipper. The bay has become extremely popular in the summer months, for news of blissful, warm-water swimming in Unwin Lake has spread.

1. The pocket anchorage in the SW corner of the bay is quiet, secluded and subject to overnight outflow winds. It should only be entered via the NW passage.

2. A cosy, 3-boat spot west of "Woodchuck Island" (named by us) has become known locally as "Three Fathom Cove" over the years. Backed by high cliffs and grassy ledges, it is also a favourite with kayakers setting up camp for the night. A drying tombolo connects the island to the mainland at LW.

3. Good protection can be found in the spacious NW cove. It provides the most secure overnight anchorage, with easy access by dinghy to the trails linking Unwin Lake with the E cove (4).

4. The convenient and popular cove below the bluff in the NE corner is exposed to the W, but it has the best sunset views and is closest to the tempting "warm baths" at Unwin Lake. Kayakers can beach their craft at the head of the cove and pitch their tents in the old orchard campsite beside a freshwater stream. Pit toilets are provided, but all garbage must be packed out. The lake trail begins at the park's information shelter and divides about halfway along. The less demanding southern route leads to the head of Unwin Lake, jammed with a wonderful variety of sunbleached logs. It is best to continue on a little way from here if you plan to swim. Hiking along the northern trail is a little more rigorous but quite lovely as you wind your way through the forest passing miniwaterfalls and deep freshwater pools en route to bathing rocks on the lake's edge. From here you can take a blissful warm-water swim, but make your presence known well in advance as skinny dipping is often the norm.

CHARTS 3538. 3312, page 9.

APPROACH

From the S. Enter the bay by leaving the rock off Bold Head to port. Watch for isolated rocks in Tenedos Bay.

ANCHOR

1. Reasonable protection can be found behind the small islets in the SW corner.

2. For all-weather protection "Three Fathom Cove" (local name) is hard to beat. Note the shallow entrance bar, approximately 1.5 m (5 ft) at chart datum.

3. Alternative anchorage is possible in the roomy NW corner.

4. The popular anchorage below the bluff in the NE corner is exposed to the W. Depths, holding and bottom condition vary. Stern lines are recommended.

Morning tranquility in the NE corner.

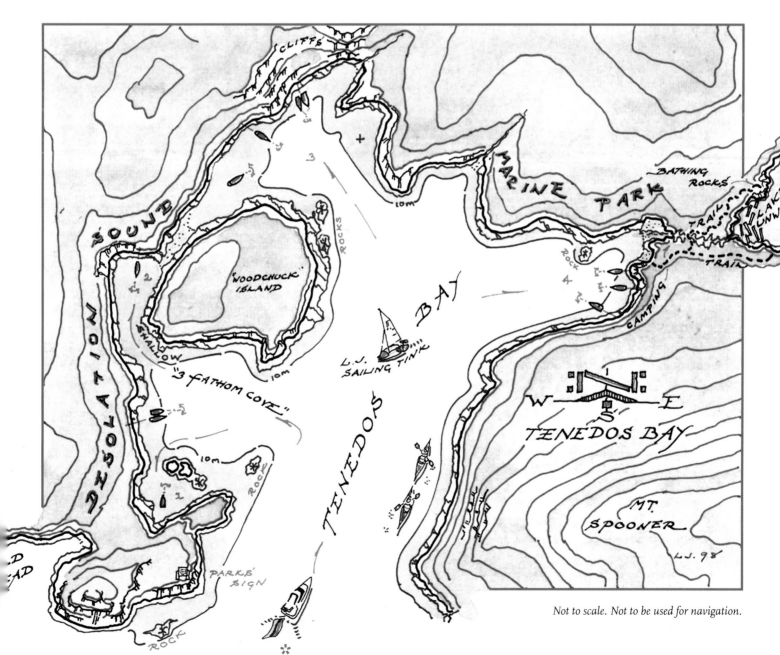

Not to scale. Not to be used for navigation.

5.12 "Otters Pool," Otter Island, Desolation Sound Marine Park

❋ 50° 7.4' N   124° 43.7' W

CHARTS 3538. 3312, page 9.

APPROACH
Slowly from the SW, out of Desolation Sound, or from the N, out of Homfray Channel.

ANCHOR
Temporary anchorage can be found within the passage between Otter Island and the mainland. Depths 4 - 8 m (13 - 26 ft), holding varies over a rocky bottom.

Note: Sky Pilot Rock lies N of Otter Island.

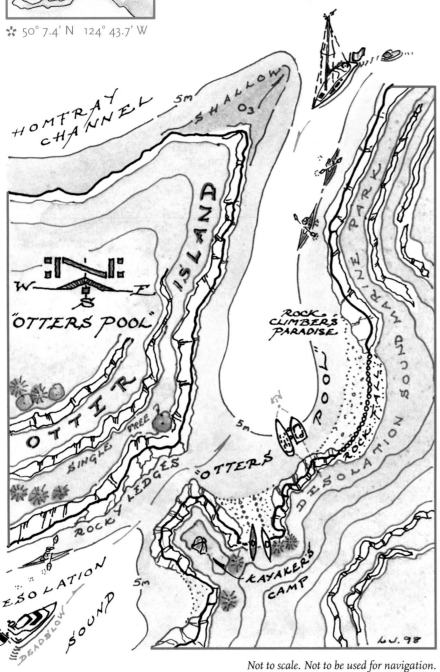

Not to scale. Not to be used for navigation.

Otters Pool" (named by us) is a lovely anchorage tucked between Otter Island and the mainland. Unfortunately it is also a convenient passage for runabouts and other speedy craft en route to or from nearby anchorages. Boaters should slow down, reduce their wake and allow the peace and solitude to be enjoyed by all.

Sheltered stern-to anchorage can be found S of the steep rocky ledges – a rock climber's paradise. Stones have also been cleared in the little nook S of the anchorage, making it possible for kayakers to beach their craft and camp on the lovely grassy spot over-looking the pass.

"Otters Pool" provides and unlikely anchorage.

CHARTS 3538. 3312, page 9.

APPROACH

This is not a recommended spot for deep-draft boats and should only be navigated on a rising tide. Beware of rocks that lie to the N, in the entrance. The head of the channel is shallow and dries on a zero tide.

ANCHOR

Temporary anchorage is possible for a small boat. Swinging or turning room is limited. Stern lines ashore are a must. Depths, holding and bottom condition unrecorded.

✳ 50° 7.1' N   124° 44.6' W

Kayakers camp above rocky beach.

The tranquil Curme Islands are a kayaker's heaven and provide a good camping base while exploring farther afield. Temporary anchorage for 1 small, shallow-draft boat is also possible. Clustered off the NE shore of Mink Island and now included in the marine park's boundaries, the islands provide flat, grassy spots for camping, rocky ledges and beaches for exploring and an abundance of trees for shade and protection. It would be easy to spend a few restful days here enjoying the simplicity of nature – or until your food and water supplies run low.

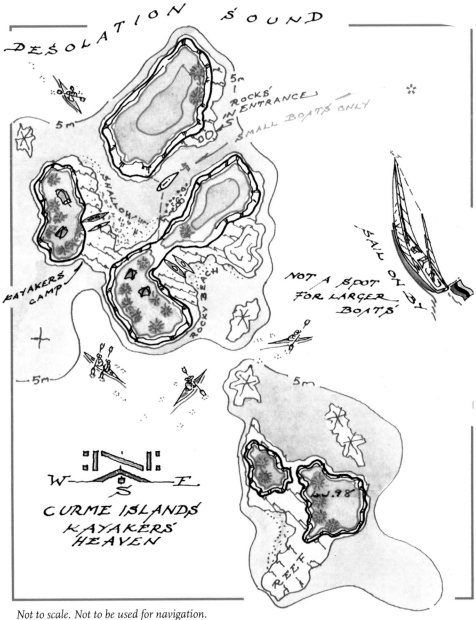

Not to scale. Not to be used for navigation.

5.14 PRIDEAUX HAVEN, MELANIE & DESOLATION SOUND MARINE PARK

Majestic, snow-capped mountains, awe-inspiring vistas and remarkably warm waters lie in wait for the cruising boater voyaging N to the three most popular anchorages in Desolation Sound Marine Park. Prideaux Haven and Melanie and Laura Coves lie snuggled between the mainland and a small string of islands that form a protective barrier from wind and seas in exposed Homfray Channel. The narrow pass between Lucy Point and Oriel Rocks off William Islands provides the only safe entrance into Prideaux Haven.

Spectacular PRIDEAUX HAVEN has become legendary for two diverse reasons: its roomy and well-protected harbour, warm and sheltered waters, open vistas, and choice of cosy nooks and crannies come first and foremost, while its reputation as the "power haven" for a large assortment of luxury yachts in the busy months of July and August takes a close second.

CHARTS 3555. 3312, page 11.

APPROACH: PRIDEAUX HAVEN

From the NW between Scobell and Eveleigh Islands. Head for the parks sign prior to turning to starboard and entering between Lucy Point and the Oriel Rocks.

ANCHOR

All-weather protection may be found throughout the haven. Depths 2 - 12 m (6.5 - 39 ft), holding good over a mud bottom.

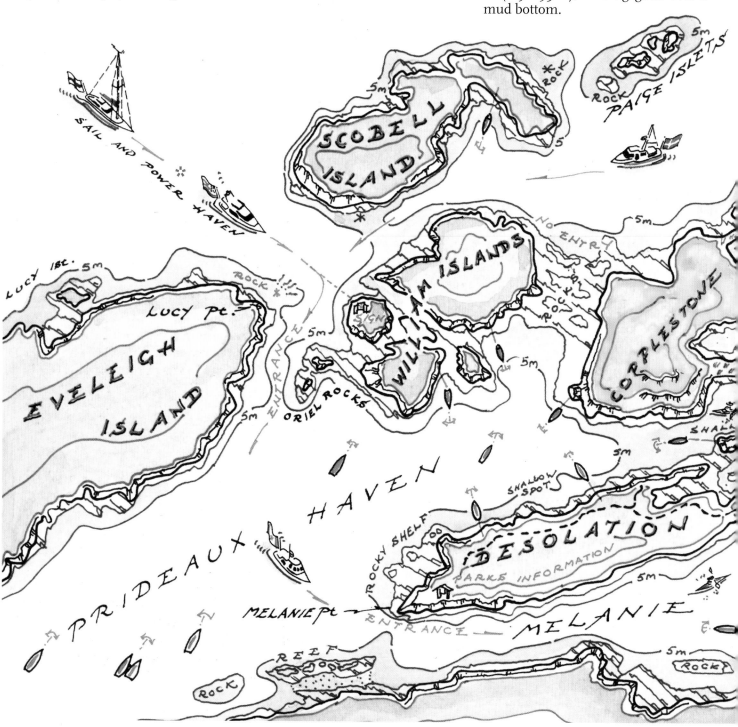

Laura Coves,

APPROACH: Melanie Cove

Melanie Cove branches E from Melanie Point within Prideaux Haven. Note the drying reef at the entrance.

ANCHOR

Good all-weather protection can be found in depths of 4 - 8 m (13 - 26 ft), holding good in mud. Note the drying rocks and mud flats at the head of the cove.

APPROACH: Laura Cove

From the N; enter between the rocky ledge off Copplestone Point and the isolated rock off Copplestone Island. Best approached at LW when the rocks are clearly visible and the isolated rock is just visible.

ANCHOR

Good all-weather protection in depths of 3 - 9 m (10 - 29.5 ft), holding good in mud.

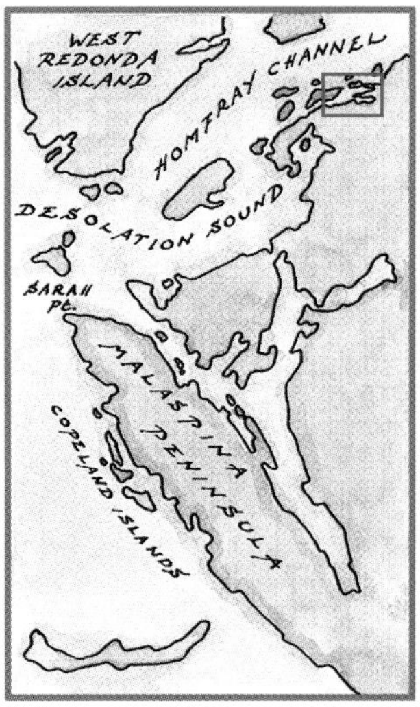

50° 8.8' N 124° 41.1' W

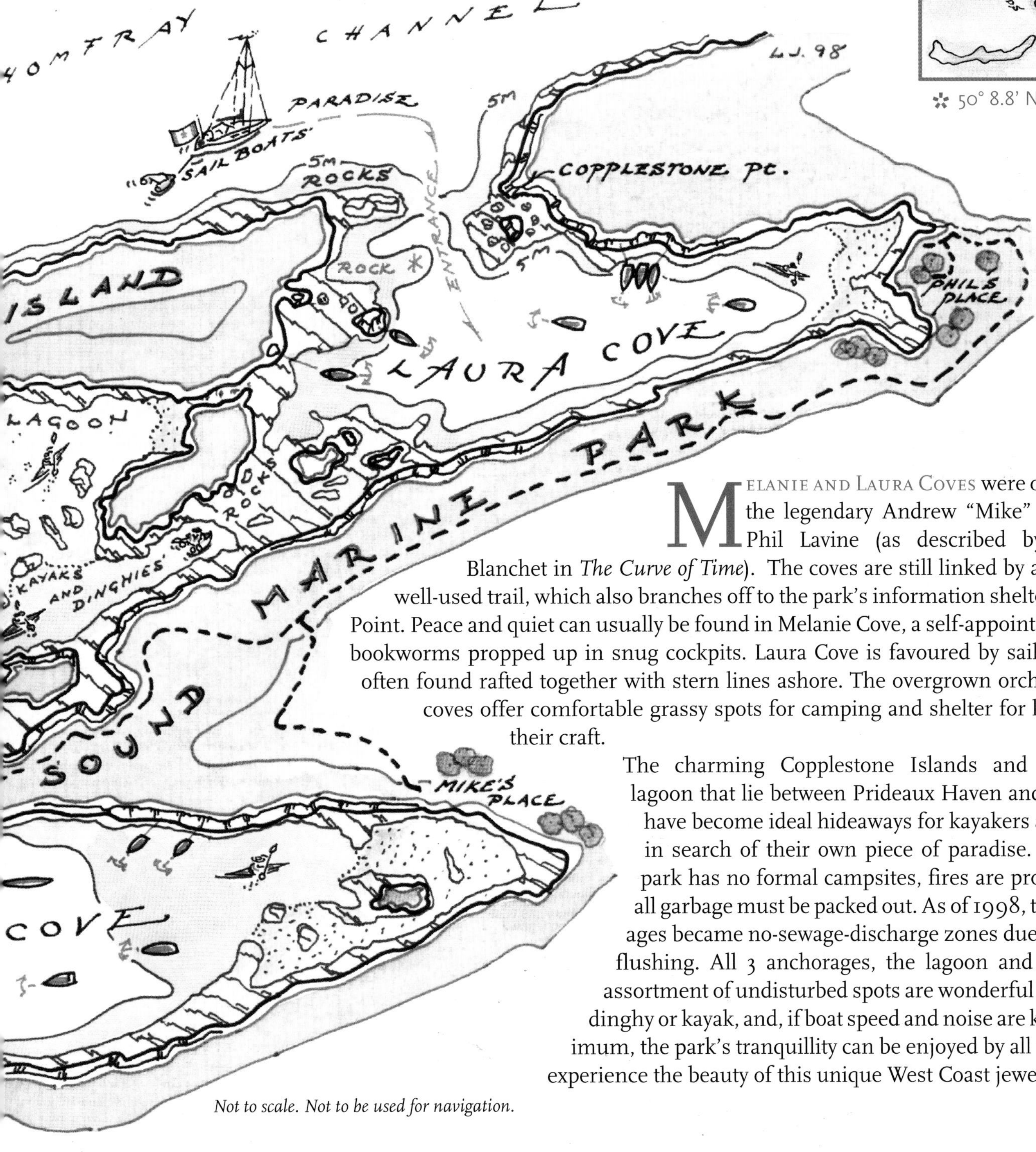

Melanie and Laura Coves were once home to the legendary Andrew "Mike" Shutter and Phil Lavine (as described by M. Wylie Blanchet in *The Curve of Time*). The coves are still linked by an unofficial, well-used trail, which also branches off to the park's information shelter at Melanie Point. Peace and quiet can usually be found in Melanie Cove, a self-appointed retreat for bookworms propped up in snug cockpits. Laura Cove is favoured by sailboat parties, often found rafted together with stern lines ashore. The overgrown orchards in both coves offer comfortable grassy spots for camping and shelter for kayakers and their craft.

The charming Copplestone Islands and warm-water lagoon that lie between Prideaux Haven and Laura Cove have become ideal hideaways for kayakers and campers in search of their own piece of paradise. Because the park has no formal campsites, fires are prohibited, and all garbage must be packed out. As of 1998, these anchorages became no-sewage-discharge zones due to poor tidal flushing. All 3 anchorages, the lagoon and a charming assortment of undisturbed spots are wonderful to explore by dinghy or kayak, and, if boat speed and noise are kept to a minimum, the park's tranquillity can be enjoyed by all who come to experience the beauty of this unique West Coast jewel.

Not to scale. Not to be used for navigation.

5.15 "Pyramid Cove," Roffey Island, Desolation Sound Marine Park

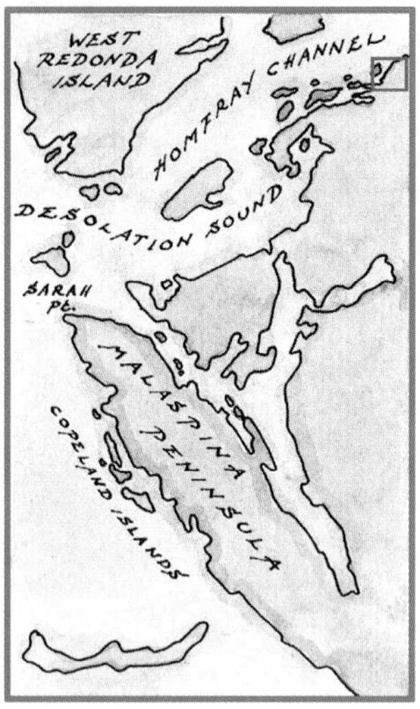

50° 9.2' N 124° 39.8' W

CHARTS 3555. 3312, page 11.

APPROACH

From the NW at LW because the shoreline is fringed by rocky ledges that extend into deep water. An alternative approach is from the S via a "tricky pass" between two prominent rocks.

ANCHOR

Temporary anchorage for 3 - 4 boats, in depths of 2 - 5 m (6.5 - 16 ft). Holding varies over a sand and rock bottom.

Note: The passage to the S is "tricky" because of a reef extending S, from the western rock.

A rocky but undisturbed hideaway for 3 or 4 boats can be found in "Pyramid Cove" (named by us), between the rocky outcrops of Roffey Island and the mainland. Those willing to venture beyond popular Prideaux Haven and navigate a somewhat tricky pass into the cove will be rewarded with quiet and solitude beneath towering mountains. The less restricted entrance into the cove is N of Roffey Island. This anchorage affords reasonable protection from prevailing summer and overnight outflow winds, with limited room to swing. A stern anchor or line ashore is advised.

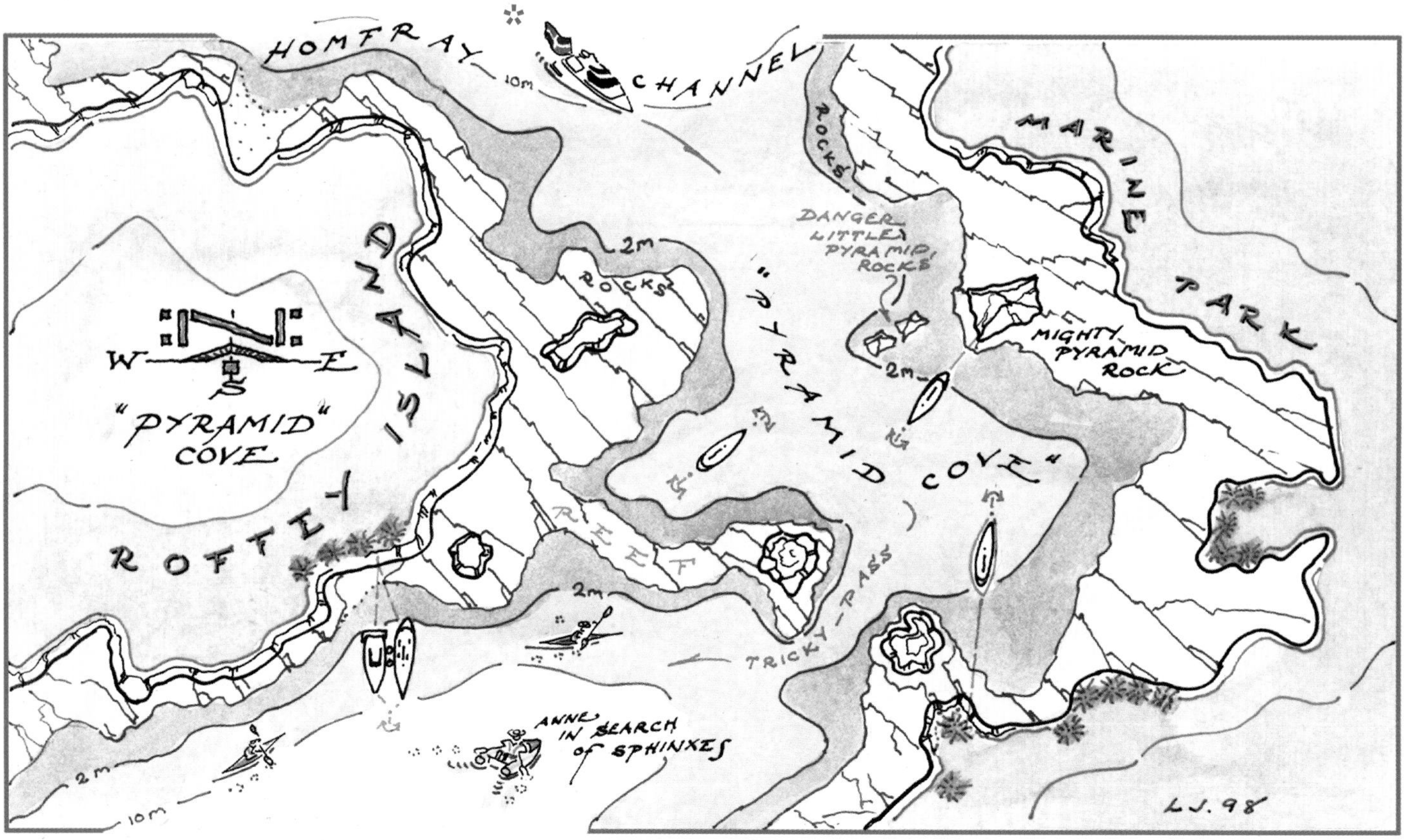

Not to scale. Not to be used for navigation.

Chapter 6
CORTES ISLAND

Driftwood sculptures line the foreshore of Sharkspit Marina Island.

Chapter 6
CORTES ISLAND

TIDES

Canadian Tide and Current Tables, Volume 5
Reference Port: Point Atkinson
Secondary Ports: Twin Islands, Gorge Harbour, Whaletown.

CURRENTS

Note: Although there are no reference and secondary current stations, tidal currents may be encountered at the entrance to Cortes Bay, Gorge Harbour, Von Donop Inlet and Squirrel Cove and at the entrances of tidal lagoons.

WEATHER

Note: No specific reporting station covers this chapter. Summer winds are usually moderate, but they tend to funnel and accelerate through the anchorages. A forecast for a strong northwesterly in Johnstone Strait or the Strait of Georgia (northern half) will equate to strong northwesterly winds over Cortes Island.

Mansons Landing (6.2).

CAUTIONARY NOTES

Three dangers to keep a keen lookout for while circumnavigating the island:

(1) rocks to the N of Three Islets as one approaches Cortes Bay;

(2) the reef off Sutil Point, the southernmost tip of Cortes Island;

(3) the rock off the southern boundary of Manson's Landing Marine Park, especially when covered at HW.

If a quick circumnavigation of the globe will just not fit into this year's busy boating schedule, consider treating yourself to a comfortable one- or two-week cruise around friendly Cortes Island – the heart of the magnificent cruising grounds encompassed in this volume.

Although Cortes is only 16 km (10 mi) across at its widest point and 32 km (20 mi) in length from north to south, its varied coastline offers easy picnic nooks, tranquil coves and safe all-weather anchorages. Excellent provisioning stops, cafés and restaurants are scattered around the island and pride themselves on being able to offer fresh and organic produce in season. White sandy beaches, warm-water swimming, crystal-clear lakes and the gentle pace of island life complete this wonderful package.

Seaplanes operate daily scheduled and chartered flights into Cortes Bay, making it a convenient pickup and drop-off point. The next stop is MANSON'S LANDING MARINE PARK, with its enticing white sandy beaches, saltwater lagoon and warm-water swimming in Hague Lake. Welcoming GORGE HARBOUR MARINA RESORT offers moorage, camping, squeaky-clean showers and a well-stocked general store. The OLD FLOATHOUSE RESTAURANT is a culinary delight and the perfect spot to while away an afternoon in the shade. Shark Spit, just a short hop north, provides an idyllic picnic anchorage and the opportunity to dig for clams, swim or simply laze on the beach.

Whaletown's gruesome history as a whaling station in the late 1800s has been replaced by its importance as a ferry terminal connecting Cortes Island with Quadra and Vancouver Islands. Farther north, three delightful fair-weather anchorages surrounded by a lush recreational reserve can be found in Carrington Bay, and Quartz Bay provides protected overnight anchorage. A quick side trip across Sutil Channel takes you to peaceful Evans Bay and its spectacular mountain views.

Protected Von Donop Inlet, with its beautiful marine park, offers a rich variety of anchorages and is still a firm favourite with cruising boaters who rendezvous to explore the lagoon or relax in the park's calm, sheltered waters. A trail leads from here to Squirrel Cove, the most popular anchorage on Cortes Island due to its proximity to Prideaux Haven and its reputation for abundant, safe anchorage. This large cove often accommodates up to 100 boats in the busy summer months of July and August. The community of Squirrel Cove, about three km (two mi) from the anchorage, has a public wharf, well-stocked general store, post office, B.C. Liquor Store outlet and shower and laundry facilities.

FEATURED DESTINATIONS

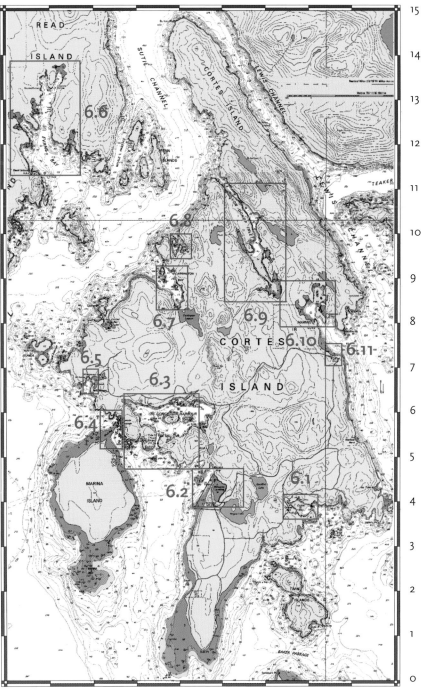

Not to be used for navigation.

6.1   CORTES BAY, CORTES ISLAND

Entrance to Cortes Bay.

❉ 50°3.8' N   124° 55.3' W

Enterprising Mr. Sewell with his local catch at the public wharf.

Distracted skippers beware: the rocks that lie between the northern shoreline and the starboard light at the entrance to Cortes Bay are well covered at HW. Be sure to enter the bay S of the distinctive red-and-white tower.

This large, lovely bay provides a convenient stopping point for boaters journeying N from Comox as well as a gentle introduction to island life for those prepared to venture farther than the public wharf. The friendly wharf manager encourages visitors to tie up for the night, as available space is not taken up by local boats in the summer months. The public wharf also offers a safe alternative to anchoring in the bay.

The Royal Vancouver Yacht Club has an extensive outstation at the head of the bay, and the Seattle Yacht Club sits comfortably on the southern shore. Seaplanes operate scheduled and chartered flights into and out of Cortes Bay, making it a convenient pickup and drop-off point for friends, family and crew.

Stretch your legs and meet the locals with a stroll along Manzanita Road to the BAREFOOT GALLERY, 250-935-6682, which features work by local artists (visitors can also tie up at the private dock on Cortes Bay's northern shore). En route visit Carol and Jim Wilson, who are often able to supply visitors with fresh vegetables and invaluable local information. Guide yourself on a tour of the fascinating WOLF BLUFF CASTLE, handcrafted by local folk artist Karl Triller, who lives next door.

For panoramic views and a little more exercise, take the Squirrel Cove road to Easter Bluff. Pop into LINNEA FARM for organic vegetables, an informal tour or a quiet wander through its beautiful gardens. For idyllic, warm-water swimming, visit HAGUE LAKE, a 30-minute walk along Bartholomew Road. A walk to GUNFLINT LAKE, NW of Cortes Bay, takes about 20 minutes.

Keep a lookout for two local fish boats tied up at the public wharf that sell freshly caught prawns, halibut and salmon. The *SEAN TODD* and the *LEE BJ* are owned and operated by Roger Sewell, a charming fisherman and entrepreneur who delivers his catch of the day to many of the island communities.

Delicious home-baked and fresh-from-the-oven pies, pastries and breads can be specially ordered from Elizabeth Anderson, 250-935-8559. Reasonable advance notice is preferred, and delivery to the public wharf is included in the price.

T'AI LI LODGE, 250-935-6749, just a 5-minute dinghy ride from Cortes Bay, welcomes kayakers and boaters to use its well-managed facilities. Take a nature tour by kayak or enjoy a home-cooked meal. Prebooking is required.

CHARTS

3538. 3312, page 8. 3311, sheet 5.

APPROACH

From the E; enter between the starboard light (red) and the cliffs on the southern shore.

ANCHOR

The bay is well protected, and anchorage is possible throughout. However, the anchorage is far from ideal because the bottom condition of loose sand and mud makes for relatively poor holding. Depths vary.

PUBLIC WHARF

Primarily used by visiting boats in the summer months. Power but no water on the float.

MARINA

The marinas are private.

BOAT LAUNCH

Public, alongside a private float for local boats.

Note: Anchors tend to drag when the winds shift in direction.

Delightful yellow house at the head of Cortes Bay.

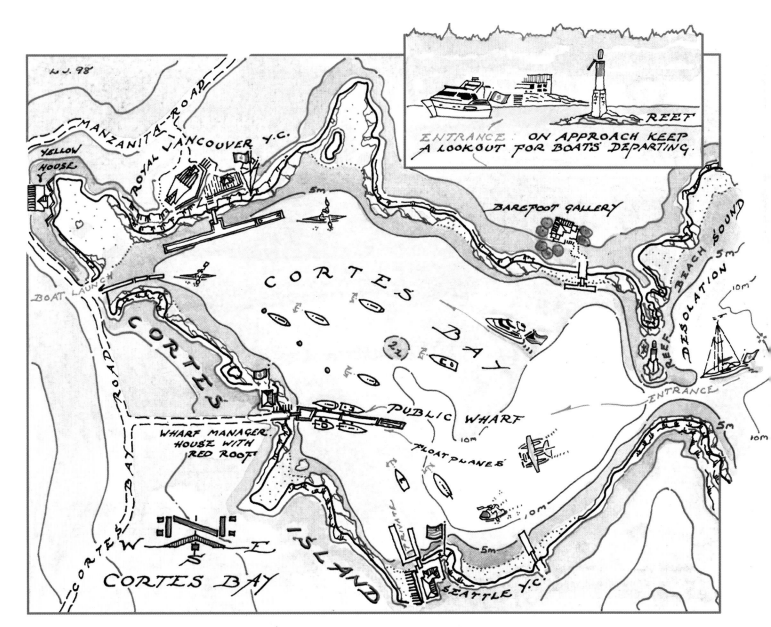

Not to scale. Not to be used for navigation.

6.2　MANSONS LANDING MARINE PARK, CORTES ISLAND

✤ 50° 3.8' N　125° 0.0' W

Approach to Mansons Landing from the SW.

Evening light in Manson Bay.

In settled weather, Mansons Landing Marine Park is the idyllic spot to drop anchor, dig out your bucket and spade and just have fun for a few days. With two inviting bathing spots – saltwater and freshwater – clean, white sandy beaches and magnificent views out to snow-capped mountains, who could wish for more?

Temporary anchorage is possible in Manson Bay, with better protection available behind "Cat & Sheep Islets." Shallow-draft boats wishing to venture into beautiful "Mansons Lagoon" and anchor in the deep basin at the S end should do so with extreme caution and good local knowledge. This saltwater lagoon is also wonderful to explore by dinghy or kayak, and at LW an abundance of clams and mussels can be collected for the pot.

The public wharf is a colourful place, with visiting boats and local runabouts all happily rafted up together. Provisioning is available at CORTES MARKET, 250-935-6626, a 15-20 minute walk up Sutil Point Road. It stocks fresh produce, organic food and hardware and is open 7 days a week from 9 a.m. - 9 p.m. A public fax service is also available, and free delivery of provisions to your boat can be arranged. The post office, QUADRA CREDIT UNION (both open Monday, Wednesday and Friday) and COMMUNITY HALL (check notice board for events) are also located here. CORTES CAFÉ, 250-935-6886, open Monday, Wednesday and Friday from 9 a.m. - 4 p.m., offers outside deck seating, wholesome breakfasts and hearty lunches. THE TACK, 250-935-8555 is open 7 days a week, year-round and serves a good variety of evening specials.

The white sandy beach and clean, warm water of HAGUE LAKE can be reached by taking the Seaford Road route (off Sutil Point Road) or by hiking along the lovely lagoon-side trail to the "Skinny-Dipping Rocks" (named by us), where sunbathing au naturel is favoured. Alternatively laze on the family beach or take an exhilarating swim to the big smooth rocks on the lake's eastern shore. Because Hague Lake provides drinking water for lakeside residents, motorboats are forbidden, the use of soap or shampoo is prohibited and dogs are not allowed on the beach or in the water.

CHARTS 3538. 3313, sheet 5.

APPROACH
From the SW, maintaining a safe distance from the Cortes shore to clear the rocks off the park's SW boundary.

ANCHOR
In Manson Bay. Good protection from NW seas. Open to the SW and summer southerly afternoon winds and sea. However, these winds are generally light and diminish in the early evening. Depths 4 - 12 m (13 - 39 ft), holding good in sand.

PUBLIC WHARF
Generally occupied by a mixture of local and visiting boats.

BOAT LAUNCH
Public and tidal into the lagoon.

Note: Manson Bay is a floatplane operations zone with a designated float at the public wharf.

The lagoon is a magical place.

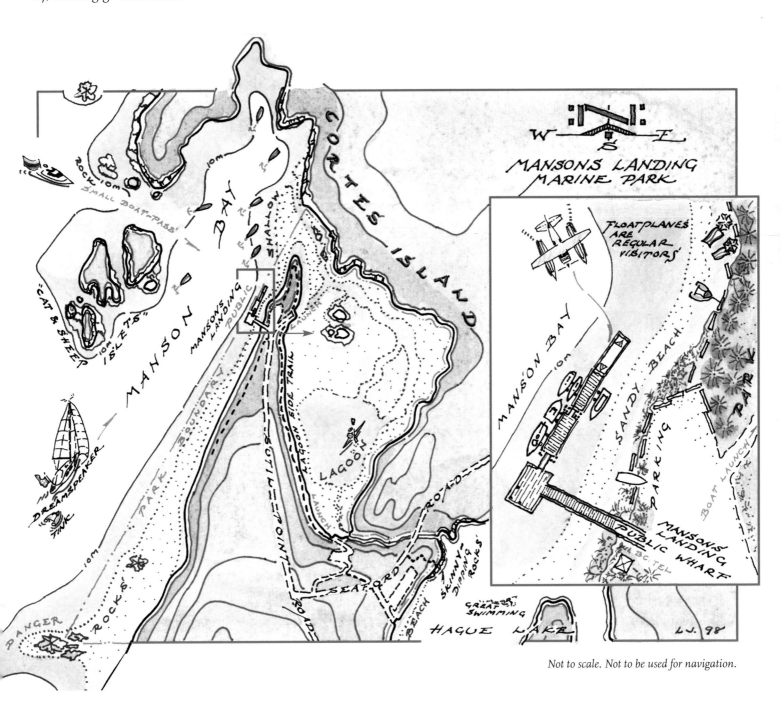

Not to scale. Not to be used for navigation.

6.3   GORGE HARBOUR, CORTES ISLAND

✳ 50° 4.6' N   125° 0.8' W

The entrance to Gorge Harbour.

Lazing in the cockpit on a sunny afternoon.

The appropriately named Guide Islets mark the bottleneck entrance to The Gorge, with its high, steep cliffs depicting First Nations rock paintings. Be sure to leave Tide Islet to starboard on entering Gorge Harbour, and keep in mind that tides can run up to 4 knots through this narrow pass.

The harbour offers good anchorage, with some secluded bights and a variety of islets and coves to explore. The large, well-appointed GORGE HARBOUR MARINA RESORT offers moorage, fuel, wonderfully clean shower facilities with no time limit (guests only during peak periods) and a 24-hour laundromat.

The resort is an ideal base for kayakers to set up camp, and tent sites in the old apple orchard come equipped with picnic tables and fire pits. Kayak rentals, RV camping and guest rooms are also available. The well-stocked store carries a good selection of basic groceries, fresh produce, excellent frozen foods and freshly baked goods. A small deli section is handy for picnic items. Marine hardware, charts, fishing licenses, propane and a public fax service are also available.

The lovely OLD FLOATHOUSE RESTAURANT, 250-935-6433 or 935-6631 (summer only), with its shaded deck and waterfront view, was transported from a logging camp near Kingcome Inlet 15 years ago. Today it is noted for its friendly service, excellent selection of unique dishes and choice display of local artwork. This is the perfect spot to while away a few hours before retiring to the cockpit for an après-lunch nap. The restaurant is licensed and open for lunch, dinner and Sunday brunch. Reservations are recommended.

Hikes from Gorge Harbour include a 2.4 km (1.5 mi) energetic walk to historic Whaletown (see page 81) and a pleasant stroll through nearby SMALL PARK on The Gorge to the rocky bluffs. Scooter, mountain bike and car rentals are available at the resort, and the "CORTES CONNECTION" operates a minibus service to Campbell River 5 times a week. (Check the schedule at the resort store.) Mitlenatch Island tours and Cortes Island nature walks are offered by naturalist-guide George Sirk, 250-935-6926, co-author of *Birds of Cortes and Mitlenatch*.

Freshly baked pastries, deliciously decadent Viennese cakes and good espresso can be found at TRUDE'S CAFÉ on Whaletown Road, just a short walk up from the Gorge Harbour Marina Resort.

CHARTS

3538. 3312, page 19. 3311, sheet 5.

APPROACH

From the S. The narrow entrance pass is conspicuous below the towering cliffs on the western side located to the N of the Guide Islets. Leave Tide Islet to the E.

ANCHOR

There are many nooks and bights throughout the harbour, but most boats anchor off the marina in the NW corner. Depths vary, holding good in a mix of mud and sand.

PUBLIC WHARF

A single float lies along the northern shore. Moorage space is usually taken up by local boats.

MARINA

The Gorge Harbour Marina Resort, 604-935-6433, has extensive visitor moorage.

BOAT LAUNCH

At the marina.

FUEL

At the marina.

Note: Tidal currents up to 4 knots may be encountered in the entrance pass.

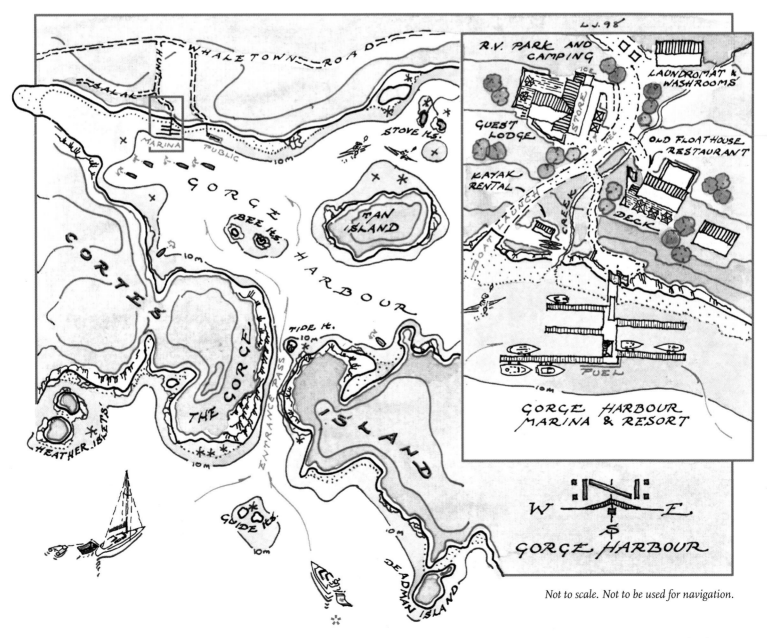

Not to scale. Not to be used for navigation.

6.4 UGANDA PASSAGE, SHARK SPIT, MARINA ISLAND

✴ 50° 5.0' N 125° 2.0' W

CHARTS

3538. 3312, page 19. 3311, sheet 5.

APPROACH

Either from the S off Heather Islets or from the W out of Sutil Channel. Uganda Passage is best transited prior to HW, when the spit is still visible.

ANCHOR

On a shallow shingle ledge to the E of Shark Spit. The spit offers good protection from NW seas while exposed at LW. Depths of 2 - 6 m (6.5 - 19.5 ft), holding good in mud and shingle.

Shark Spit looking out to Uganda Passage.

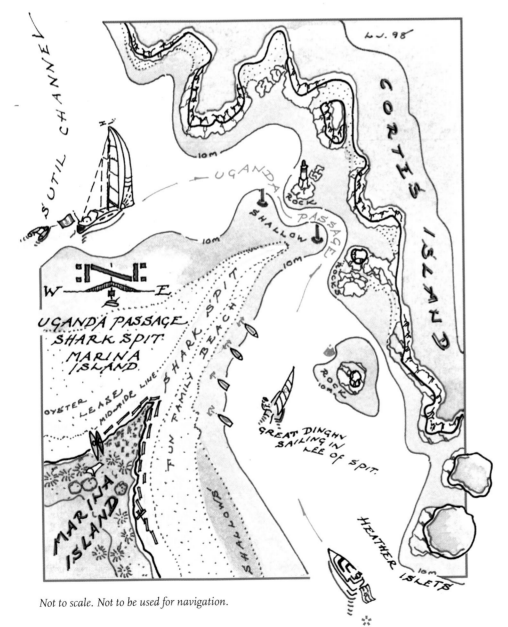

Not to scale. Not to be used for navigation.

The rather narrow and sinuous Uganda Passage is well marked as it twists around the shallows off Shark Spit and the scattered rocks and shoals off western Cortes Island. The long, fin-shaped gravel-and-shell beach that forms Shark Spit extends out from the northern tip of Marina Island, creating an idyllic picnic anchorage with crystal-clear waters and mountain views. Many relaxing hours can be spent swimming, digging clams, beachcombing or collecting driftwood for the design of beach encampments and sculptures. Excellent dinghy sailing can be found in the lee of the spit, and walks to the tip of the spit at LW can prove exhilarating when boats navigating Uganda Passage pass closely by.

Whaletown's charming little Post Office.

CHARTS

3538. 3312, page 19. 3311, sheet 5.

APPROACH

Either from the S midway between the starboard (red) buoy and the Cortes shore or from the W between the same buoy and the porthand light.

ANCHOR

NE of the porthand day beacon off the public wharf. Depths 2 - 6 m (6.5 - 19.5 ft). Holding good in thick, sticky mud.

PUBLIC WHARF

Well used by local boats.

Note: Whaletown Bay is the terminus for the ferry from Heriot Bay, Quadra Island. Stay well clear of its channel and terminal.

✳ 50° 6.2' N   125° 3.3' W

A regular ferry service to and from Heriot Bay on Quadra Island operates from sleepy Whaletown Bay, well worth a visit if your craving for a double-scoop cone cannot be put aside. Temporary anchorage is available at the head of the bay, and moorage at the public wharf is possible if you can find a spot between the local runabouts or are prepared to raft up.

The family-run WHALETOWN GEN-ERAL STORE, 250-935-6562, above the wharf carries delicious ice cream flavours as well as basic provisions, hardware, propane, fishing licenses and local gifts and cards. Freshly baked bread and pastries are delivered to the store every Friday, and vegetables and fresh produce arrive twice weekly (Tuesdays and Fridays).

A short walk up Whaletown Road will take you to the charming little post office (open Monday, Wednesday and Friday) and mailbox, the local library and the picturesque white mission church, ST. JOHN THE BAPTIST. A public notice board listing local events can be found at the store and the post office.

In season, and if you are in luck, juicy blackberries can be found nearby, so take a container just in case.

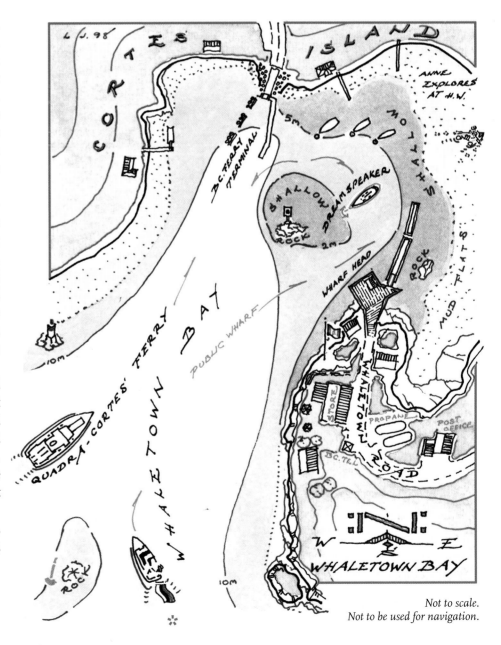

Not to scale.
Not to be used for navigation.

6.6 EVANS BAY, READ ISLAND

CHARTS 3538. 3312, page 19.

APPROACH
From the SE.

EVANS BAY: Has numerous small coves to anchor in, all temporary because they are exposed to the S. However, in prevailing northwesterly winds, they form snug overnight anchorages. Depth, holding and bottom condition vary.

✳ 50° 11.0' N 125° 4.3' W

View out to Sutil Channel from the public wharf.

The temporary anchorages along the eastern shore of Read Island, S of Evans Bay, are currently occupied by fish farms (as of 1998), although the peaceful nooks and coves scattered around Evans Bay remain relatively lease-free. All the anchorages in the bay are open to the S.

The small public wharf offers good moorage and access to the island's main road, which connects the bay with Surge Narrows public wharf and general store, if you're up for an energetic hike or mountain bike ride (see page 145). The cabins behind the wharf are for sale, and the oyster farm is abandoned (as of 1998), but you can pop into the small dock office to sign the visitors' log book and read a few interesting tales.

A charming 2-boat anchorage N of the public wharf provides spectacular mountain views, a lovely pink gravel beach, easy access to the main road and delightful LAMBERT'S BEACH PARK. There are islets and rocky ledges to explore, and although the bay loses its light early the sunset's afterglow creates a wonderful backdrop to this tranquil spot.

The property surrounding Bird Cove is privately owned, although the drying mud flats at the head of the cove are wonderfully peaceful and fun to explore by dinghy or kayak at HW. A more sheltered anchorage can be found N of Bird Cove, tucked behind 3 charming islets, and 2 other temporary spots are available at the head of Evans Bay in either the western or the eastern arm.

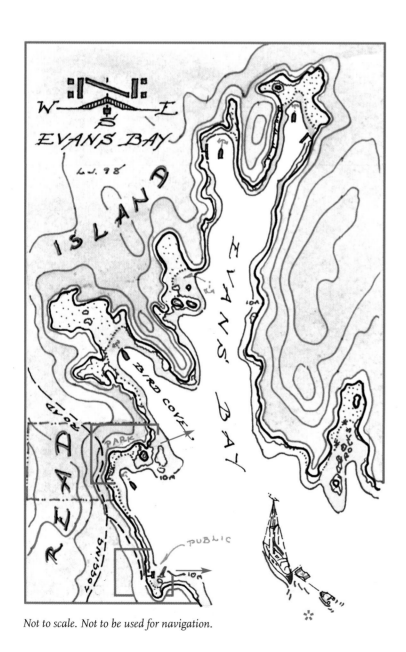

Not to scale. Not to be used for navigation.

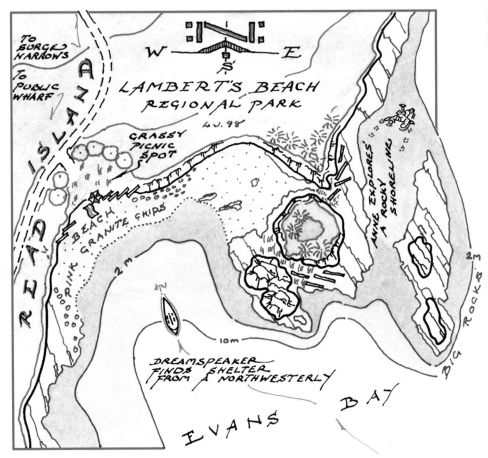

To SURGE NARROWS

To PUBLIC WHARF

READ ISLAND

W N E S

LAMBERT'S BEACH REGIONAL PARK

ω.J. 98

GRASSY PICNIC SPOT

BEACH GRANITE CHIPS

DRINK

2m

10m

ANNE EXPLORES A ROCKY SHORELINE

2M

BIG ROCKS

DREAMSPEAKER FINDS SHELTER FROM A NORTHWESTERLY

EVANS BAY

Not to scale. Not to be used for navigation.

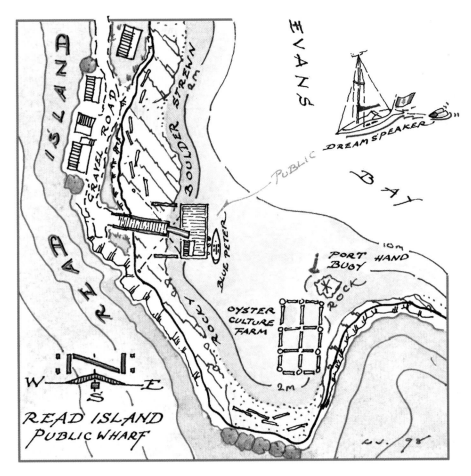

READ ISLAND

EVANS

GRAVEL ROAD

BOULDER STREWN 2M

EVANS BAY

PUBLIC DREAMSPEAKER

2M

BLUE PETER

PORT HAND BUOY

ROCK

10m

OYSTER CULTURE FARM

2M

W N E S

READ ISLAND PUBLIC WHARF

ω.J. 98

Not to scale. Not to be used for navigation.

Delightful Lambert's Beach Park.

LAMBERT'S BEACH PARK, READ ISLAND: A small park and picnic spot fringed by a rocky islet make for a reasonable anchorage with good protection from the NW. Depths 4 - 6 m (13 - 19.5 ft), holding good over a gravel and mud bottom.

READ ISLAND PUBLIC WHARF: A small public wharf lies in the SW corner of Evans Bay. Well used by visiting boats in the summer.

Approach to Evan Bay public wharf.

6.7 CARRINGTON BAY, CORTES ISLAND

‡ 50° 8.8' N   125° 1.0' W

CHARTS 3538. 3312, page 19.

APPROACH

From the NW. Jane Islet may be passed via the northern channel or by the southern passage, but watch for the unmarked rocks that lie due S of the islet.

ANCHOR

Carrington Bay offers good protection from the SE but is relatively open to prevailing northwesterly winds. Protection from the NW can be found behind Jane Islet or between "Lucy & Ronnie Islets" (named by us) and the Cortes shore. Depths 8 - 12 m (26 - 39 ft), holding fair over a rock and mud bottom.

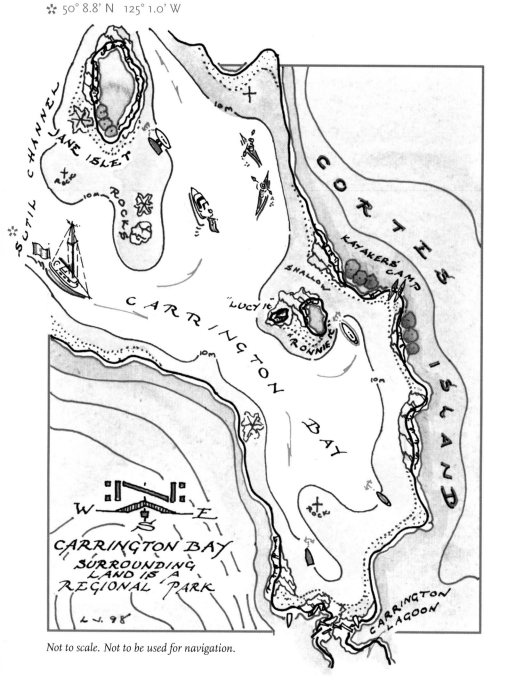

Not to scale. Not to be used for navigation.

Surrounded by a provincial recreational reserve, 3 delightful fair-weather anchorages await the intrepid explorer willing to take a detour into Carrington Bay on Cortes Island's western shoreline.

The 2 ideal spots to drop your anchor are behind "Lucy and Ronnie Islets" (named by us) or Jane Islet, as they afford some protection from the northwesterly winds known to spring up in the late afternoon or early evening. The 3rd anchorage, at the head of the bay, is the most exposed, although in settled weather it provides easy access to Carrington Lagoon, which is fun to explore by dinghy or kayak if you don't mind a tricky portage over piled-up driftwood. Carrington Bay is also known for its glorious sunsets.

Carrington Bay is fun to explore.

CHARTS 3538. 3312, page 19.

APPROACH

From the NW out of Sutil Channel. The passage into the inner anchorage between the peninsula and the islets is deep.

ANCHOR

Good all-weather protection can be found in this snug anchorage. Depths 8 - 14 m (26 - 46 ft), holding good in mud.

✳ 50° 9.7' N 125° 0.3' W

If you need a little more protection than Carrington Bay offers in a strong northwesterly, take a short hop N to Quartz Bay. Sheltered anchorage is possible behind the islet and drying isthmus in the bay's westernmost arm. An oyster farm occupies the NW end of the arm, and private homes look down from the eastern shoreline, making the anchorage more suitable for a quick overnight stop than an extended stay.

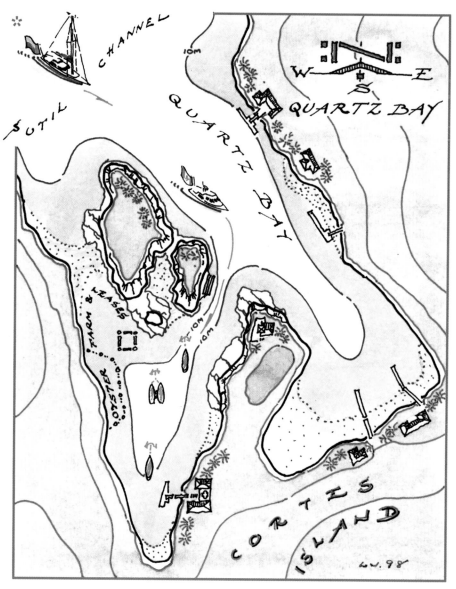

Not to scale. Not to be used for navigation.

6.9   HÀTHAYIM MARINE PARK, VON DONOP INLET, CORTES ISLAND

✳ 50° 11.0' N   124° 58.8' W

CHARTS 3538.3312 page 19

APPROACH

From the NW. The most conspicuous landmark is the park's sign on the NE shore. Although the entrance appears narrow and shallow, there is more than adequate width (50 m / 164 ft) and depth (4.3 m / 14 ft) in its narrowest part. However, danger lurks in the form of a rock with less than 2 m (6.5 ft) of water above it, a rock only visible at LW. Favour the western shoreline to clear.

ANCHOR

Good all-weather anchorage exists throughout the length of the inlet in depths of 4 - 12 m (13 - 39 ft), holding good in sticky mud. There are two excellent anchoring options.

Von Donop Inlet is almost 5 km (3 mi) in length and rather narrow in spots as it twists and turns, almost dividing Cortes Island. B.C. Parks, in partnership with the Klahoose First Nation, declared the inlet and surrounding lands a marine park in 1994 and preserved this magical spot for all to enjoy.

Although sheltered Hàthayim Marine Park can become crowded in the summer months, it still offers a rich variety of nooks and crannies to anchor in as well as peaceful lagoons to explore and forested trails to hike.

The most popular anchorage is at the head of the inlet, where a trail leads to Squirrel Cove and the shaded deck of MARILYN'S SALMON restaurant (see page 88). The small lagoon is enchanting to explore at HW.

"Lagoon Falls" (named by us), just E of the inlet's narrow entrance, is a favourite rendezvous at HW as dinghies and kayaks get ready to enter Von Donop Lagoon. Passage into the lagoon at any other time is hindered by swift currents and a profusion of boulders.

"Buccaneer Cove" (named by us), one of the most serene anchorages in the inlet, has a shallow bar at its entrance, dries at the southern end at LW and can only fit 2 - 3 boats comfortably. Once settled, you could spend a few blissful days walking the trails, lazing in the cockpit or dining al fresco at the two lovely picnic spots provided. The picnic table at the entrance to the cove comes with an excellent view of the inlet.

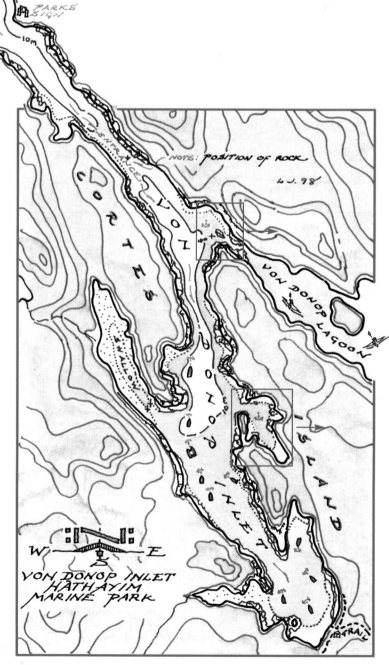

Not to scale. Not to be used for navigation.

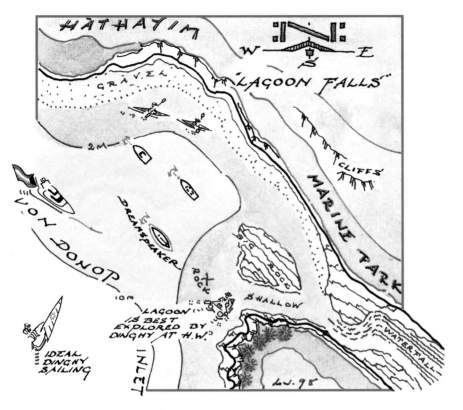

Not to scale. Not to be used for navigation.

ANCHOR

"Lagoon Falls" (named by us)
Just inside the entrance. Anchor in depths of 3 - 9 m (10 - 29.5 ft).

Note: Passage into the lagoon is only possible at HW by dinghy or kayak.

Lagoon Falls sparkle on a sunny day.

ANCHOR

"Buccaneer Cove" (named by us)
On the eastern shore midway down the inlet. A bar guards the entrance, charted at 1.8 m (6 ft). Depths of 2-3m (6.5 - 10 ft).

Note: The wind funnels and accelerates throughout the inlet.

Two 'buccaneers' ships' in "Buccaneer Cove".

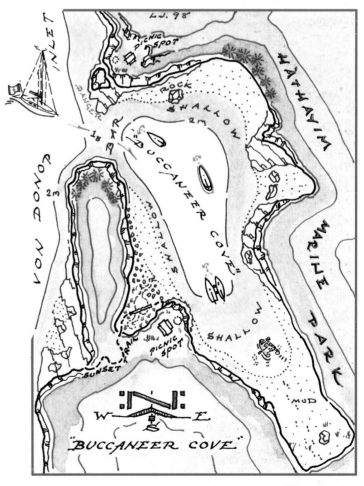

Not to scale. Not to be used for navigation.

6.10 Squirrel Cove, Cortes Island

50° 7.7' N 124° 55.1' W

Entrance to Squirrel Cove anchorage.

A not-too-busy September day.

Be sure to enter the anchorage of Squirrel Cove W of Protection Island, as the eastern passage is strewn with rocks and boulders. This large and protected cove can accommodate up to 100 boats in the busy summer months, with its northern portion being the most popular. Safe alternative anchorage can be found W of Protection Island. If you are determined to find a little more privacy and are prepared to keep a sharp lookout for rocks, tuck into the NE end of Protection Island. "Squirrel Cove Lagoon" provides entertainment on an ebbing tide as dinghies and kayaks prepare to shoot the tidal rapids at the mouth of the lagoon. The small islet in the centre of the cove is also interesting to explore, but visitors should be aware that property surrounding the cove is either private or part of the Klahoose First Nation Reserve.

For many years, cruising boaters and visitors to Squirrel Cove were able to enjoy a special treat thanks to Bill Rendall and his famous cinnamon buns. Although Bill and his small, rustic bakery are no longer found in the cove, his legend will certainly live on.

A trip to Marilyn's Salmon, the only restaurant in the anchorage, is well worth the short adventure, where dining is mainly al fresco on a wooden deck overlooking the cove. Equipped with her own smokehouse, Marilyn serves traditional Native food and organizes special seafood feasts, barbecued-salmon dinners and cultural entertainment on Friday and Saturday evenings. She also offers breakfast, local baked goods, ice cream and special coffees. Call her on VHF channel 68 or at 250-830-7059 for takeout orders and reservations. The restaurant is open in July and August only, 7 days a week, 8 a.m. - 8 p.m.

Stretch your legs or work up an appetite with a pleasant half-hour walk. The trail begins at Marilyn's Salmon and ends at the head of Von Donop Inlet and Hàthayim Marine Park (see page 86).

CHARTS 3555. 3312, page 10.

APPROACH

From the SE, having given the starboard day marker off Boulder Point a wide berth. A sign indicating the Klahoose First Nation is a conspicuous landmark that overlooks the entrance.

ANCHOR

Good all-weather protection can be found throughout the cove. However, chop from SE seas does penetrate into the anchorage. Both northwesterly and southeasterly winds whistle through. Depths of 4 - 14 m (13 - 46 ft), holding good in sticky mud.

Great views from the community of Squirrel Cove. (6.11)

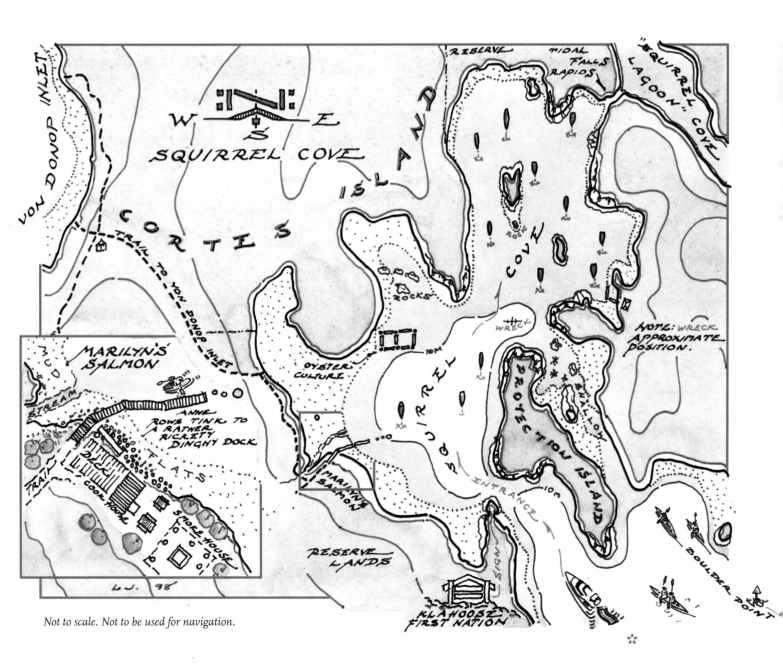

Not to scale. Not to be used for navigation.

6.11 COMMUNITY OF SQUIRREL COVE, CORTES ISLAND

✳ 50° 7.2' N 124° 54.6' W

CHARTS 3555. 3312, page 10.

APPROACH

From the NE, the Squirrel Cove General Store and community buildings being the most conspicuous landmarks.

ANCHOR

If the public wharf has no available moorage, temporary anchorage can be found to the NW of the wharf. Depths of 4 - 6 m (13 - 19.5 ft), holding good in mud. For all-weather anchorage, see 6.10 (page 88).

PUBLIC WHARF

Extensive moorage is available at 2 floats, but they are very busy and used as temporary moorage by islanders and visitors going ashore for provisions.

Note: The convenient dinghy dock located W of the public wharf allows quick access to the community but is surrounded by mud at LW.

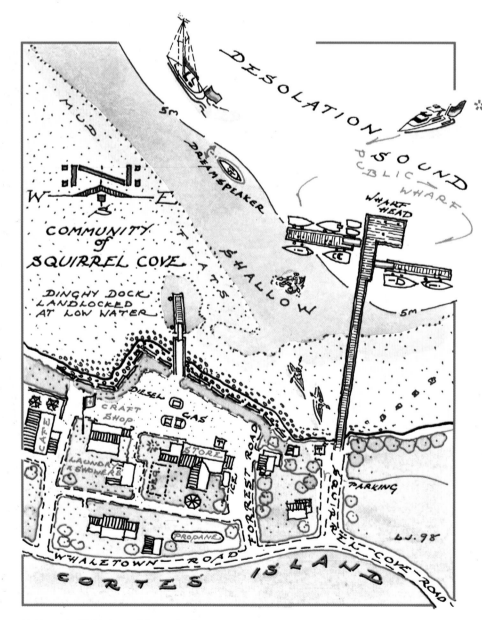

Not to scale. Not to be used for navigation.

The public wharf and SQUIRREL COVE GENERAL STORE (open year-round, 250-935-6327), which houses the post office and a B.C. LIQUOR STORE outlet, are located at the entrance to Squirrel Cove but are at least 3 km (2 mi) from the anchorage at the head of the cove. The well-stocked store carries everything you might need, including freshly baked "Cortes Island Bread," fresh and organic produce, propane, ice, charts and an excellent variety of hardware. It even offers a fax machine and film-developing service. Laundry and shower facilities are available, and garbage disposal ($3 per bag) is provided at the end of the public wharf.

The CORTES CRAFT SHOP, a co-op of island artists and craftspeople, carries a wonderful variety of unique handmade works. CAFÉ SUZANNE, 250-935-6866, reputed for its eclectic bistro food, is open daily throughout the summer, and you can watch the boat traffic entering and exiting Squirrel Cove from its shaded deck. It is licensed and often requires dinner reservations in peak season.

Chapter 7

THE
REDONDA
ISLANDS

Roscoe Bay, a landlocked paradise at LW

Chapter 7
THE REDONDA ISLANDS

Breathtaking Toba Inlet.

TIDES

Canadian Tide and Current Tables, Volume 5
Reference Port: Pt. Atkinson
Secondary Ports: Prideaux Haven, Channel Islands

CURRENTS

Although there are no reference and secondary current stations covering the waters in this chapter, tidal currents stream through the inlets and channels at rates of 1 - 2 knots. Currents of 3 knots may occur at the northern entrance to Waddington Channel.

WEATHER

No specific reporting station covers this chapter. Summer winds tend to be moderate and take their directions from the inlets or channels through which they funnel. Nightly outflow winds can wake one in the early hours but are usually absent by daybreak.

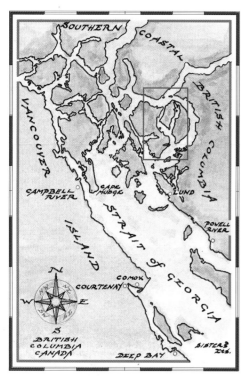

CAUTIONARY NOTES

Anchoring is in predominantly deep water with a stern line ashore. Be well experienced in this technique. If you need direction, ask some of the old salts for advice.

The steep-sided inlets and channels create barriers for both VHF and cellular coverage, which are poor in Waddington Channel, Pendrell Sound and Toba Inlet and nonexistent in Roscoe Bay.

If you are in search of cascading waterfalls, freshwater lakes, warm-water swimming, energetic hikes and the serene beauty of coastal wilderness, then this chapter is for you. From spectacular "Cassel Lake Falls" to the warm waters of Pendrell Sound and the wild beauty of Toba Inlet, these often bypassed spots have so much to offer the more enterprising boater and kayaker.

Teakerne Arm Marine Park offers the perfect picnic stop and a chance to stretch your legs and indulge in a warm-water wash and brush-up in Cassel Lake. Refuge Cove, a major provisioning stop, welcomes boaters with reasonably priced moorage, provisions and friendly island hospitality and service. Regular seaplane service is also available from here.

The surprise anchorage in Roscoe Bay Marine Park turns into a tranquil, land-locked paradise at LW. The warm waters of Black Lake offer excellent bathing and diving rocks and a fun day of paddling for those energetic souls willing to portage their dinghies or kayaks along the well-worn trail.

The warmest water can be found in Pendrell Sound, designated a shellfish reserve as it provides the perfect location for producing Pacific oyster spat. Visiting boaters are requested to maintain a wake-free speed within the sound. Serene "Oyster Cove" (named by us) provides protected anchorage, a delightful picnic spot with a view atop a rocky bluff and an enticing saltwater lagoon just waiting to be explored.

Breathtaking Toba Inlet lures you to its head with the promise of ice fields, roaring waterfalls and open vistas – and you won't be disappointed. The easiest way to explore the inlet is by setting up base at the TOBA WILDERNEST MARINA & RESORT at the mouth of the inlet, where rustic charm, the convenience of modern facilities and the welcoming hospitality of Ed and Mary Schlote can be enjoyed to the full.

Finally charming Walsh Cove Marine Park, the last protected anchorage in Waddington Channel, offers you the opportunity to hunt for hidden petroglyphs, fine warm-water swimming and great views of the East Redonda Mountains.

FEATURED DESTINATIONS

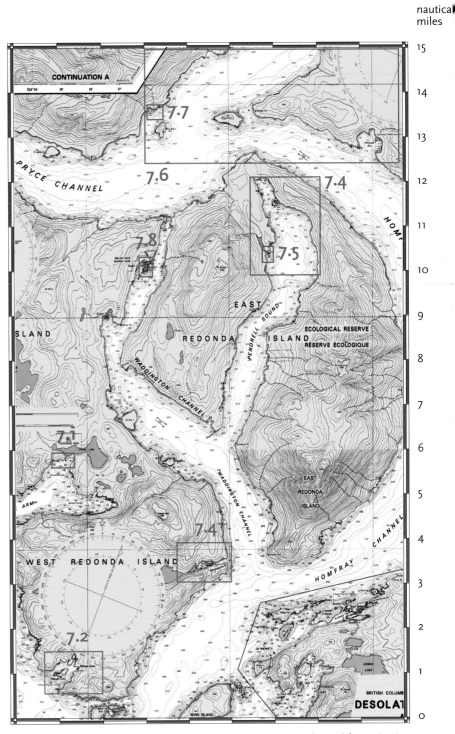

Not to be used for navigation.

7.1 "Cassel Lake Falls," Teakerne Arm Marine Park, W Redonda Islani

✷ 50° 11.7' N 124° 50.9' W

Anchoring is possible along the N.W. shore.

A lucky boat beside the waterfall.

The main attractions of Teakerne Arm Marine Park on West Redonda Island include the invitingly warm waters of Cassel Lake and its spectacular, cascading falls.

This is the perfect place to picnic and treat yourself to a freshwater wash and brush-up. A full-pressure shower under "Cassel Lake Falls" is for the adventurous only, and good footwear is advised as the rocks are very slippery. For an energetic hike and a more relaxing bath, follow the well-worn trail that leads from the dinghy dock to a ledge of smooth, clean bathing rocks on the lake's southern shore. A helpful haul-out rope has also been placed here for your convenience.

It's difficult to anchor close to the falls as water is very deep right up to the rocky shoreline. The first lucky boats can tie up to 2 rings provided on the eastern side, and stern-to anchorage is possible in the popular nook SW of the falls or along part of the SE shoreline, though both are subject to afternoon chop. A more protected 2-boat anchorage can be found farther W of the falls, and kayakers can beach their craft and set up camp atop the rocky spine or the dry grassy spots farther behind.

The southern shoreline of Teakerne Arm affords splendid sunsets, and rafting alongside a log boom is always acceptable, but be prepared to untie at a moment's notice and at any hour of the day or night. It should be noted that although log booms appear to be sturdy and are rather tempting, they are extremely dangerous to walk or play on. Temporary, fair-weather anchorage can also be found in Eastern Teakerne Arm or at the head of Talbot Cove, but take care to avoid the drying rock near the centre of the cove.

CHARTS 3538. 3312, page 8.

APPROACH

From the SW. The park's sign on the rocky promontory W of the waterfall is the most conspicuous landmark.

ANCHOR

Temporary anchorage can be found along the NW shore with a stern line ashore. The deep water shelves rapidly to shallow water. Depth, holding and bottom condition vary.

Note: Not recommended as an all-weather anchorage because Teakerne Arm tends to funnel northwesterly and southeasterly winds and chop into its upper reaches. In settled summer weather, though, afternoon winds tend to die off in the early evening, leaving glassy water for a peaceful night.

Rafting alongside a log boom.

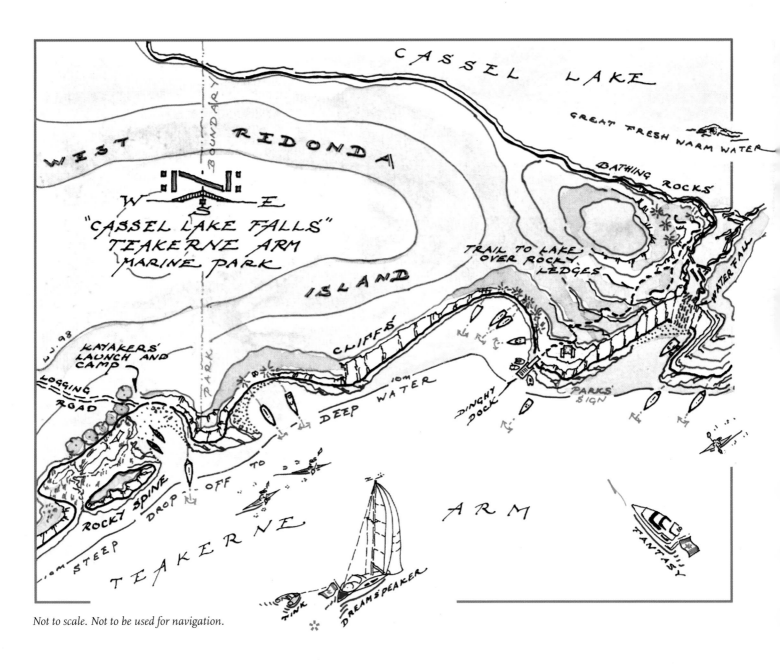

Not to scale. Not to be used for navigation.

7.2   REFUGE COVE, W REDONDA ISLAND

The community of Refuge Cove, complete with General Store.

❉ 50° 6.9' N   124° 51.2' W

A friendly pioneering charm prevails.

Welcoming Refuge Cove is cooperatively owned and operated and certainly lives up to its name. This friendly, enterprising community happily accommodates many visiting boats in the summer months and then leads a quiet, secluded life the rest of the year.

Reasonably priced moorage is available at the public wharf and marina, both operated by the GENERAL STORE. Water and power are available on the docks, and shower and laundry facilities are located at the top of the ramp. The well-stocked store carries fresh and frozen produce, baked goods, ice, propane, charts, books and fishing supplies. It also houses a B.C. LIQUOR STORE outlet and post office (mail drop and pickup on Monday, Wednesday and Friday). Open June 1 - Sept. 15, 9a.m. - 5p.m. (9 - 6 July and August).

Don't pass up the opportunity to sample a delicious, freshly made hamburger at THE HAMBURGER STAND or a frothy Starbucks cappuccino while visiting the cove. UPCOAST SUMMERS stocks a carefully selected medley of crafts and specialty books, and its café serves pastries and coffee on the shaded deck overlooking the cove.

Deep anchorage is possible in the cove opposite the wharf and marina or in a more protected minicove to the N, but watch for 2 rocks at its narrow entrance.

Refuge Cove is a popular rendezvous for cruising boaters and a convenient location to pick up or drop off family, friends and crew because seaplanes operate regular chartered and scheduled flights to and from Vancouver and Campbell River (see page 168).

Note: Fuel is available after Sept. 15 on Mondays, Wednesdays and Fridays 1pm-3pm.

CHARTS 3538. 3555. 3312, page 10.

APPROACH

From the SW. Deep-water channels exist to both the N and the S of the unnamed island in the centre of the cove.

ANCHOR

To the W of the public wharf and marina. Depth is approximately 15 m (49 ft), holding good in mud. Alternative anchorage may be found at the head of the cove, but many local boats occupy this spot during the summer.

PUBLIC WHARF & MARINA

The wharf and marina offer extensive visitor moorage. Power and water are available. Moorage and the collection of fees are administered by the GENERAL STORE. 250-935-6659

FUEL

Available from the float operated by the general store.

Note: In summer the public wharf and marina are a hive of activity. Anchoring off is fine. Rumours of "old logging equipment fouling the bottom" are, locals say, untrue.

Approaching the marina.

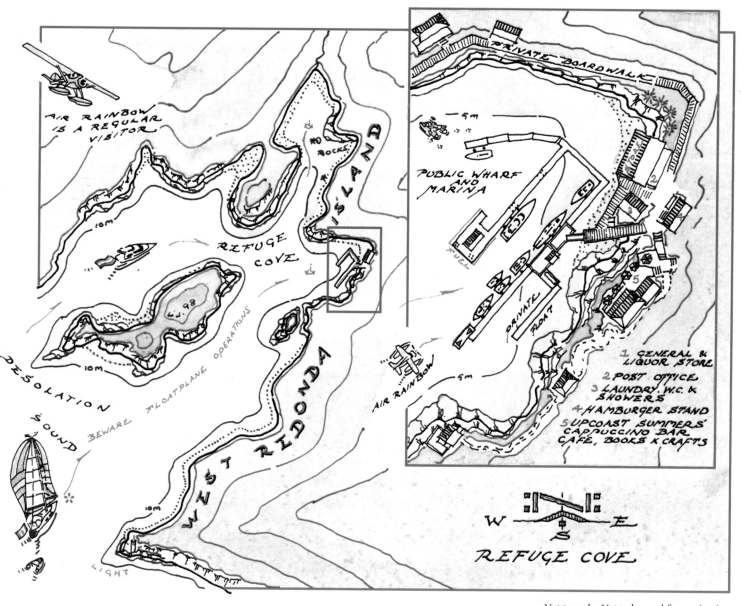

1 GENERAL & LIQUOR STORE
2 POST OFFICE
3 LAUNDRY. W.C. & SHOWERS
4 HAMBURGER STAND
5 UPCOAST SUMMERS' CAPPUCCINO BAR CAFÉ, BOOKS & CRAFTS

REFUGE COVE

Not to scale. Not to be used for navigation.

7.3 ROSCOE BAY MARINE PARK, W REDONDA ISLAND

✻ 50° 9.7' N   124° 44.7' W

With a stern line ashore, it's time to relax in Roscoe Bay.

A good breeze in Waddington Channel.

The safest time to enter or exit Roscoe Bay is at HW and preferably on a rising tide as the shallow bar at the entrance turns this surprise anchorage into a landlocked paradise at LW. To ensure ultimate tranquillity, ROSCOE BAY MARINE PARK is also surrounded by steep, forested slopes and fed by a freshwater lake.

Once inside the bay, visitors are presented with a large, all-weather anchorage that affords reasonable depths, a flat, grassy spot to beach kayaks or set up camp and warm-water swimming at its best. These factors have contributed to the popularity of the park, making it a favoured rendezvous in the busy summer months, but unlike other sought-after destinations the peace and quiet of the bay is highly respected, and any form of noise is considered an intrusion.

The trail to BLACK LAKE is reasonably easy to hike, so you can portage a light dinghy or kayak for a fun day of paddling. Excellent bathing, swimming and rocks for diving can be found just beyond the mouth of the lake, usually jammed with logs, and farther along the trail more private beaches lie in wait for the adventurous. An energetic hike along the grassy ledges on the bay's NW shore will take you to a mossy picnic spot with a bird's-eye view of the activities below.

A few blissful days could certainly be spent exploring this lovely marine park and its hidden history or just lazing in the cockpit, a book in one hand and a cool drink in the other.

A special note for those who missed the HW deadline: safe anchorage is possible just outside the shallow bar, with good views of Waddington Channel and an extra half-hour of light at sunset.

CHARTS 3538. 3312, page 9.

APPROACH

The outer entrance lies N of Maryle-bone Point. The park's sign on the northern shore is the most conspicu-ous landmark. A bar that dries on a zero tide creates a tidal gate to the inner bay and anchorage.

ANCHOR

Good all-weather anchorage, room for numerous boats. Depths of 3 - 9 m (10 - 29.5 ft), holding good in sticky mud.

Note: Time arrival and departure according to your draft. As a general rule, enter on a rising tide as close to HW as possible. Post a bow lookout, and initially favour the south-ern shore and then the centre channel prior to entering the inner bay.

The outer entrance from Waddington Channel.

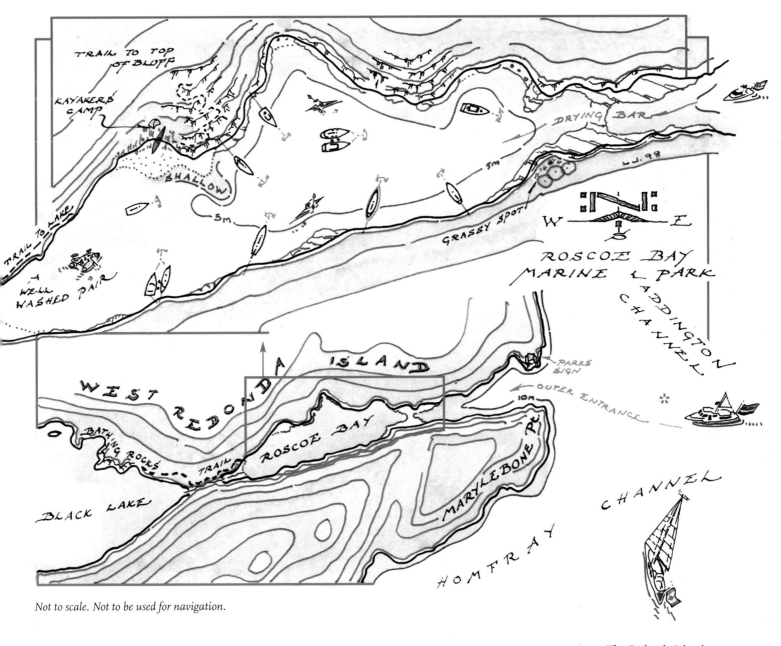

Not to scale. Not to be used for navigation.

7.4   HEAD OF PENDRELL SOUND, E REDONDA ISLAND

CHARTS 3541. 3312, page 16.

APPROACH

At a wake-free speed. The water is deep and free of obstructions.

ANCHOR

Temporary anchorage is possible in numerous nooks. Deep-water anchoring with a stern line ashore is recommended. Depth, holding and bottom condition vary.

An exhilarating spinnaker run.

✳ 50° 16.0' N 124° 42.8' W

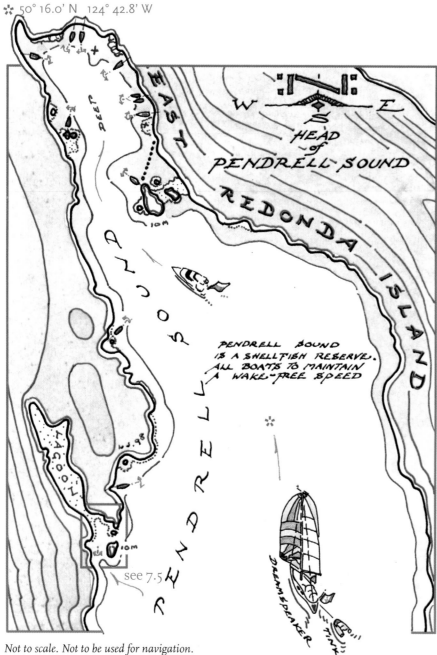

Not to scale. Not to be used for navigation.

Pendrell Sound intersects with Waddington Channel and almost divides East Redonda Island in half. The island's eastern side has a unique ecosystem and is protected as an ecological reserve, enabling scientists to preserve and study its stunning variety of natural vegetation.

The waters of Pendrell Sound are extremely deep, with little tidal exchange and practically no currents, helping water temperatures to reach 20° C (78° F) in the summer months. The sound is also protected from prevailing winds by majestic, snow-capped mountains, making these waters the perfect location to produce Pacific oyster spat (seed). This important and exceptionally vulnerable industry relies on visiting boaters to maintain a wake-free speed within the sound, as delicate oyster spat can be destroyed by excessive motion. Any activity causing pollution is also prohibited and sound has been officially designated a no-sewage-discharge zone (as of 1998).

A trip to the head of the sound will reveal a temporary anchorage filled with booms and rafts used for spat collection along with spectacular views of snow-capped mountains. Because of the deep water, stern lines ashore are essential.

Spectacular vistas from "Oyster Cove."

CHARTS 3541. 3312, page 16.

APPROACH
"Oyster Cove" (named by us) lies on the western shore of Pendrell Sound.

ANCHOR
Temporary anchorage with the best protection in Pendrell Sound. A stern line ashore is recommended because the water is deep and swinging room is limited. Depths of 6 - 8 m (19.5 - 26 ft), holding fair over a shingle and mud bottom.

✳ 50° 16.2' N   124° 43.5' W

Protected anchorage in relatively shallow water can be found behind "Shell Island" in lovely "Oyster Cove" (both named by us). From here you can simply lounge in your cockpit, taking in the serene mountain views, or jump into your trusty dinghy to explore the saltwater lagoon at HW.

The cove is definitely stern-line territory, enabling a good number of boats to tuck in for the night and enjoy the natural delights of Pendrell Sound. Mount Bunsen towers over the anchorage's western shore, where views out to mighty Mount Addenbroke are wonderfully uninterrupted. A hike along the northern shore's rocky bluff leads up to a charming picnic spot with a backdrop of the glacier and twin peaks of Mount Whieldon and Mount Grazebrooke. On your return, stop to pick fresh sea asparagus growing haphazardly alongside "Spatt Islet" (again, named by us).

Because Pendrell Sound was officially designated as a no-sewage-discharge zone in 1998, holding tanks are mandatory in "Oyster Cove."

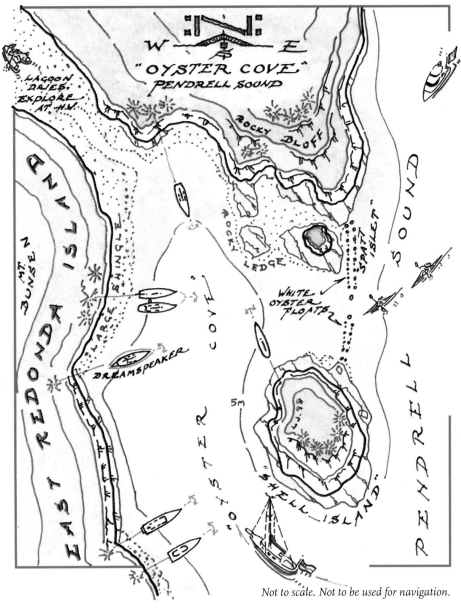

Not to scale. Not to be used for navigation.

7.6   TOBA INLET

✳ 50° 19.2' N 124° 46.2' W

CHARTS

3541. 3312, pages 16 & 29.

APPROACH

Toba Inlet extends 32 km (20 mi) N from Channel and Double Islands. The inlet is very deep and steep-sided with no navigational obstruction.

ANCHOR

There is no all-weather anchorage within the inlet, but there are a few spots where the experienced cruiser can find temporary shelter in settled summer weather. Depth, holding and bottom condition vary.

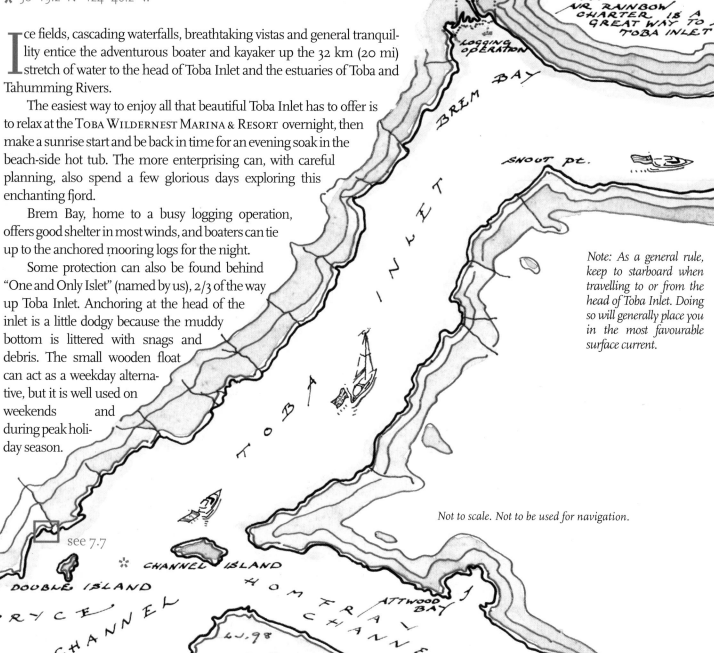

Ice fields, cascading waterfalls, breathtaking vistas and general tranquillity entice the adventurous boater and kayaker up the 32 km (20 mi) stretch of water to the head of Toba Inlet and the estuaries of Toba and Tahumming Rivers.

The easiest way to enjoy all that beautiful Toba Inlet has to offer is to relax at the TOBA WILDERNEST MARINA & RESORT overnight, then make a sunrise start and be back in time for an evening soak in the beach-side hot tub. The more enterprising can, with careful planning, also spend a few glorious days exploring this enchanting fjord.

Brem Bay, home to a busy logging operation, offers good shelter in most winds, and boaters can tie up to the anchored mooring logs for the night.

Some protection can also be found behind "One and Only Islet" (named by us), 2/3 of the way up Toba Inlet. Anchoring at the head of the inlet is a little dodgy because the muddy bottom is littered with snags and debris. The small wooden float can act as a weekday alternative, but it is well used on weekends and during peak holiday season.

Note: As a general rule, keep to starboard when travelling to or from the head of Toba Inlet. Doing so will generally place you in the most favourable surface current.

Not to scale. Not to be used for navigation.

see 7.7

APPROACH

The resort lies due N of Double Island and can be approached from the S or SE.

ANCHOR

Temporary deep anchorage is possible in the bight W of the resort. Depths, holding and bottom condition unrecorded.

MARINA

The resort has visitor moorage, with power and water on the floats; call 250-286-8507.

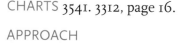

TOBA WILDERNEST MARINA & RESORT 7.7

Tucked inside Double Island at the mouth of Toba Inlet lies TOBA WILDERNEST MARINA & RESORT This welcoming outpost, lovingly built by Mary and Ed Schlote, combines the authentic, rustic charm of an early coastal homestead with the convenience of modern facilities.

In the summer months, the Schlotes offer moorage and guest cabins as well as fishing and hiking trips, and visitors often fly thousands of kilometres to experience the wild beauty of Toba Inlet. Power and water are provided on the docks, and washrooms, showers and a hot tub are available onshore. Mary's ministore stocks basics, ice, snacks and a selection of ice cream flavours.

An invigorating 20-minute hike along the well-used trail will take you past Ed's pride and joy (the hydro plant), across the ravine and up to the spectacular waterfall (although the log bridge isn't for the squeamish). Call 250-286-8507 or 604-597-5280 for more information.

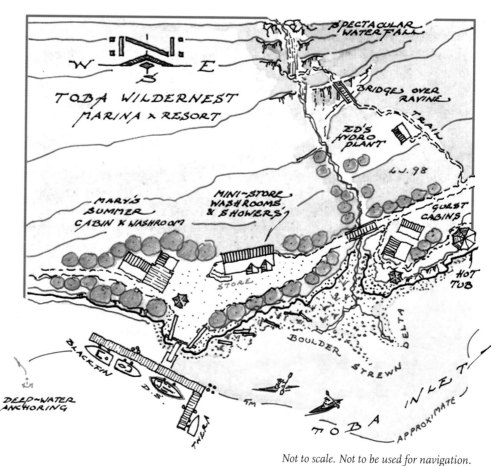

Not to scale. Not to be used for navigation.

7.8 WALSH COVE MARINE PARK, WADDINGTON CHANNEL, W REDONDA ISLAND

✳ 50° 15.9' N   124° 48.1' W

CHARTS 3541. 3312, page 16.

APPROACH

From the S, the park's sign on the Gorges Islets, atop Bluff Point, is the most conspicuous landmark.

ANCHOR

The cove offers reasonable protection, but the winds do whistle through it. Depths of 5 - 15 m (16 - 49 ft) over a mixed bottom of shingle, mud and rock.

Note: False Pass is navigable by recreational craft, but this is best done at LW when the rocks on either side of the passage are visible.

A serene moment, alone in Walsh Cove.

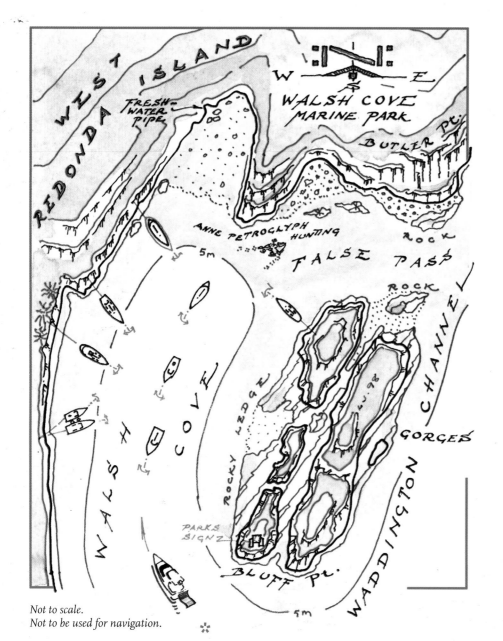

Not to scale.
Not to be used for navigation.

Boaters planning an expedition up breathtaking Toba Inlet should note that the last protected anchorage available in Waddington Channel is tucked in behind Gorges Islands, in lovely Walsh Cove Marine Park. The alternative is moorage at TOBA WILDERNEST MARINA & RESORT (see page 103), where deep-water anchorage is also possible.

Safe entrance to steep-sided Walsh Cove can be found W of Bluff Point. False Pass should only be attempted at LW and with careful navigation. Once you are inside, this charming marine park offers adequate stern-to anchorage, an opportunity to hunt for petroglyphs at Butler Point, fine warm-water swimming and great views over to the East Redonda mountains. Take some time to explore the enchanting wooded islets, where wild onion and thyme still grow and sun-heated rock ledges provide excellent warm-water swimming as the tide rises.

Clean and piped fresh water can be found at the head of the small, drying nook on the western side of the cove, which comes as a nice surprise if you are beginning to run a little low and don't plan to leave the delights of Walsh Cove for another day or two.

Chapter 8

CALM
CHANNEL
TO BUTE
INLET

Avocet moored at Waddington Harbour, Bute Inlet.
Lynn Ove Mortensen photo

The view up Calm Channel from Rendezvous Lodge.

Chapter 8
CALM CHANNEL TO BUTE INLET

TIDES

Canadian Tide and Current Tables, Volume 5
Reference Port: Pt. Atkinson
Secondary Ports: Redonda Bay, Orford Bay & Waddington Harbour (Bute Inlet)

CURRENTS

Although there are no specific reference and secondary current stations, weak tidal currents (usually less than 2 knots) can be encountered in Whiterock Passage. A perpetual southerly surface current, which can attain 2 knots, exists in Bute Inlet.

WEATHER

In the summer months, Calm Channel tends to be in a wind shadow, from the prevailing Northwesterlies. However, Bute Inlet funnels the daytime inflow wind and nighttime outflow wind along its length. Strong outflow winds are more common in winter, early spring and late fall than in summer. These winds can often reach gale force.

CAUTIONARY NOTE

If venturing up Bute Inlet, check your stock of provisions and top up with fuel and water. To date no minimall exists in Waddington Harbour to replenish supplies.

In the busy summer months, Calm Channel turns into a bustling water highway filled with pleasure boats and commercial craft because it provides a safe and convenient link between the two most popular cruising areas: Desolation Sound and the Discovery Islands. This chapter invites boaters to slow down and discover a few enchanting but lesser-known treasures before continuing with their voyages.

At first glance, the low-lying Rendezvous Islands seem to hold little excitement; on closer inspection, they offer two charming picnic anchorages, a community nature park, hiking trails and a welcoming lodge offering delicious patio lunches. Undeveloped South Rendezvous Island has been preserved as a provincial park.

A detour up the small, steep-sided inlet of Ramsay Arm is well worth the effort, and protected overnight anchorage can be found nearby in peaceful Frances Bay. Bute Inlet offers few protected anchorages and has no marina, but the adventurous boater will find the beauty of this tranquil 65 km (40 mi) fjord irresistible. In settled weather, a few days spent exploring the inlet's spectacular shoreline will prove both worthwhile and memorable. "Leask Cove" (named by us), tucked below Fawn Bluff, is a short way up from the mouth of Bute Inlet and provides an inviting picnic stop or overnight anchorage in settled weather. Laze in your cockpit surrounded by green glacial waters or stretch your legs with a hike to secluded Leask Lake for a freshwater skinny-dip.

Included in this chapter is Whiterock Passage, which provides a convenient shortcut to the reopened and well-stocked Surge Narrows Store on Read Island and the enticing anchorages along Quadra's eastern shoreline. The well-dredged but narrow boat passage can be successfully navigated on a rising tide with the aid of a lookout and the large leading marks provided, although both skipper and crew need their wits about them as there is little margin for error in this boulder-lined pass.

Featured Destinations

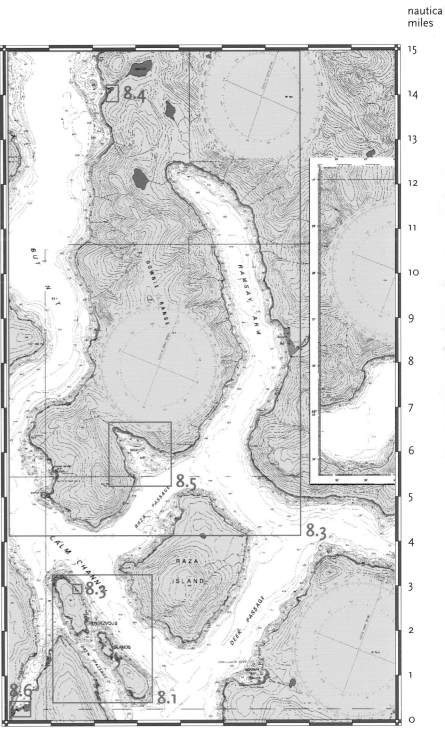

nautical
miles

Not to be used for navigation.

8.1 Rendezvous Islands, Calm Channel

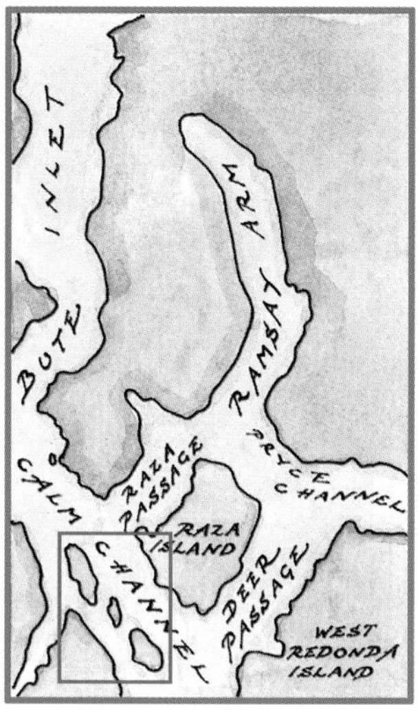

50° 16.2' N 125° 1.4' W

CHARTS 3541. 3312, page 17.

APPROACH

The waters of both Calm Channel and Drew Passage are deep right up to the shoreline. Navigation between the middle and S Rendezvous Island is possible with local knowledge.

ANCHOR

Temporary anchorage is possible in the spots as indicated on the shoreline plan below; stern lines ashore are required. Depths, holding and bottom condition unrecorded.

Note: Boaters are requested to slow down and minimize wake when transiting Calm Channel, especially when passing the community docks of the Rendezvous Islands.

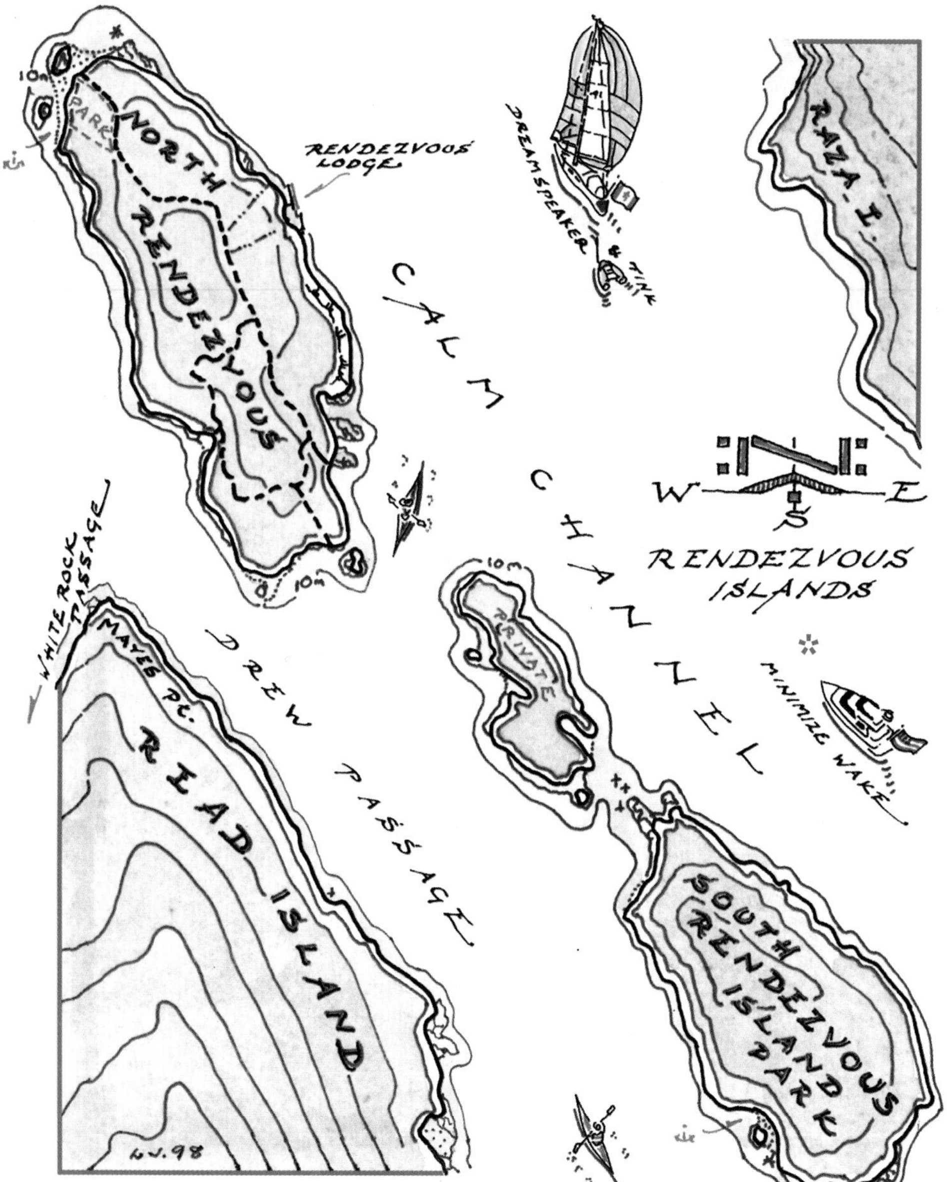

Not to scale. Not to be used for navigation.

At first glance, the Rendezvous Islands seem to offer little excitement for the cruising boater heading N. Yet a few tempting surprises lie in wait for those willing to slow down and take a little time to explore the hideaway picnic anchorages or stop in for lunch at the welcoming Rendezvous Lodge.

Undeveloped S Rendezvous Island has been set aside as a provincial park with 112 hectares of upland and 51 hectares of foreshore to explore. Temporary anchorage is possible on the SW shore, tucked in behind an islet. The middle island is private, and space in the small cove is taken up by a private mooring buoy.

In the early 1900s, the population of N Rendezvous Island was large enough to support a school and post office. Today the island is home to a small, enterprising community of people who wish to preserve the enchantment of island life. Temporary anchorage is possible in a nook below the Community Nature Park at the northern end of the island, and a fairly well-developed road and trail system circles the island and provides excellent hiking opportunities. Kayakers can set up camp on the islet, joined to the park at LW.

An unexpected treat in Calm Channel.

APPROACH

From the E out of Calm Channel. The lodge and flags comprise the most conspicuous landmark.

MARINA

The lodge has limited moorage for visitors, preferably patrons of the lodge, restaurant and facilities. Call 250-287-0318.

✻ 50° 17.5' N   125° 3.7' W

The inviting, shaded deck of the RENDEZVOUS LODGE provides the perfect spot for a get-together with boating friends while exploring Calm Channel and Bute Inlet.

Primarily a "wilderness vacation lodge," it also offers moorage, and visiting boaters can tie up at the private dock to enjoy a patio lunch or fireside dinner. You'll be rewarded with friendly service, glorious views across Calm Channel and some tasty home cooking accompanied by a bottle of house wine. Darlene's memorable desserts and Ray's melt-in-the-mouth smoked salmon (produced in the small smokehouse out back) certainly make this side trip worthwhile. Well-mannered pets are welcome, and overnight guests can stretch their legs on the local hiking trails or relax in the outdoor hot tub.

Note: The dock float is exposed to the wash from passing boats, (a floating breakwater was added in 1999) and although lunch is "drop-in" reservations are suggested for dinner and overnight moorage. Contact Ray or Darlene Bugeaud at 250-287-0318.

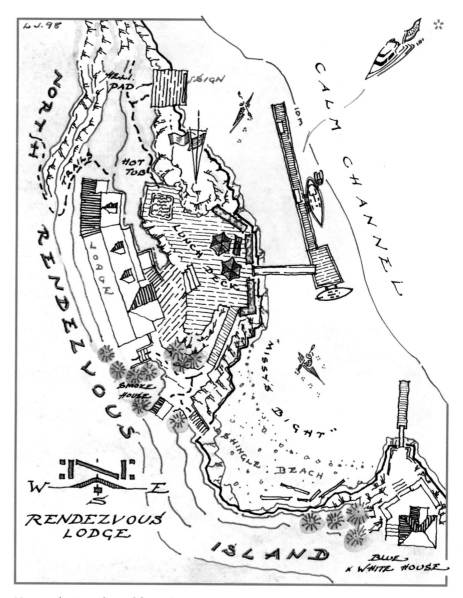

Not to scale. Not to be used for navigation.

❋ 1) 50° 21.2' N   125° 6.6' W Bute Inlet
❋ 2) 50° 20.5' N   124° 58.8'
        W Ramsay Arm

Looking up Bute Inlet from Mt. Muehle, Stuart Island.

Entrance to the Southgate River, head of Bute Inlet.
Lynn Ove Mortensen photo

The 65 km (40 mi) stretch of glacial water to the head of Bute Inlet and the Homathko River estuary is often considered out of bounds by the cruising boater in search of convenient marinas, safe anchorages and predictable weather. Bute Inlet's reputation for being somewhat daunting and forever shrouded in mist is not unfounded, but if the forecast calls for settled weather and you find yourself within close proximity, treat yourself to a few memorable days exploring the inlet's spectacular shoreline and experiencing its isolated tranquillity. The great beauty of Bute Inlet is difficult to appreciate fully unless you are prepared to take the plunge and venture to its upper reaches, where you'll find yourself surrounded by breathtaking vistas of snow-capped mountains and the dazzling expanse of Homathko Glacier.

Temporary deep-water anchorages are available en route, and an overnight stop in Waddington Harbour is possible if you are able to tie up at one of the logging floats or alongside an anchored log boom. Although depths are suitable for anchorage, the open exposures, murky waters, shifting silt and hidden debris make anchoring hazardous. It's possible to explore the 2 glacial rivers by dinghy, but be aware that hazards are often obscured by the opaque waters. Study the tide tables carefully, beginning and ending your journey on a rising tide.

Peaceful "Leask Cove" (named by us), below Fawn Bluff, provides good anchorage in settled weather and is a convenient overnight stop for boaters planning a dawn start up Bute Inlet. This charming picnic spot shouldn't be missed, even if the full journey up Bute Inlet isn't on your cruising itinerary this year (see page 112).

The small inlet of Ramsay Arm, with its towering cliffs and eerie solitude, is interesting to explore by boat if you have the time, although the only protected anchorage available is off Raza Passage in secluded Frances Bay (see page 113). In settled weather, drop your anchor in nearby Quatam Bay. Picnic or dig for clams at LW.

CHARTS 3541. 3542. 3312, pages 17, 27, 28.

APPROACH

From Calm Channel, both Bute Inlet and Ramsay Arm are deep-water channels.

ANCHOR

The spots as indicated on the adjacent shoreline plan below are temporary and require careful sounding close to shore. These locations are remote and require careful preplanning. Depth, holding and bottom condition vary.

Note: Strong outflow winds can be experienced in the inlet during the summer months, when the weather pattern is about to change.

Afternoon inflow winds occur during settled, sunny weather. They are generally light but can be accelerated by the inlet's length and steep-sided shoreline. Surface currents of up to 2 knots flow S and are only marginally affected by the flood and ebb tides.

Temporary moorage at commercial docks and floats is possible with permission from local logging operations.

Majestic undergrowth at Frances Bay.

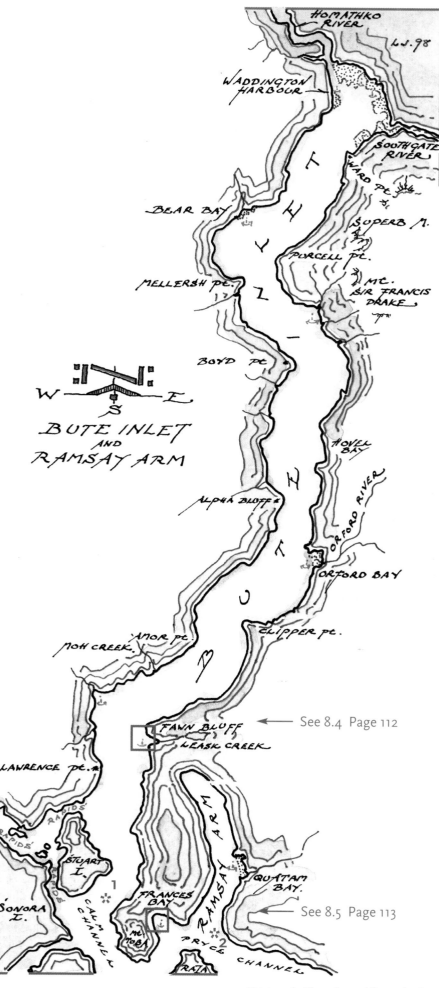

See 8.4 Page 112

See 8.5 Page 113

Not to scale. Not to be used for navigation.

8.4 "LEASK COVE," LEASK CREEK, BUTE INLET

CHARTS 3542. 3312, page 27.

APPROACH
From the SW. "Leask Cove," Leask Creek, lies about 1 km (2/3 mi) S of Fawn Bluff.

ANCHOR
The cove is one of the better protected anchorages off Bute Inlet. Fawn Bluff shields the cove from the brunt of out-flow winds. Depths of 4 - 6 m (13 - 19.5 ft), with stern line ashore. Holding over a mixture of rock and mud.

Wash and brush-up facilities at the stream.

Tucked away below Fawn Bluff on the eastern shoreline of Bute Inlet, charming "Leask Cove" (named by us) is the perfect picnic stop, although in settled weather you could easily idle away a few days here. Once a flourishing homestead, all that remains of the Leask brothers' innovative workmanship are crumbling terraces and wild fruit trees.

This pocket paradise is surrounded by green glacier water, and the small pebble beach and sheltered "campsite" face the setting sun. A freshwater stream provides an excellent wash and brush-up facility, and the well-cleared trail leads half a mile up to secluded LEASK LAKE.

Not to scale. Not to be used for navigation.

Dreamspeaker and shrimp boat in "Leask Cove."

FRANCES BAY, "FANNY BAY," RAZA PASSAGE 8.5

CHARTS 3541. 3312, page 17.

APPROACH

From the SE. Frances Bay lies at the confluence of Raza Passage and the mouth of Ramsay Arm.

ANCHOR

Temporary anchorage can be found at the head of the bay. Deep-water swinging or stern lines ashore. Depth, holding and bottom condition vary.

Note: Exposed to the SE, although winds tend to be light from this direction in summer. Overnight outflow winds, however, do swirl down from the surrounding mountains.

✳ 50° 20.8' N 125° 2.2' W

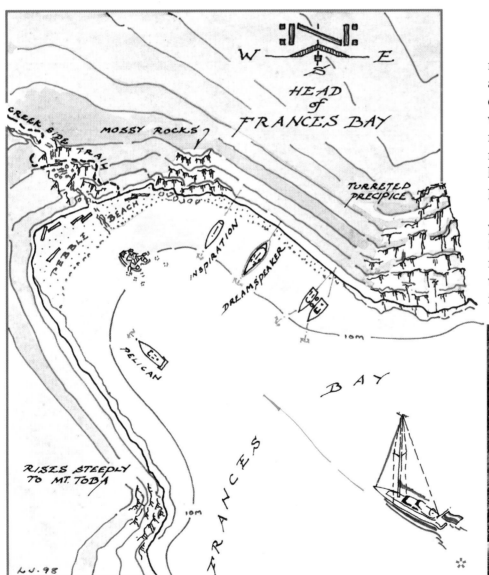

Not to scale. Not to be used for navigation.

Peaceful Frances Bay (known locally as "Fanny Bay") is a natural wonderland offering a turreted precipice, mossy picnicking rocks and a small pebble beach. The short creek trail leads into a cool forest retreat where decaying "nurse logs" form miniature gardens, and ferns and moss-covered rocks share space with huge old-growth stumps, which support new trees.

From the comfort of your cockpit, you can identify Toba Mountain to the SW and the Downie Range rising majestically to the NW. The stunning view down Pryce Channel is included in the package.

The head of Frances Bay.

APPROACH

The approach bearings as indicated on the shoreline plan below are true bearings and refer to entering the passage from the southern and northern ends respectively. A lookout armed with binoculars is an added bonus because the dog-leg turn in the centre of the passage requires a quick change of position from bow to stern.

Whiterock Passage from the South.

✳ 1) *50° 14.5' N   125° 6.9' W
✳ 2) *50° 15.2' N   125° 5.8' W

Boulder-strewn Whiterock Passage provides a convenient short-cut S to the reopened SURGE NARROWS GENERAL STORE on Read Island (see page 145) and the inviting anchorages tucked into Quadra Island's eastern shore-line.

The dredged boat passage between the boulders can be successfully navigated on a rising tide by using the large leading marks ranges provided on the Read Island shore.

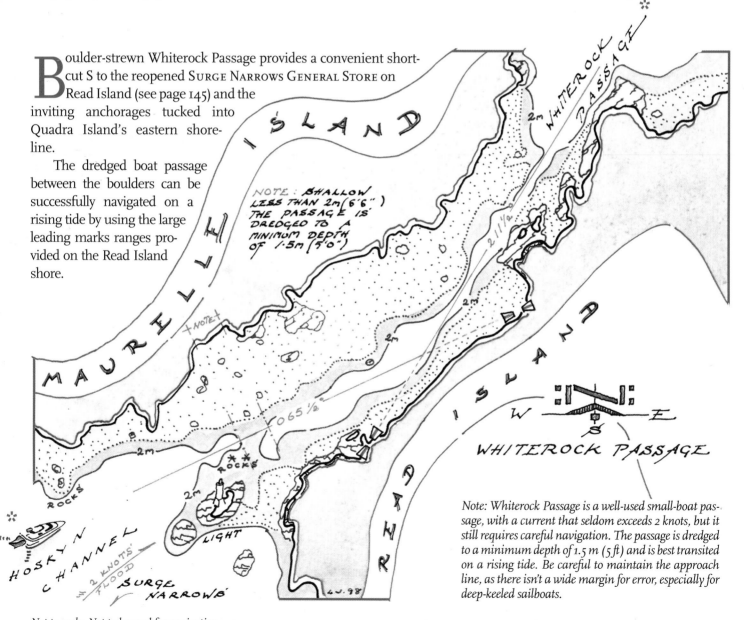

Note: Whiterock Passage is a well-used small-boat passage, with a current that seldom exceeds 2 knots, but it still requires careful navigation. The passage is dredged to a minimum depth of 1.5 m (5 ft) and is best transited on a rising tide. Be careful to maintain the approach line, as there isn't a wide margin for error, especially for deep-keeled sailboats.

Not to scale. Not to be used for navigation.

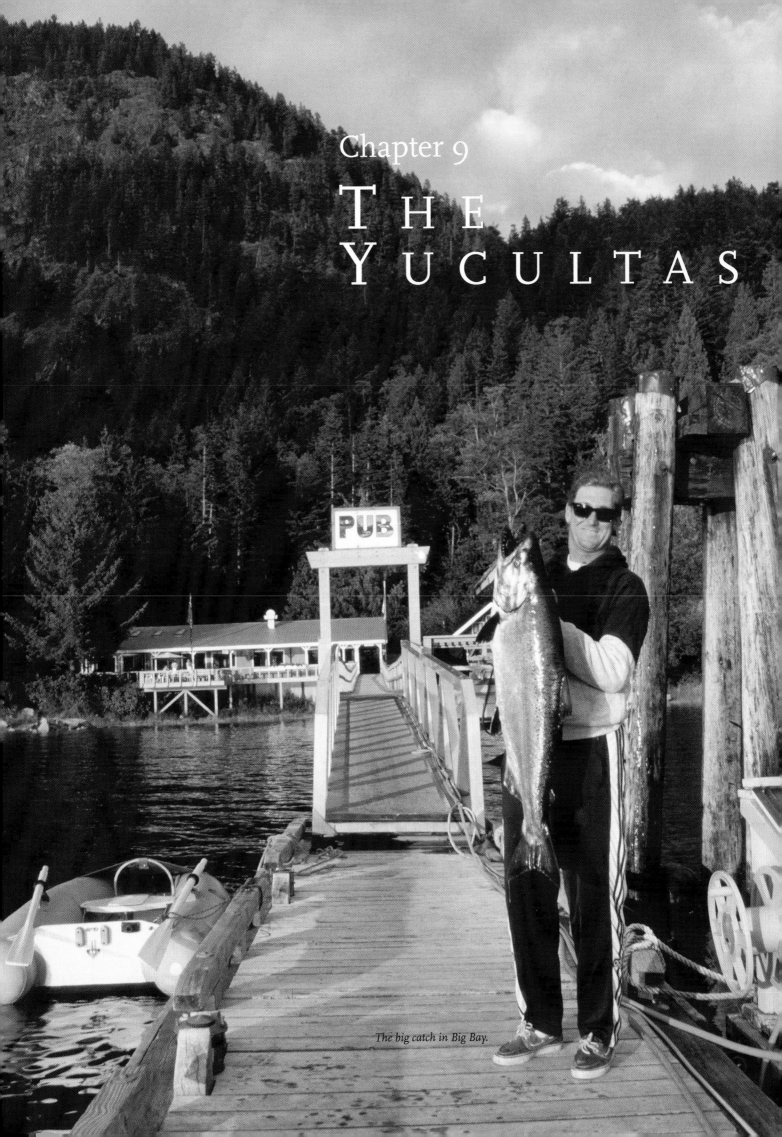

Chapter 9
THE YUCULTAS

The big catch in Big Bay.

Chapter 9
THE YUCULTAS

Patio and view from Dent Island Lodge.

TIDES

Canadian Tide and Current Tables, Volume 6
Reference Port: Campbell River
Secondary Port: Big Bay
Reference Port: Owen Bay
Secondary Port: Mermaid Bay

CURRENTS

Reference Station: Gillard Passage, Arran Rapids
Secondary Stations: Yuculta Rapids, Dent Rapids

Note: See 9.4 (page 122) for details of the Yucultas, which include the Yuculta and Dent Rapids as well as Gillard and Barber Passages.

WEATHER

No specific reporting stations. The boater is entering an area where the topography has a big effect on wind and wind direction. In summer, in periods of high pressure, the mornings are usually overcast, but by midday the sun breaks through, having burned away the cloud cover.

CAUTIONARY NOTES

The prudent navigator should always transit the rapids at or close to slack water. Big engines below may be no match for nature. Don't be caught in the wrong place at the wrong time, because these rapids are exceedingly hazardous, especially to small craft.

This essential chapter serves as a gateway to the inviting cruising grounds that lie beyond the delights of Desolation Sound in the cooler, more challenging waters of the Discovery Islands. From here on, the all-important Canadian Tide and Current Tables should always be studied diligently and kept close at hand.

The legendary Yucultas, almost always pronounced "Uke-la-taws" or jokingly called "Yuks," are a string of rather daunting rapids that require careful navigation when journeying north from Calm Channel (Chapter 8) to Cordero Channel (Chapter 10). They are comprised of the Yuculta Rapids proper, the Dent Rapids and Gillard and Barber Passages, and they present a fearsome obstacle at all times except on or close to slack water. The exceptionally strong tidal currents that flow through all four passes come with associated overfalls and whirlpools, and the freshwater overlays and aerated boils also reduce the buoyancy of a displacement hull. Boaters should keep in mind that these passes are still the preferred route for tugs towing log booms south, resulting in partly submerged debris often in the form of dreaded deadheads. To top it all, some thoughtless skippers are determined to storm through these rapids at top speed, causing unnecessary wakes and added turbulence, sometimes more frightening and dangerous than the mighty rapids themselves.

With careful planning, you can transit all three rapids in one go, but we recommend a more relaxed approach and encourage boaters to take the rapids one at a time, enjoying the hospitality and amenities offered in featured destinations along the way.

The friendly community of Big Bay offers moorage, guided sport-fishing tours and the tastiest fish and chips on Stuart Island. If time doesn't permit a trip through the Arran Rapids at slack water, hike along Stuart Island's northern shore, where a truly awesome whirlpool, known locally as "The Drain," can be viewed from Arran Point. The Dent Island Lodge, located at the eastern end of Cordero Channel, offers comfortable moorage, friendly service and excellent home cooking. The hot tub overlooking "Canoe Pass" is the perfect spot to unwind and soak your weary muscles. Historic Mermaid Bay, in Cordero Channel, has a wonderful collection of tugboat names above the rocks and high in the trees and is an interesting spot to while away a few hours waiting for slack water.

Featured Destinations

nautical miles

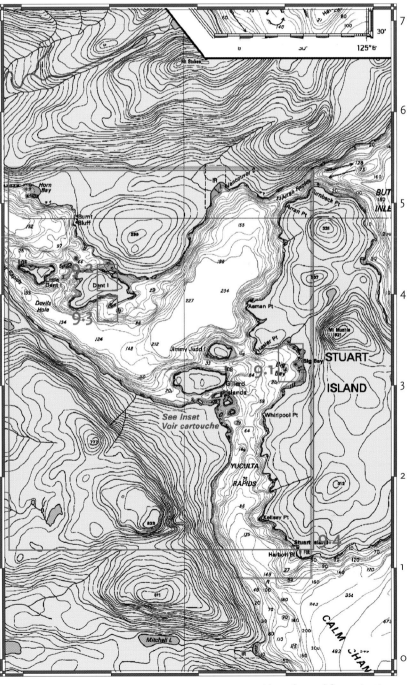

Not to be used for navigation.

9.1 BIG BAY, STUART ISLAND

✳ 50° 23.5' N   125° 8.3' W

Big Bay looking north from the public wharf.

Big Bay Marina & Resort restaurant.

Note: Please respect private boundaries of homes on the island as this is a "fenceless" community.

Accessible by floatplane, helicopter or boat, the friendly community of Big Bay takes full advantage of its focal position and natural resources in the summer months. It offers moorage and resort facilities, professional sport-fishing guides, ecotours and the opportunity for boaters to relax before continuing N or S through the turbulent waters of Gillard or Barber Passage and the reputed Yuculta or Dent Rapids. Moorage is available at the BIG BAY MARINA & RESORT, the MARTINS' DOCK, the WHEELHOUSE PUB float and the local public wharf – each with something special to offer (see phone numbers on following page).

Efficiently run by the Knierim family since 1977, the BIG BAY MARINA & RESORT also includes cabin and lodge facilities, a restaurant and a general store with an on-site bakery and small B.C. LIQUOR STORE outlet. The store carries good basic provisions, frozen foods, a limited selection of fresh produce, ice, charts, books and local crafts, but don't expect mainland prices! You can also specially order homemade cakes and pies or indulge in a freshly made latté. Public phones are operated via satellite and credit card. Fuel is available on the dock, but power and water are limited, and garbage is not accepted. The shower and laundry facilities are well maintained.

THE MARTINS' DOCK and the local post office are run by an enterprising and creative couple. Don and Deb Martin also offer professional fishing-guide services, personalized ecotours and private moorage, which sometimes includes a large home-grown zucchini. Water is limited, and power and garbage drop-off aren't available.

For the tastiest fish and chips and the liveliest conversation on Stuart Island, tie up at the WHEELHOUSE PUB float and saunter up to the patio deck. Here you can enjoy a fine sunset view while catching up on island gossip over a cold beer. You never know whom you might bump into here, as the owners, Tom and Barbara Thompson, attract an eclectic mix of visitors. Along with their son, Tom Jr., they also run a successful sport-fishing guide service.

The BIG BAY PUBLIC WHARF has a good amount of space for small craft and is a friendly, laid-back spot to tie up for the night.

A trail behind the marina takes you to nearby "Eagle Lake," which offers warm-water swimming and 2 or 3 small rowboats for general use. For a more energetic walk to view the Arran Rapids, ask the locals for directions, as certain public-access points have now become private property.

CHARTS 3543. 3312, page 26.

APPROACH

The community of Big Bay lies E of Hesler Point below the slopes of Mount Muehle. Avoid the large kelp bed over the 4 m (13 ft) patch in the centre of the bay.

ANCHOR

Anchoring is possible off the floats but isn't recommended because the waters are in a constant state of movement, either from the strong back eddies or from the sport boats zooming by. Depth, holding and bottom condition unrecorded.

PUBLIC WHARF

A U-shaped float with moorage for visiting craft lies S of a timber breakwater.

MARINA

The Big Bay Marina & Resort, 250-286-8107, has extensive visitor moorage. In busy July and August, it is essential to book ahead. Additional moorage can be obtained at the Martins' Dock, 250-287-0264, or at the Wheelhouse Pub float, 250-830-8622.

FUEL

At the marina.

Note: The bay is a zone for floatplane operation.

Wheelhouse Pub and float.

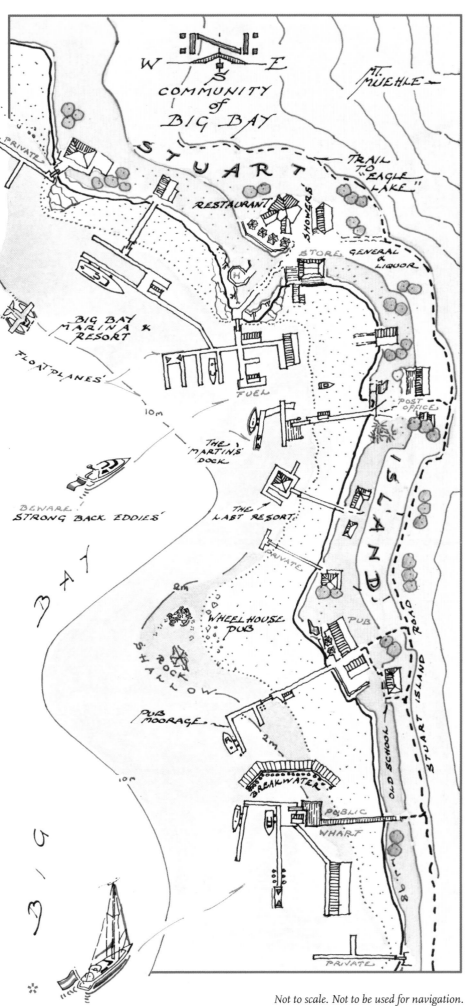

Not to scale. Not to be used for navigation.

9.2 THE DENT ISLAND LODGE, "WEE DENT ISLET," CORDERO CHANNEL

❈ 50° 24.4' N   125° 10.9' W

CHARTS 3543. 3312, page 26.

APPROACH

From the SE. The Dent Island Lodge's marina lies between Dent Island and the mainland, at the head of a small cove.

NOTE: Canoe Pass is a small boat passage only.

ANCHOR

Good protected anchorage can be found in the cove. Boats at anchor will swing to the current that flows through "Canoe Pass." Depth, holding and bottom condition unrecorded.

MARINA

The DENT ISLAND LODGE has generous visitor moorage and is very popular in the summer months, so making reservations is essential; call 250-286-8105.

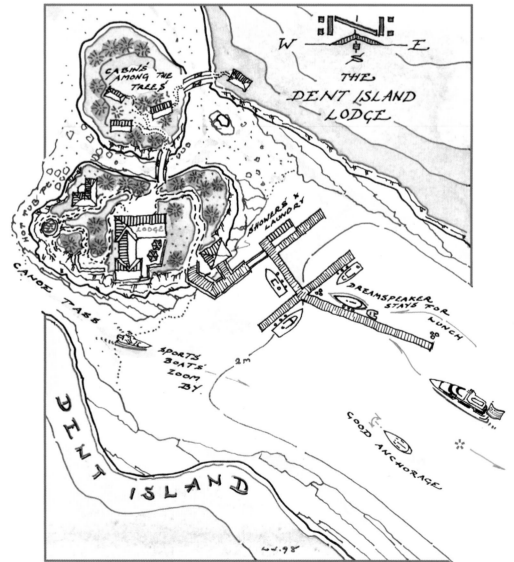

Not to scale. Not to be used for navigation.

Built in harmony with its natural surroundings, the DENT ISLAND LODGE on "Wee Dent Islet" offers its guests deluxe log cabins and comfortable moorage with magnificent views out to "Canoe Pass" and the turbulent Dent Rapids. The lodge's laid-back luxury, friendly service and excellent home cooking can be enjoyed by the cruising boater and discriminating angler alike. Moorage comes with power, water and access to all lodge facilities, including a state-of-the-art fitness room. The chef's lavish dinner menu includes a platter of fresh hors d'oeuvres served at your chosen location – try the hot tub and its view, built above the rocky shoreline of "Canoe Pass." Lunch and dinner are by reservation.

Excellent facilities at the Dent Island Lodge Marina.

120 – The Yucultas

CHARTS 3543. 3312, page 26.

APPROACH

From the S, by rounding the wooded peninsula.

ANCHOR

Temporary anchorage is possible off a small shingle beach. Depths of 6 - 12 m (19.5 - 39 ft), holding good in shingle and mud.

Note: If you've missed slack water, it's prudent to wait for the following slack water. If Mermaid Bay is taken up with a log boom, ask for permission to tie up alongside it or visit the Dent Island Lodge (see page 120) a short distance away.

❈ 50° 24.1' N   125° 11.3' W

Tucked neatly into the southern end of Dent Island, Mermaid Bay provides a convenient temporary or emergency anchorage and is a pleasant spot to while away a few hours waiting for slack water. Historically it was used by tug skippers as a "waiting place," especially when both the Dent Rapids and Gillard Passage had to be attempted in one go. Generations of tugboat names have been painted onto driftwood or old planks and wedged into the rocks or nailed to the trees, but no mermaids have been spotted to date! Because space in the bay is limited, be prepared to tie up alongside a log boom if necessary.

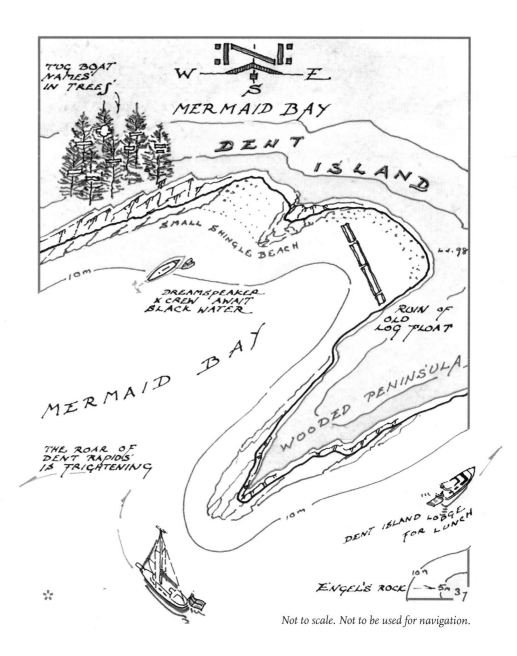

Not to scale. Not to be used for navigation.

Generations of tugboat names in Mermaid Bay.

9.4   THE YUCULTAS

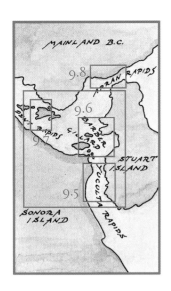

NORTHBOUND (INCLUDES YUCULTA RAPIDS, GILLARD PASSAGE & DENT RAPIDS)

If you are heading N, approach the Yucultas off Kellsey Point on the Stuart Island shoreline an hour prior to the turn to ebb, cross over, take advantage of the northerly current that prevails along the Sonora Island shore and transit Gillard Passage. It's approximately 5 nautical miles from Kellsey Point to the turbulent free waters in Cordero Channel N of Little Dent Island. A sailboat at 6 knots should be able to transit Dent Rapids before the ebb has had time to build to full force.

SOUTHBOUND (INCLUDES DENT RAPIDS, GILLARD PASSAGE & YUCULTA RAPIDS)

If you are heading S, the cruising plan is easier because the Dent Rapids turn to flood 15 minutes earlier than Gillard Passage. It's approximately 2 nautical miles from the Dent Rapids to Gillard Passage, so approach the Dents 15 minutes prior to the turn. At a speed of 6 knots, you should reach Gillard Passage at the turn and thus make it through the Yuculta Rapids safely.

9.5 THE YUCULTA RAPIDS

These rapids extend N from Harbott Point to Big Bay, Stuart Island, with maximum current velocities being encountered between Kellsey Point and Whirlpool Point. The secondary station lies centre channel, SW of Whirlpool Point, attaining maximum strengths of 10 knots flood and 8 knots ebb. Dangerous whirlpools and overfalls form off Whirlpool Point.

Reference current station: Gillard Passage
Direction of flood: S
Times of slack water as follows:
- turn to flood plus (+) 25 minutes
- turn to ebb plus (+) 5 minutes

9.6 GILLARD & BARBER PASSAGES

These rapids extend W and N from Big Bay through Gillard and Barber Passages respectively. Maximum current velocities encountered in the passages are recorded at the current station situated in the centre of Gillard Passage between Gillard and Jimmy Judd Islands, with a maximum flood of 13 knots and an ebb of 10 knots. Dangerous whirlpools and overfalls form between Hesler Point and the Gillard light.

Reference current station: Gillard Passage
Direction of flood: E and S
Note: Don't forget to add 1 hour in periods of daylight-savings time.

9.7 Dent Rapids

These rapids extend NW from the western tip of Dent Island, with maximum current velocities encountered in Tugboat Passage and between Little Dent Island and the Sonora Island shoreline. The secondary station, S of Little Dent Island light, has recorded a maximum of 11 knots on the flood and 10 knots on the ebb. Dangerous whirlpools and overfalls form in Devils Hole.

Reference current station: Gillard Passage
Direction of flood: SE
Times of slack water as follows:
 • turn to flood minus (–) 15 minutes
 • turn to ebb minus (–) 25 minutes

9.8 Arran Rapids

These rapids extend through the very eastern end of Cordero Channel as the passage narrows between the mainland and the Stuart Island shoreline. Maximum current velocities of 14 knots on the flood and 13 knots on the ebb can be encountered between Arran Point and Turnback Point, Stuart Island. A truly fearsome whirlpool forms off Arran Point.

Reference current station: Arran Rapids
Direction of flood: NE
Note: Don't forget to add 1 hour in periods of daylight-savings time.

Not to scale. Not to be used for navigation.

Chapter 10
CORDERO CHANNEL

A frequent sight – fog lies above Cordero Channel.
Lynn Ove Mortensen photo

Public wharf at Shoal Bay.

Chapter 10
CORDERO CHANNEL

TIDES

Canadian Tide and Current Tables, Volume 6

Reference Port: Owen Bay

Secondary Ports: Shoal Bay, Cordero Islands, "Blind Channel," Chatham Point

CURRENTS

Reference Station: Seymour Narrows

Secondary Station: Greene Point Rapids

WEATHER

Area: Johnstone Strait

Reporting Stations: Helmcken Island, Chatham Point

Note: The relentless currents and strong to gale-force afternoon and evening winds that plague Johnstone Strait S seldom penetrate into Cordero Channel to the same intensity.

CAUTIONARY NOTES

Once you are clear of the Dent Rapids, Cordero Channel itself is relatively free of turbulent water, but currents remain strong, especially in the western half of the channel. It's therefore advisable to travel with the prevailing tidal stream.

Don't forget, "Blind Channel" (the local name for Mayne Passage) has rapids and turbulent water in its northern reaches. Both "Blind Channel" and Greene Point Rapids shouldn't be attempted other than at or near slack water.

In this chapter, we explore a diverse selection of destinations between the Dent and Greene Point Rapids, in Cordero Channel, in Mayne Passage (known locally as "Blind Channel") and in the less travelled Nodales Channel. Should you plan to stop over or refuel at the BLIND CHANNEL RESORT, keep in mind that the "Blind Channel Rapids" extend as far north as Shell Point in Mayne Passage.

Historic Shoal Bay on East Thurlow Island provides a convenient base while you explore the "Gut" (as it's known locally) and Estero Basin in Frederick Arm or while you take a side trip up Phillips Arm. Tie up at the peaceful public wharf and treat yourself to a relaxed supper at the rustic SHOAL BAY LODGE. Bickley Bay, just around the corner, offers a pleasant alternative anchorage.

Tucked in behind Lorte Island, the family-run CORDERO LODGE, with its hearty German cooking, comes as a wonderful surprise as you near the end of Cordero Channel. Snuggled between the Cordero Islands and the mainland shore lies a lovely, quiet anchorage, an ideal hideaway for just lazing in the cockpit and watching the world rush by.

The efficiently run BLIND CHANNEL RESORT provides the only fuelling and provisioning stop for the area covered in this chapter, and it is a welcome sight to the cruising boater running low on supplies. Family owned and operated, the resort has built an excellent reputation over the years by offering comfortable moorage, a cosy restaurant with tasty, home-cooked meals and a well-stocked store that offers delicious loaves of home-baked bread. Take a walk along the well-maintained trail to the 800-year-old cedar, or picnic on the pebble beach in Charles Bay, a short hop across Mayne Passage.

Peace and solitude can be found in undeveloped Thurston Bay Marine Park, where you can dig for clams, pick blackberries and wild mint or just idle away a few blissful days surrounded by wilderness. The head of Hemming Bay on East Thurlow Island offers you sheltered anchorage, great sunsets and the opportunity to relax and explore at your leisure.

FEATURED DESTINATIONS

nautical miles

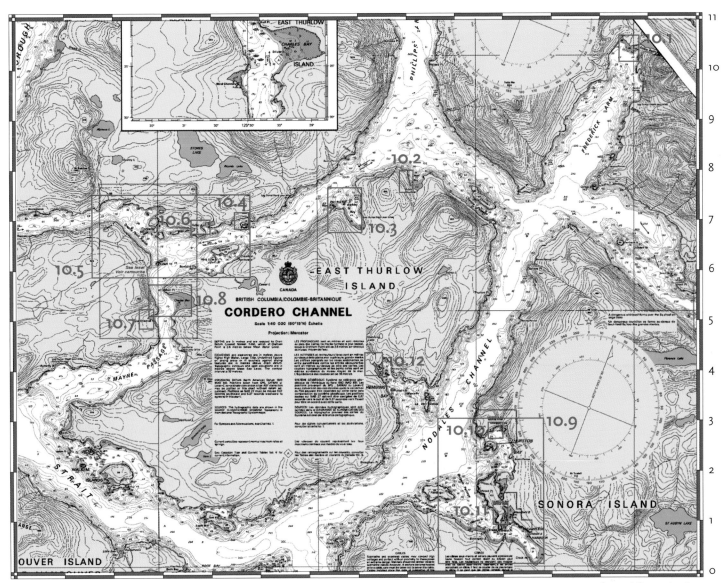

Not to be used for navigation.

10.1 The "Gut" to Estero Basin, Frederick Arm

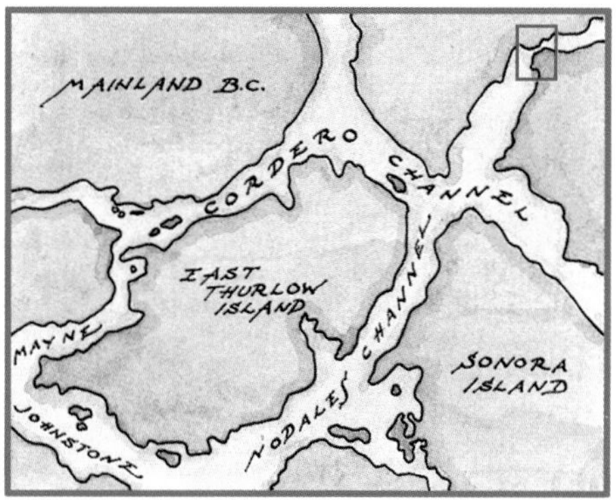

✲ 50° 29.9′ N 125° 15.1′ W

CHARTS 3543. 3312, page 25.

APPROACH

Use caution as you approach the head of Frederick Arm because a shallow delta extends out from the "Gut" to Estero Basin. The entrance to the "Gut" is also obscured by overhanging greenery.

ANCHOR

Temporary anchorage is possible below a cliff of bare rock. Depths of 10 - 15 m (33 - 49 ft), holding good in shingle and rock.

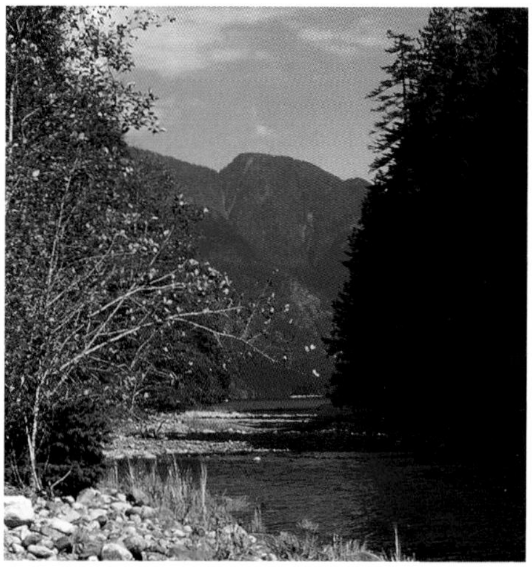

The "Gut" to Estero Basin.

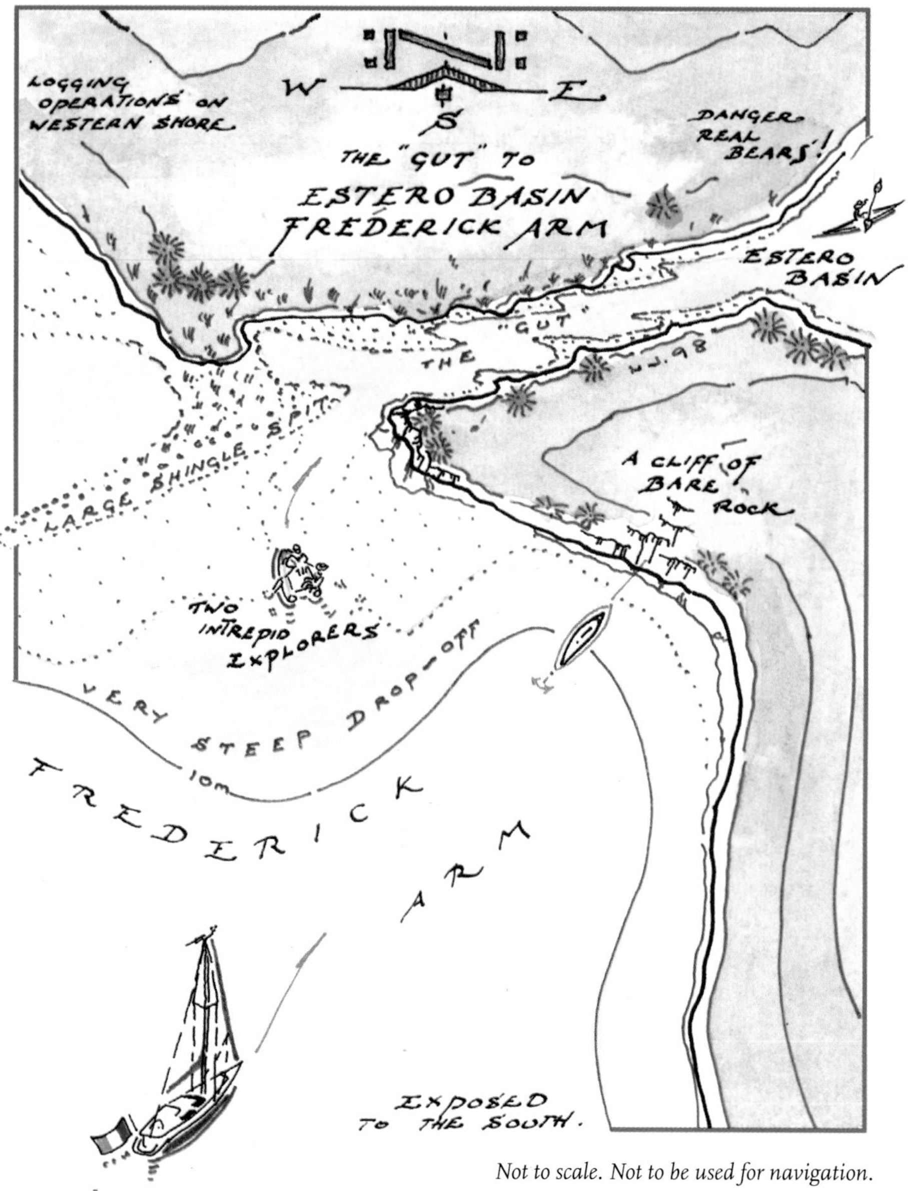

Not to scale. Not to be used for navigation.

✲

The temporary, deep-water anchorage at the head of Frederick Arm makes an excellent day stop, as from here you can easily adventure into beautiful Estero Basin by dinghy or kayak. The tidal waters flow rapidly in and out of the basin, so timing your trip around slack water is essential unless you plan to shoot the rapids or are prepared to beach or portage your dinghy at some point. Although tugboats have been using the "Gut" (as it's known locally) for years, ascending the narrows in a deep-draft boat, even at HW slack, isn't advisable without detailed local knowledge. Take advantage of the clear, freshwater stream that flows down into Estero Basin from the lakes on the northern shore, and pack your soap and swimsuit. Boaters should keep in mind that this is bear country and take the usual precautions when exploring beyond the shoreline.

Note: Afternoon inflow winds can make the head of Frederick Arm choppy and sometimes untenable for safe anchorage by small craft. If you time it right, you can take the last of the flood into the basin, enjoy a 2-hour excursion, then return on an early ebb and settle into Shoal Bay (see page 129) for the night.

CHARTS 3543. 3312, page 25.

APPROACH

From the N out of Cordero Channel. The wharfhead and jetty are the most conspicuous landmarks.

ANCHOR

Anchorage is possible to the NE and NW, within the vicinity of the public wharf. Depths, holding and bottom condition unrecorded.

PUBLIC WHARF

Popular with visitors in the summer months. There is no power on the floats, and water is restricted.

Note: Shoal Bay experiences overnight out-flow winds emanating from Phillips Arm, making the anchorage a lee shore. Ensure that your anchor is well set prior to an overnight stay.

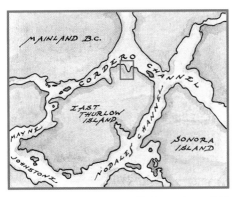

✣ 50° 27.6' N   125° 21.9' W

Shoal Bay provides a convenient base while you explore Phillips and Frederick Arms or while waiting for slack water at Dent and Greene Point Rapids. Although the peaceful public wharf in Shoal Bay has limited amenities, it's in good repair and has a great view across Cordero Channel, up Phillips Arm. It's hard to imagine now that this bay was a boom town in the early 1900s, claiming a community larger than the new city of Vancouver.

A long jetty across the shallows takes you past the abandoned 100-year-old store and post office, where a boardwalk leads you to the SHOAL BAY LODGE, 250-286-6016. Ice is available and showers can be arranged. The lodge serves an informal breakfast or lunch on the patio, but dinner reservations are needed a few hours in advance. This relaxed and rustic lodge offers fishing, kayaking, ecotours, comfortable family accommodation, a cosy pub and good home cooking. There is a 45-minute hike to the DOUGLAS PINE MINE, which once produced gold, copper and iron – just ask the managers of the lodge for directions. (The lodge was up for sale when we visited it in 1998.)

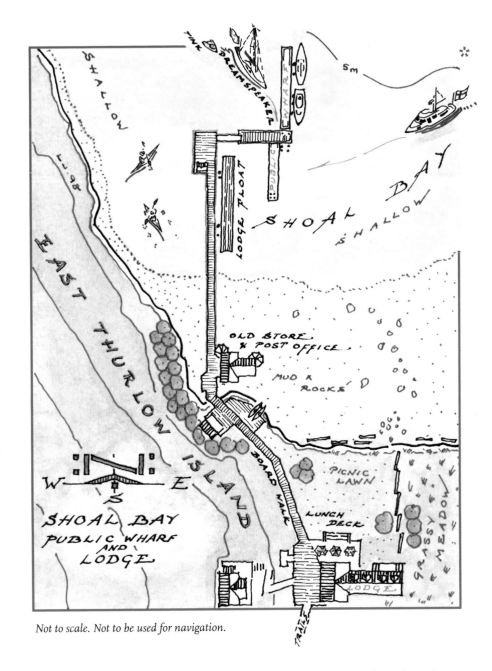

Not to scale. Not to be used for navigation.

10.3   BICKLEY BAY, E THURLOW ISLAND

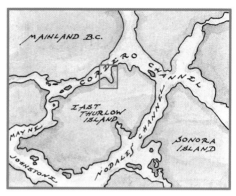

❋ 50° 27.3' N   125° 24.0' W

CHARTS 3543. 3312, pages 24 & 25.

APPROACH
From the N, between Peel Rocks and a large fish farm.

ANCHOR
Reasonably protected anchorage can be found at the head of the bay. Depths of 5 - 10 m (16 - 33 ft), holding good in mud.

Note: Overnight outflow winds from Phillips Arm make the bay a lee shore. In summer, however, the relatively light wind is offset by good holding. Ensure that your anchor is well set prior to an overnight stay.

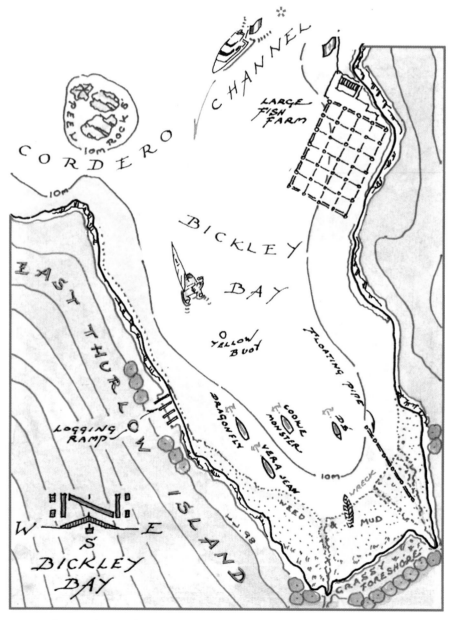

Not to scale. Not to be used for navigation.

Just around the corner from Shoal Bay lies well-protected Bickley Bay. It is a pleasant place to anchor overnight or use as a base while you explore Phillips Arm. It is backed by a grassy foreshore and fed by a freshwater stream. If you have a kayak on board and the tide is up, take the opportunity to paddle at leisure and observe the wildlife. When we visited one August, the stream was so low that the restless salmon were jumping around our boat but unfortunately not onto our hooks. Perhaps they were escapees from the nearby fish farm celebrating their successful getaway!

The floating Cordero Lodge.

CHARTS 3543. 3312, page 24.

APPROACH

Either from the S, out of Cordero Channel, or from the W, between the mainland and Lorte Island.

ANCHOR

W of the lodge, where reasonable protection can be found between Lorte Island and the mainland. Depths, holding and bottom condition unrecorded.

MARINA

CORDERO LODGE, 250-287-0917, has moorage exclusively for its guests and visitors. It monitors VHF channel 73 and requires summertime booking.

Note: Plan your approach to the lodge's floats with caution because the current swirls around Lorte Island, making docking precarious at times.

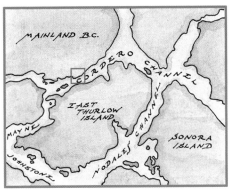

❖ 50° 26.7' N 125° 27.1' W

Please reduce speed when you see the "SLOW" sign near the entrance to this picturesque floating lodge, bedecked with hanging baskets of flowers in the summer months.

Visitors have returned for over 15 years to enjoy the good fishing, warm hospitality and hearty German cooking provided by Reinhardt and Doris Küppers and their family. Doris's famous schnitzel dishes come stuffed, fried, topped or sautéed, the seafood is fresh and regulars claim that the apple strudel is out of this world. The restaurant, with a lounge and piano, seats 22 but has been known to squeeze in 25 hungry guests and boaters, so count on dinner being a lively affair. To avoid disappointment, reserve in advance.

The lodge offers overnight moorage, with water and limited power on the docks, and accommodation for up to 8 guests. Because the family believes in a good night's sleep, the running of generators is restricted at night.

NOTE: The lodge is just a short hop from the anchorage in Bickley Bay.

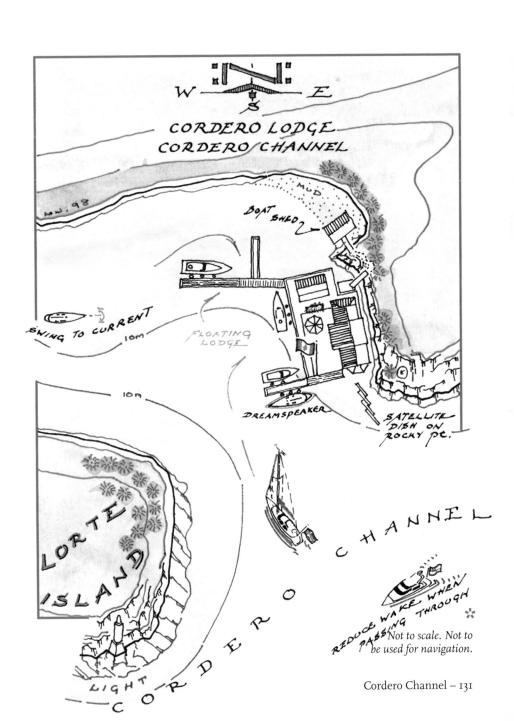

Not to scale. Not to be used for navigation.

10.5 Greene Point Rapids & W Cordero Channel

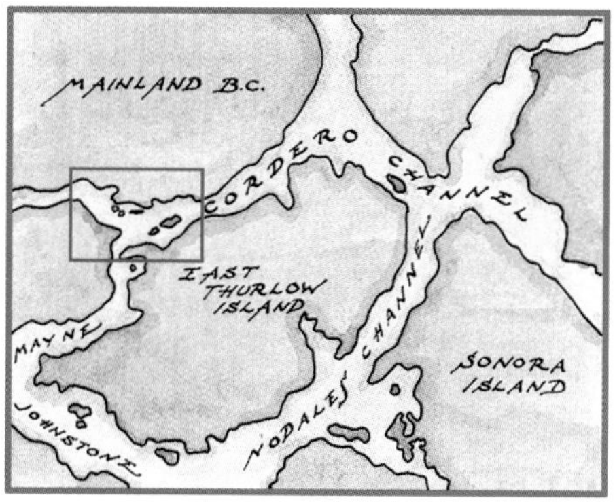

✲ 50° 26.0' N 125° 29.5' W

CHARTS 3543. 3312, page 24.

GREENE POINT RAPIDS

Approach the rapids at or near slack water and with the current turning in your favour.

Reference current station: Seymour Narrows
Direction of flood: SE
Times of slack water as follows:

- turn to flood:
  minus (–) 1 hour 25 minutes
- turn to ebb:
  minus (–) 1 hour 35 minutes

W CORDERO CHANNEL

Listed are 4 handy anchorages in Cordero Channel to overnight or await the turn of the tide.

1. "CORDERO COVE," see 10.6 (page 133)
2. LORTE ISLAND, see 10.4 (page 131)
3. TALLAC BAY, on the mainland shore, offers a comfortable temporary anchorage on its western shore. Backed by a grassy meadow, it offers good holding and is fun to explore.
4. CRAWFORD ANCHORAGE, in a cosy nook on the southern shore of Erasmus Island

These rapids extend both E and W from Greene Point. Strong currents of up to 5 knots are found off Erasmus Island, but they dissipate to 3 knots past Lorte Island. Maximum current velocities encountered in the rapids are recorded at the current station, situated centre channel between the Cordero Islands and W Thurlow Island, with a maximum flood of 7 knots and an ebb of 5 knots. Dangerous overfalls and turbulent water form SW off the Cordero Islands, with whirlpools and upwellings W of Greene Point and N of Edsall Islets.

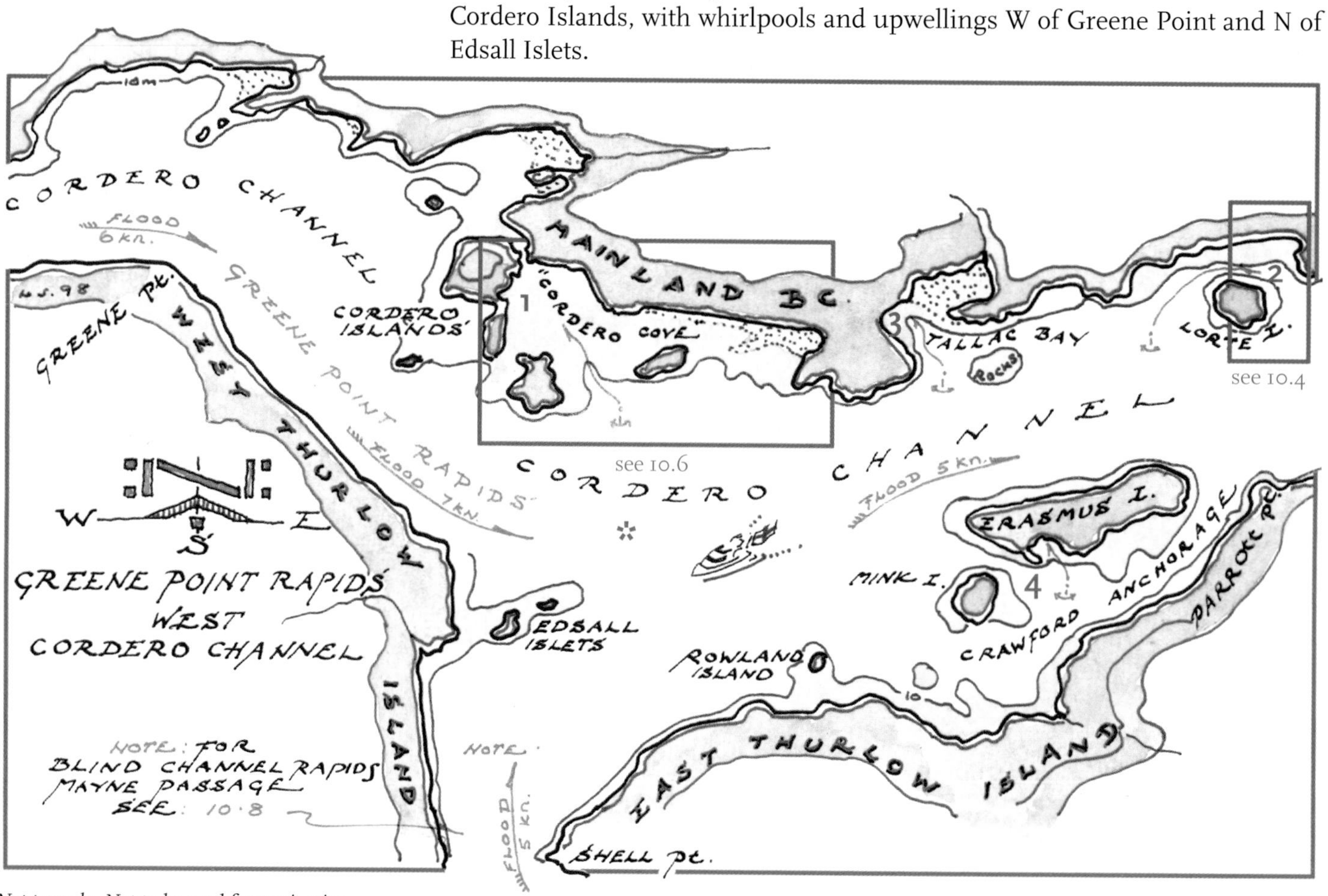

Not to scale. Not to be used for navigation.

CHARTS 3543. 3312, page 24.

APPROACH

From the S; the channel between the southern islands is fringed by kelp. A rock lies off the western tip of the easternmost island.

ANCHOR

Good sheltered anchorage, away from the turbulence and eddies in Cordero Channel, can be found in the cove. Depths of 6 - 12 m (19.5 - 39 ft), holding over a mud, sand and weed bottom.

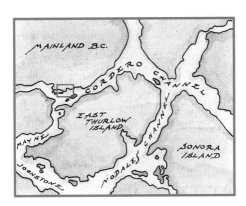

✳ 50° 26.4' N   125° 29.6' W

Smooth rocks for a lazy afternoon nap.

This surprise anchorage is protected from northwesterly winds and the swift current in Cordero Channel by 3 charming islands. The SE basin also affords some protection in a southeasterly.

  With a pleasant view out to bustling Cordero Channel, "Cordero Cove" (named by us) is an ideal spot for exploring, picnicking, shell collecting and just lazing in the cockpit. Many tranquil hours can be spent basking on the smooth-rock islet in the cove's NW corner. You'll be lulled by water music as water gushes through the narrow gap and tumbles over rocks at HW. The best spot to spread your picnic blanket is on the downy moss and grass patch on the western-most island with a great view over to the Greene Point Rapids.

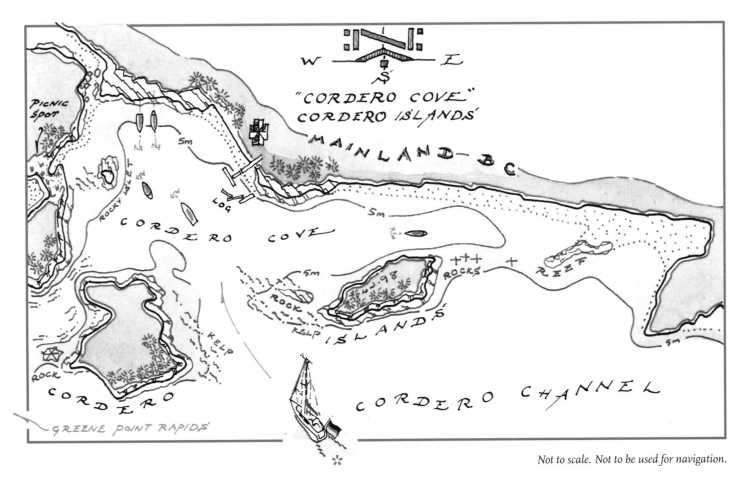

Not to scale. Not to be used for navigation.

10.7 Blind Channel Resort, W Thurlow Island

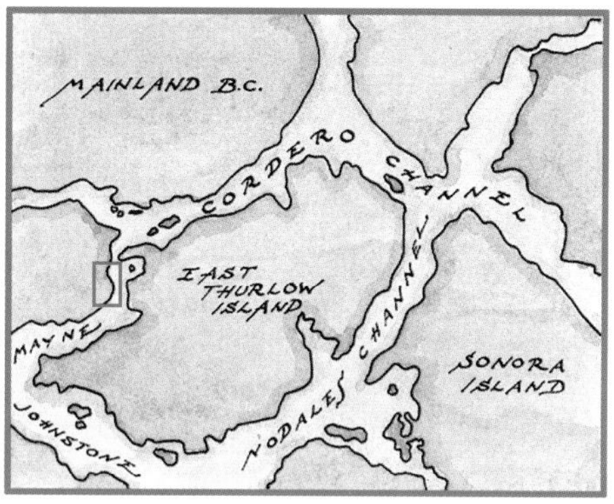

50° 24.9′ N 125° 29.9′ W

CHARTS 3543. 3312, page 24.

APPROACH

With caution, because a back eddy, running counter to the current in Mayne Passage, creates a strong current setting into the marina facility.

MARINA

The Blind Channel Resort marina, 250-830-8620, VHF 73, has extensive visitor moorage. A fuel dock is operated by the resort.

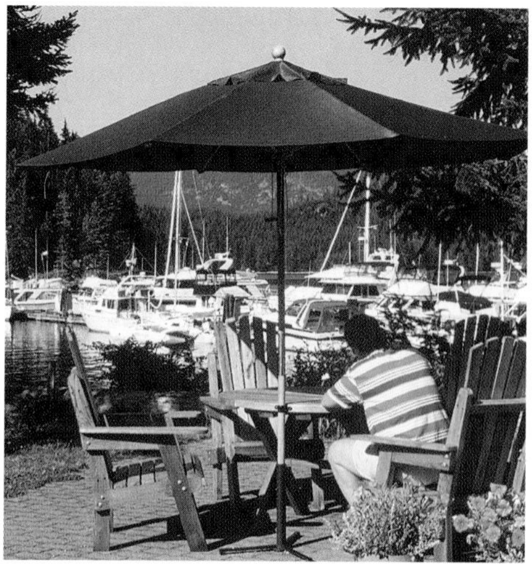

The deck at Blind Channel Resort.

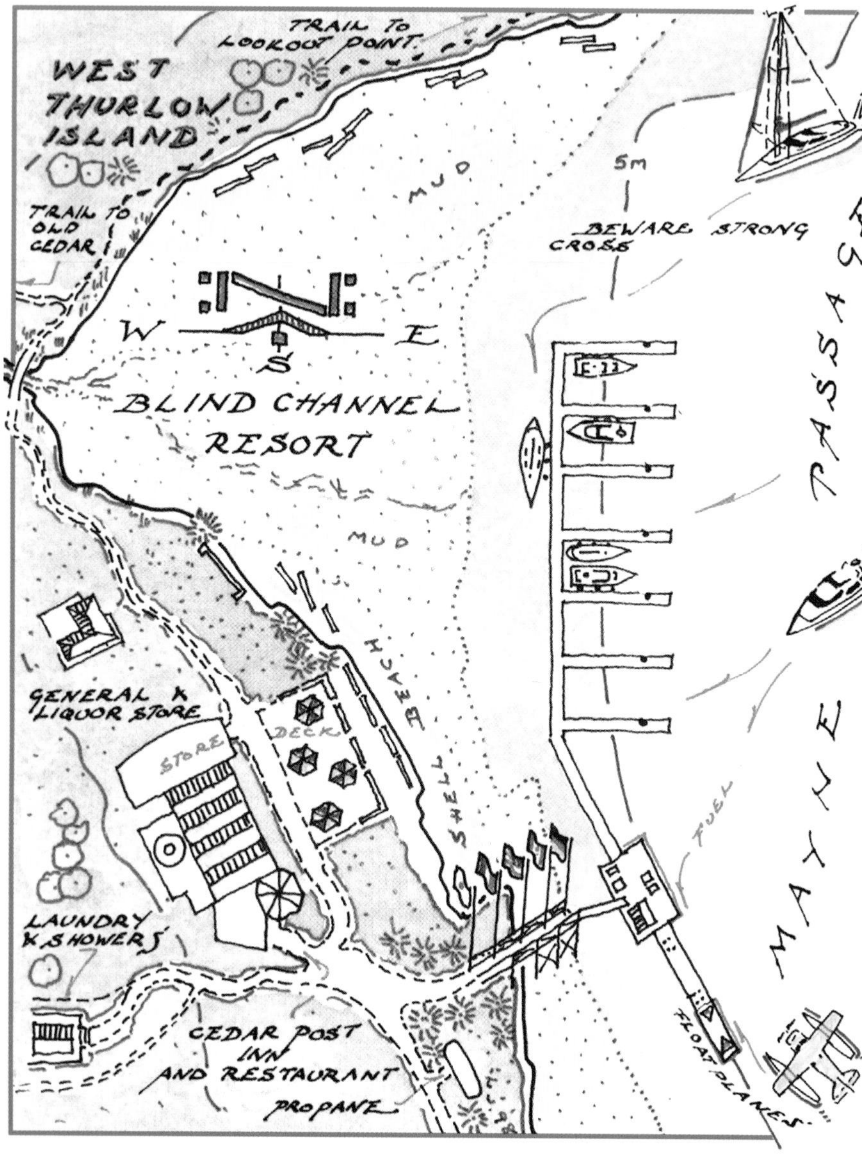

Not to scale. Not to be used for navigation.

Pristine docks, colourful artwork and terra cotta pots spilling over with flowers welcome you to the efficiently run Blind Channel Resort. Owned and operated by 3 generations of the Richter family since 1970, this self-contained resort has a restaurant and patio, store, post office, B.C. Liquor Store outlet and waterside cottage with full facilities. It also sells fuel and propane, and moorage comes with 24-hour power and piped spring water. Free moorage of 2 hours is given to boaters while they shop or dine at the resort. Shower and laundry facilities are also available. The well-stocked store offers delicious, freshly baked bread and muffins, a variety of basic provisions, frozen meats and an adequate selection of fresh produce. "Spring water ice" is produced on site, and fishing licenses, charts, books and unique gifts are also sold. Pick up a hiking trail map and visit the 800-year-old cedar in the forest behind the resort.

Evidence of Edgar and Annemarie Richter's artistic talents can also be seen in the Cedar Post Inn, where excellent home-cooked, Bavarian-style meals are served along with an interesting selection of wines. Reservations are essential, so phone or fax 250-830-8620.

Charles Bay, "Blind Channel Rapids," E Thurlow Island 10.8

CHARTS 3543. 3312, page 24.

APPROACH: Charles Bay

From Mayne Passage at LW slack.

ANCHOR

Due N of Eclipse Islet, and swing in back eddies. Depths of 2 - 4 m (6.5 - 13 ft), holding good in mud.

Note: The bay, although open to Mayne Passage, lies in the wind shadow of W Thurlow Island and is therefore well protected from the prevailing summer westerlies.

APPROACH: "Blind Channel Rapids"

On or near slack water.

Reference current station: Seymour Narrows
Direction of flood: N
Times of slack water as follows:

- Turn to flood: minus (–) 20 minutes
- Turn to ebb: minus (–) 1 hour

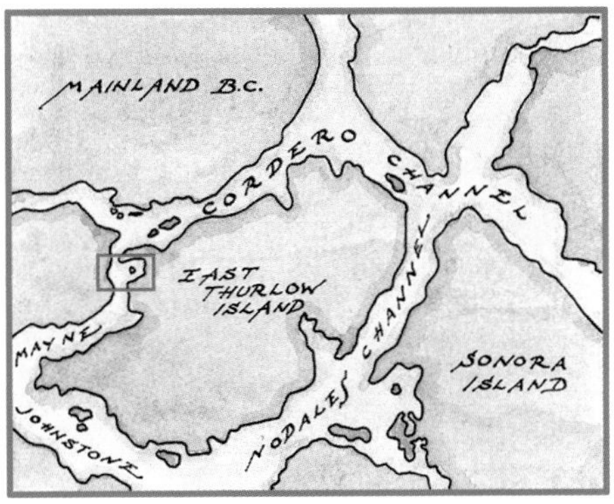

50° 25.2' N 125° 29.6' W

Good crabbing and well-protected anchorage can be found across the way from Blind Channel Resort (see page 134) in secluded Charles Bay. Sheltered from southeasterly and northwesterly winds and the effects of the Greene Point and "Blind Channel Rapids", this small haven offers peace. Beautiful Eclipse Islet, circled by clear water, provides an idyllic picnic spot. You can pick fresh sea asparagus, poke around the rocks or just laze on the colourful pebble beach watching boat traffic in Mayne Passage challenge the "Blind Channel Rapids."

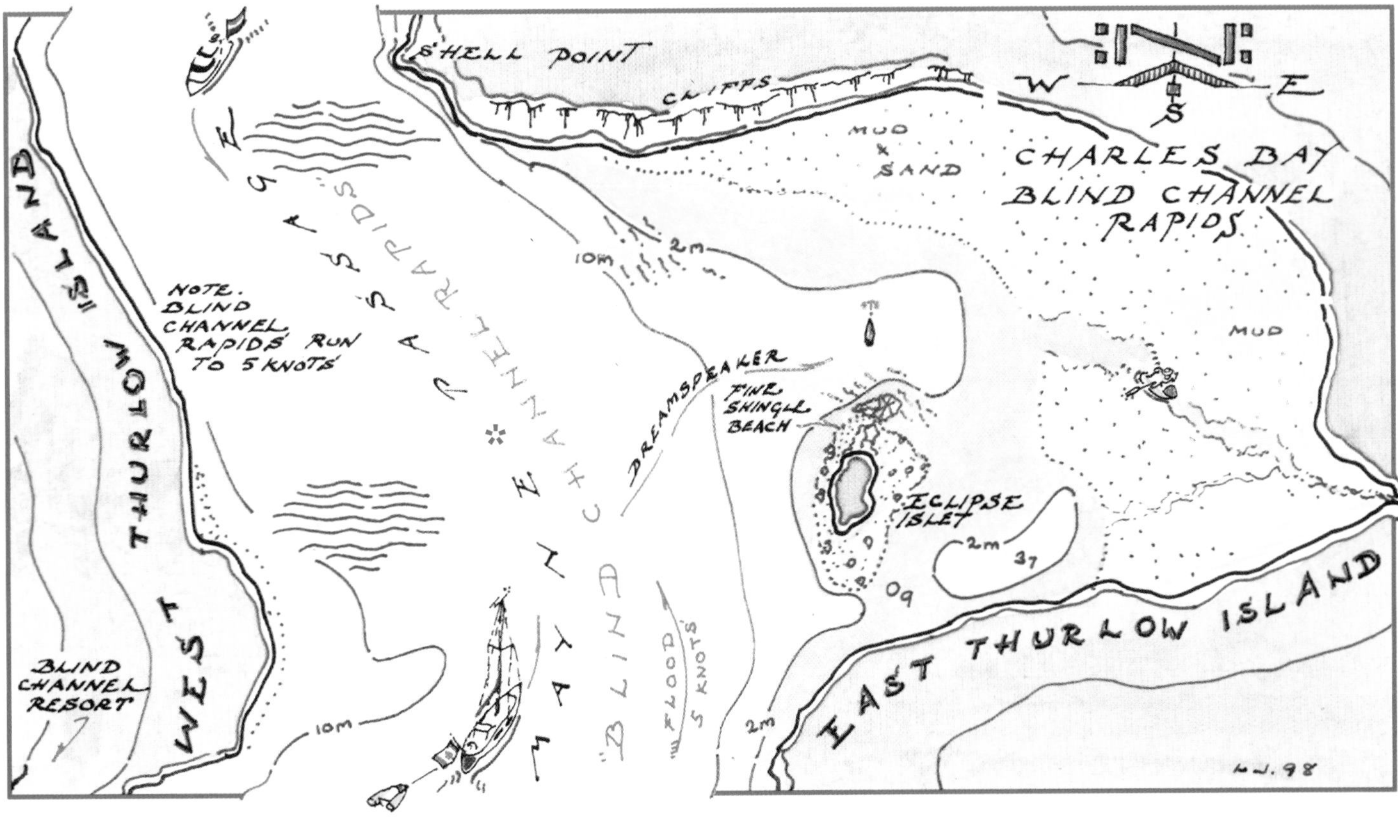

Not to scale. Not to be used for navigation.

10.9 THURSTON BAY MARINE PARK & CAMELEON HARBOUR, SONORA ISLAND

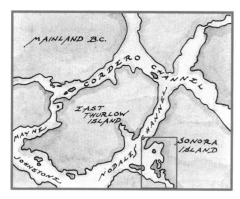

CHARTS 3543. 3312, page 25.

ANCHOR

THURSTON BAY: See 10.10 (page 137).

"ANCHORAGE LAGOON": Snug, all-weather protection, but the entrance is shallow, 0.6 m (2 ft), and requires careful navigation. Depths, holding and bottom condition unrecorded.

HANDFIELD BAY: See 10.11 (page 137).

❊ 50° 22.1' N   125° 20.4' W

CAMELEON HARBOUR: Anchorage is possible throughout the harbour. Depths vary, holding good in sticky mud. However, if a strong westerly is forecast for Johnstone Strait, the same wind will whistle through the harbour. When entering be sure to keep clear of Douglas Rock off Bruce Point, and avoid the rocky ledges that extend out from Greetham Point.

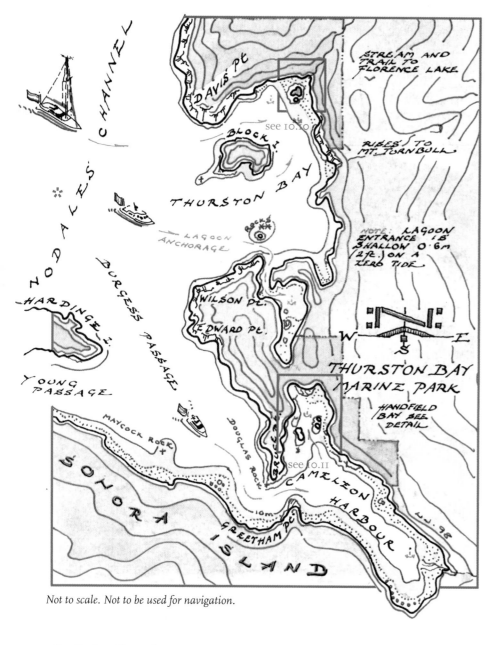

Not to scale. Not to be used for navigation.

THURSTON BAY MARINE PARK is peaceful and undeveloped, although its middle section is private property (as of 1998). There are, however, plans to acquire this central portion. The northern section of the park is in Thurston Bay itself and offers partly protected, temporary anchorage behind Block Island, especially if you tuck into the western side of "Hook Islets" (named by us). Snug but very shallow and restricted anchorage can be found in "Anchorage Lagoon" at the southern end of the bay. Almost landlocked, it should be navigated with caution as submerged rocks guard the entrance. From the marshy southern portion of the lagoon, you can hike the overgrown trail leading to Handfield Bay (see page 137) and Cameleon Harbour.

CAMELEON HARBOUR is a protected anchorage that also catches the last rays of the evening sun, so following local advice we dropped our hook in the SE corner of the harbour. This secure and peaceful spot overlooks a creek and the grassy foreshore of a long-deserted homestead. Wind can funnel down into the harbour, but the holding is excellent in sticky mud.

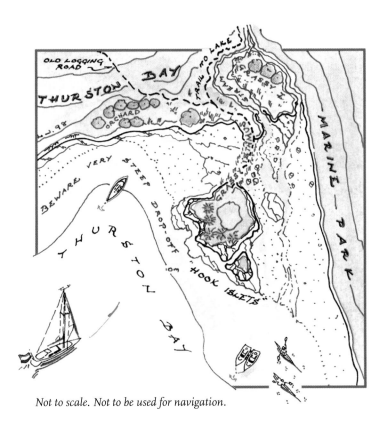

Not to scale. Not to be used for navigation.

HANDFIELD BAY 10.11

APPROACH

From the S out of Cameleon Harbour. Best approached at LW when the rocks and drying foreshore are visible.

ANCHOR

All-weather protection, best with a stern line ashore. Depths of 2 - 4 m (6.5 - 13 ft), holding moderate over a mix of rock, shell and mud.

Quiet and solitude welcome you to this lovely pocket bay, where a few idle days can be spent digging clams, picnicking on Tully Island, swimming or exploring the rocky shoreline by dinghy or kayak. The bay's narrow entrance should be navigated with caution. An overgrown trail leads through the park forest, connecting Handfield Bay with Anchorage Lagoon. A smooth sunbathing rock in the NE corner of the bay fronts a mossy glen shaded by wild fruit trees where signs of visiting deer and bears are evident. Any form of disturbance will be unappreciated in this secluded anchorage.

APPROACH

A safe approach can be made either to the N or to the W of Block Island.

ANCHOR

Temporary anchorage can be found to the NW or S of "Hook Islets" (named by us). Depths of 5 - 10 m (16 - 33 ft), holding good over sand and mud.

Note: If a strong westerly is forecast for Johnstone Strait, the wind will penetrate into the bay. Block Island gives no real protection.

Partly protected, temporary anchorage can be found behind Block Island and E or W of the "Hook Islets" (named by us), the larger Islet being connected to Sonora Island by a narrow, grassy isthmus. The islets are fun to explore, and you can relax and dip your toes in the clear water from the comfortable sunbathing rocks. En route to the stream that flows down from Florence Lake, you can pick pears and blackberries in season, and the wild mint that grows along the trail makes a great addition to a "boater's salad."

Overgrown trails beside the stream and behind the bay take you to the old B.C. FOREST SERVICE STATION site, which served for over 25 years as the regional marine headquarters, and to Florence Lake, 2.4 km (1.5 mi) inland.

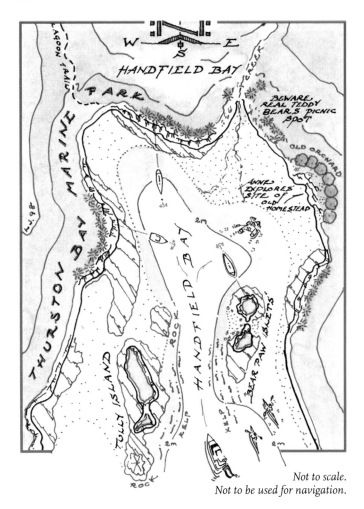

Not to scale. Not to be used for navigation.

10.12 The Head of Hemming Bay, E Thurlow Island

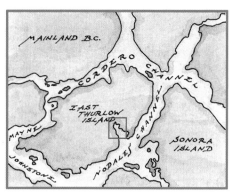

✳ 50° 23.6' N 125° 22.7' W

CHARTS 3543. 3312, page 25.

APPROACH

Leave the 6 rocky islets to port as you approach the head of the bay.

ANCHOR

There is all-weather protection for 1 or 2 boats W of the private buoy. An alternative anchorage more open to the S, but well protected from the prevailing westerlies, lies N of the private buoy. Depth, holding and bottom condition vary.

Not to scale. Not to be used for navigation.

Sheltered overnight anchorage is available for 1 or 2 boats W of the private buoy, with a stern line to the grassy islet. While deeper anchorage, exposed to the S, can be found at the head of the bay. The lagoonlike haven NW of the islets is perfect for exploring by dinghy or kayak. It has a stunning, sheer rock face at its narrow NW entrance, a freshwater stream and a lovely sunset view through the gap.

A small private float, bridge and trail lead to the Hemming Bay Community Lodge and to Hemming Lake. Signs request that visitors respect the lodge's privacy and the community's freshwater supply.

Rock bluff, head of Hemming Bay.

Chapter 11

NORTHERN
QUADRA
ISLAND

Anne and Tink explore Bodega Point.

Chapter 11
NORTHERN QUADRA ISLAND

Octopus Islands Marine Park (11.7)

TIDES

Canadian Tide and Current Tables, Volume 5 & 6
Reference Port: Pt. Atkinson
Secondary Port: Surge Narrows

CURRENTS

Reference Stations: Beazley Passage (previously Surge Narrows), Hole in the Wall (West end), Seymour Narrows
Secondary Station: Okisollo Channel (Upper Rapids)

WEATHER

Area: Johnstone Strait
Reporting Stations: Chatham Point, Campbell River

Note: The strong westerly winds in Johnstone Strait, which can reach 30 - 35 knots during summer evenings, will continue, although with reduced strength, through Discovery Passage and into Kanish Bay. These winds are also felt in Granite Bay and Hoskyn Channel prior to diminishing overnight.

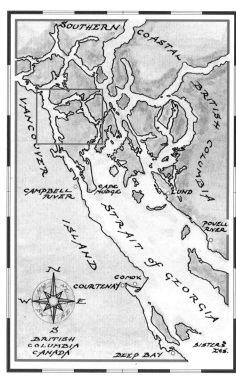

CAUTIONARY NOTES

Although the Surge Narrows-Okisollo Channel route is considered less daunting than Seymour Narrows or the Yucultas, all tidal rapids require diligent use of the Canadian Tide and Current Tables *and careful cruise planning.*

The currents in Beazley Passage, Lower Rapids, Upper Rapids and Hole in the Wall are extremely hazardous and present a real danger to all craft.

This chapter takes you north to the head of Hoskyn Channel and through the Settlers Group of islands, a route known locally as "Surge Narrows." It also includes Okisollo Channel with the Upper and Lower Rapids, Hole in the Wall and Northern Discovery Passage. Beginning with the quiet, historic anchorage in Village Bay on Quadra Island's eastern shore, the boater can choose from a good cross-section of quiet hideaway anchorages, scenic picnic stops and popular summer spots along the way.

A cosy refuge can be found in "Boulton Bay" with its smooth picnic rocks and breathtaking views down to Rebecca Spit. Don't miss the opportunity to visit Surge Narrows General Store before transiting Beazley or Whiterock Passage. Treat yourself to an ice cream on the shaded outside deck or stock up on local organic produce and freshly baked bread. The enchanting "Diamond Islets" (named by us) in Okisollo Channel invite you to stay for a while and enjoy their tranquillity. From here a mossy viewpoint looks over to the alluring Octopus Islands, where sheltered coves are neatly tucked into the northeast corner of Waiatt Bay. Although these islands are extremely popular in the summer months, they still provide you with the opportunity to take it easy and enjoy life's more simple pleasures. The spacious and well-protected waters of Waiatt Bay offer a less crowded alternative.

Protected anchorage can be found throughout Owen Bay and opposite the small public wharf. Backed by a wild apple orchard, this unassuming spot has a laid-back charm all its own. Although a good portion of Kanish Bay is occupied by fish farms, there's a delightful picnic anchorage behind Bodega Point. Historic Orchard Bay is backed by a grass-covered midden and an overgrown orchard laden with edible fruit in season. Sheltered Granite Bay once supported a thriving community of over 500 people, but today locals visit their rustic summer cabins to enjoy its out-of-the-way peace and solitude.

The all-weather anchorage found inside Small Inlet's restricted channel is surrounded by lush forest. Abundant with wildlife, it is ideal to explore by dinghy or kayak or by hiking the portage trail to the pebble beach at Waiatt Bay.

Protected from westerly winds and seemingly unaffected by the tidal turmoil in Discovery Passage, Otter Cove provides a convenient spot to stop and relax while you wait for slack water or calmer wind conditions in bustling Johnstone Strait.

Featured Destinations

Not to be used for navigation.

CHARTS 3539. 3312, page 19.

APPROACH
From the SE out of Hoskyn Channel.

ANCHOR
Temporary anchorage at the head of Village Bay on either side of "Castle Islet" (named by us). Exposed to the SE, although provides good protection from westerly and northwesterly winds. Depths of 4 - 6 m (13 - 19.5 ft), moderate holding in shingle and rock.

Village Bay, once a sizeable Indian village.

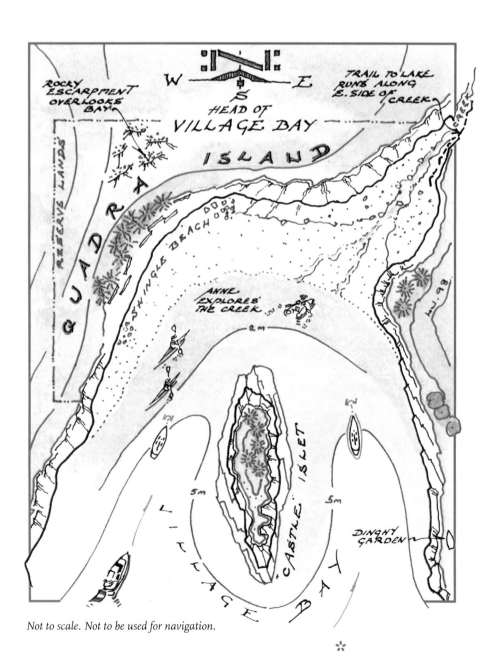

Not to scale. Not to be used for navigation.

In fair weather, you can anchor on either side of "Castle Islet" (named by us), at the northern end of this quiet hideaway. Covered with a medley of shrubs, grasses and windswept trees, the islet provides a great adventuring playground for those in need of a little exercise.

Village Bay was once the site of a sizeable Indian village, and a log "flume" was constructed in the late 1800s to transport lumber from the southern end of Village Bay Lake downstream into the bay. A natural, warmwater swimming pool can be found a short distance up from the mouth of the creek. From here a shady trail meanders alongside the stream and ends above a grassy cliff, overlooking Village Bay Lake. Although the path is on private land, as of 1998 the owners had refrained from posting "No Trespassing" signs, and we urge boaters and kayakers to respect the property. Village Bay Lake joins with Main Lake, making this freshwater waterway the largest in the Gulf or Discovery Islands.

Access to the newly completed SHELLALLIGIN PASS TRAIL is possible from the SW shoreline of Village Bay.

The sheer cliffs of "Boulton Bay."

CHARTS 3539. 3312, page 19.

APPROACH
From Hoskyn Channel by rounding Sheer Point.

ANCHOR
Temporary anchorage is possible at the head of the bay. Open to the S, but it provides good protection from westerly and northwesterly winds. Depths of 6 - 12 m (19.5 - 39 ft), holding good in mud and shingle.

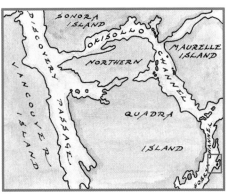

✻ 50° 11.8' N 125° 7.6' W

Steep cliffs on the western shore of "Boulton Bay" form a spectacular backdrop to this quiet refuge. Open to the S but protected from northwesterly winds, it provides temporary anchorage for 2 or 3 boats. Kayakers can beach their craft and find some shelter at the head of the bay, although overnight camping on crown land is available farther N, at "Freedom Point" (local name). A freshwater creek flows down to the log-strewn pebble beach, and a sign posted beyond the big tree stump reads "You are welcome to the water – take a rest – but beyond this point you are TRESPASSING."

There are smooth sun-basking rocks below a sign that reads "Shellfish Lease – No Pickin' Please." The picnic rocks at "Sunset Point" (named by us) are ideal for catching the last rays of the setting sun while taking in the breathtaking views down to Rebecca Spit.

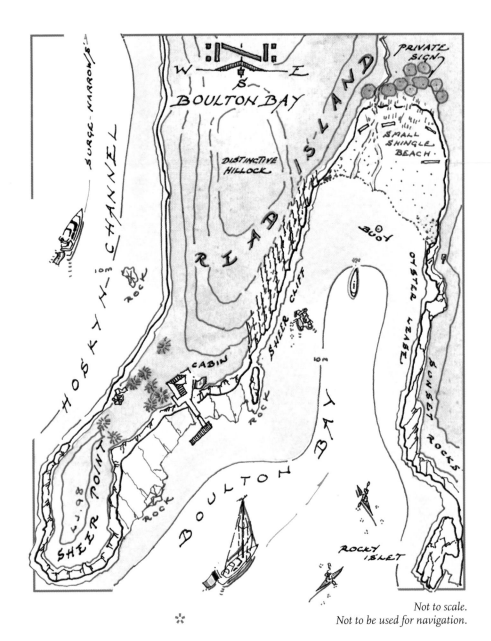

Not to scale.
Not to be used for navigation.

11.3   SURGE NARROWS

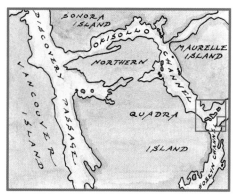

✤ 50° 13.4' N   125° 8.1' W

CHARTS 3537. 3312, page 20.

APPROACH

Beazley Passage on or near slack water. Beazley Passage is the only safe passage through or around the Settlers Group of islands.

Reference current station: Beazley Passage
Direction of flood: SE
Slack water (turn): 5 - 11 minutes

ANCHOR

Anchorage in the vicinity of the Settlers Group of islands isn't recommended because of the strong tidal streams and poor holding.

Note: Beazley Passage is wider than it appears, 60 m (197 ft), but most craft file through one at a time in the centre channel. Beware of Tusko Rock, well defined by a kelp bed when the rock is submerged.

The name "Surge Narrows" is applied locally to the entire route from Hoskyn Channel, through Beazley Passage, to Okisollo Channel. It has become the chosen scenic route N and is exceedingly popular with recreational boaters in the summer months. Because it's best to transit the narrows with the tidal turn to your advantage, be courteous and give priority to craft taking the last of a tide.

The southern tip of Maurelle Island, Peck & Goepel Islands in the Settlers Group and a small portion of Quadra Island are provincial parks, ideal for kayakers who practise low-impact camping. A small parks day float is planned for 1999 and will allow small craft access to Maurelle Island and Antonio Point.

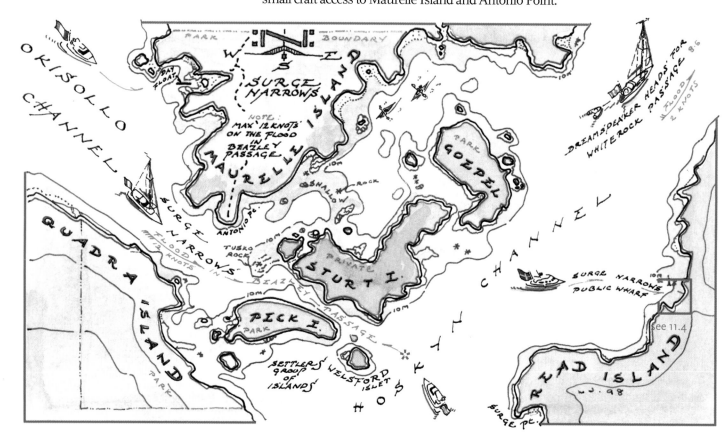

Not to scale. Not to be used for navigation.

CHARTS 3537. 3312, page 20.

APPROACH

From the W out of Hoskyn Channel. Leave the porthand (green) buoy to the N when approaching the public wharf.

PUBLIC WHARF

A small facility mainly used by locals, but visitors are always welcome.

Note: Take care while docking because strong back eddies swirl around the wharf. There are plans for private moorage at the store.

Surge Narrows store.

Locals and cruising boaters alike are delighted that the Beyerstein family has reopened the historic SURGE NARROWS GENERAL STORE (as of 1998); telephone: cell/fax 250-287-6962. With careful renovations, the store's original interior has been enhanced but still retains its old-world charm. The store offers an excellent selection of basic provisions, specialty items, local and organic produce and crafts, frozen meat (from Gunther Bros.), dairy products, ice and a refreshing choice of books. The freshly baked bread is delicious, and the seasonal homemade jams are worth stocking up on. Hardware, fishing tackle, charts and *Canadian Tide and Current Tables* are also available, as is a fax machine.

Plans for private moorage facilities and additional deck seating are proposed for 2000.

On the sunny deck, colourful flower boxes and a shaded table invite you to relax for a while, enjoy an ice cream cone and catch up on local cruising news while waiting for slack water in Whiterock or Beazley Passage. Mail is delivered to and collected from the dock post office each Monday, Wednesday and Friday. Daily store hours are from 8 a.m. until dark.

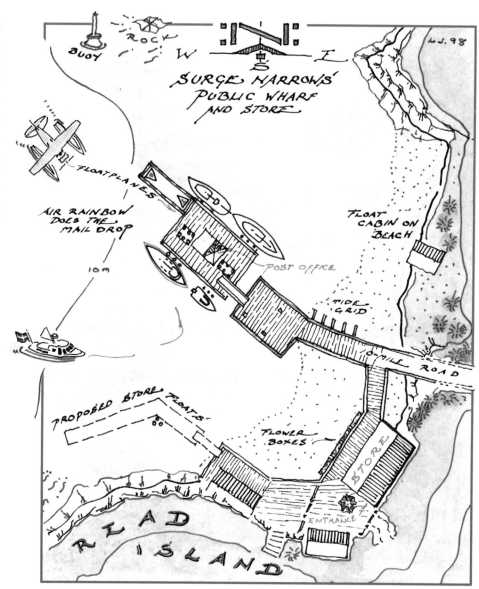

Not to scale. Not to be used for navigation.

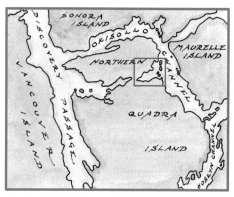

CHARTS 3537. 3312, page 21.

APPROACH

If you are approaching from the E, S of Octopus Islands, the entrance is best transited at LW when the rocks and reefs are visible. For an alternative approach from the N, see 11.7 (page 148).

❖ 1) 50° 16.1' N   125° 12.8' W
❖ 2) 50° 17.1' N   125° 13.2' W

ANCHOR

Protected anchorage can be found throughout the bay or in one of its numerous coves and nooks. Depth, holding and bottom condition vary, but holding is generally good in mud.

Note: To protect the portage trail's natural heritage and beauty, B.C. Parks is endeavouring to acquire the land between Waiatt Bay and Small Inlet. However, the majority of the southern shoreline in Waiatt Bay is now part of Octopus Islands Marine Park.

During summer months, the numerous nooks and crannies in spacious Waiatt Bay offer a peaceful alternative to the more popular anchorages in Octopus Islands Marine Park. The bay's waters are also a Parks Protected Area set aside for recreational use only.

"Cabin Cove" (named by us) on Waiatt Bay's northern shore offers good holding and will accommodate 5 or 6 boats comfortably. The rock and pebble beach is backed by a grassy foreshore and the overgrown ruins of an old cabin. Land beyond the HW mark is private. (Note that logging was in progress N of the cove in 1998.)

"Trail Cove" (named by us) at the head of the bay has clear water, a smooth pebble beach and plenty of room to swing. It's worth spending a little extra time here to explore the Waiatt Bay-Small Inlet parkland. The shaded portage trail takes you on a leisurely half-mile ramble through tranquil, second-growth forest and concealed middens to the head of Small Inlet (see page 147). From here you can take the path to Newton Lake for a refreshing, warmwater swim or a more energetic hike to Granite Bay (see page 156).

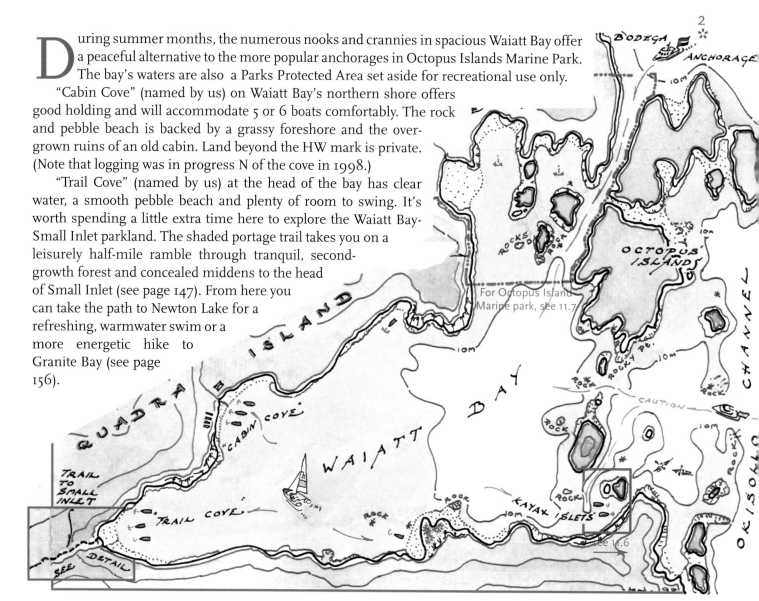

Not to scale. Not to be used for navigation.

"KAYAK ISLETS," WAIATT BAY 11.6
OCTOPUS ISLANDS MARINE PARK

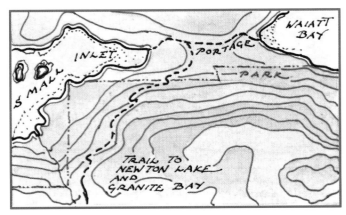

The portage trail between Waiatt Bay & Small Inlet.

CHARTS 3537. 3312, page 21.

APPROACH
See 11.5 (page 146), Waiatt Bay.

ANCHOR
Temporary anchorage, exposed to westerly winds. Depths of 3 - 6 m (10 - 19.5 ft), holding good in mud.

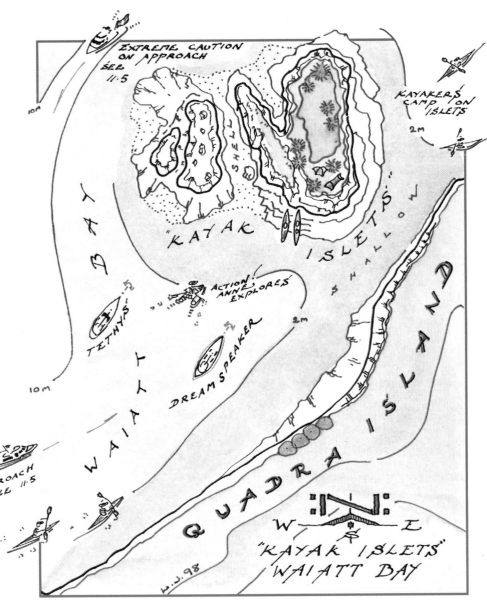

Not to scale. Not to be used for navigation.

"Kayak Islets" (named by us) are now part of Octopus Islands Marine Park, and provide a peaceful haven for kayakers and boaters alike. They are best navigated at LW to avoid the numerous submerged rocks. Outboards and generators are definitely not welcome in this back-to-nature retreat populated by a variety of intriguing wildlife and the colourful tents of fellow campers. The flat sunbathing rocks on the SW shore also provide a convenient ramp to beach a kayak or dinghy. For the longest evening light, drop your hook in the small cove SE of "Kayak Islets."

A boat gets lucky in "Kayak Islets."

11.7 OCTOPUS ISLANDS MARINE PARK, QUADRA ISLAND

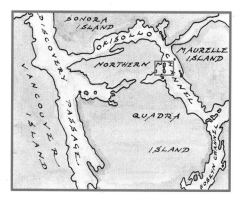

✤ 50° 17.1′ N   125° 13.2′ W

Find a nook, drop the hook, and take a line ashore.

Waiatt Bay to Octopus Islands.

The sheltered coves of OCTOPUS ISLANDS MARINE PARK are neatly tucked into the NE corner of Waiatt Bay and offer the cruising boater refuge between the tidal passes and an opportunity to take it easy while enjoying life's more simple pleasures.

Although extremely popular in the summer months, with boats rafted together and tied back to every available tree, the anchorages empty out rapidly each day as boaters on tight schedules then move on to the next desirable location. If you have the time, stay a while and explore the rocky islets by dinghy or kayak. Most boaters try to avoid the use of noisy outboards and generators within the park, thereby making life more relaxing and wildlife spotting far easier.

"Osprey Cove," the larger of the 2 coves, was named by us after a pair of local birds performed an incredible diving routine. The cove can accommodate a good number of boats, especially when stern lines are used. Shoal-draft anchorage is possible in a cosy nook to the W, where drying mud flats, a freshwater creek and an open grassy area provide the perfect facilities for kayakers to set up camp. An alternative campsite with a view is concealed above the rocky point in a secluded mossy glen.

There is certainly no room to swing in "Tentacle Cove" (named by us), but there are many choice, snug spots to drop your anchor, and the rocky perimeter of the cove is backed by lush forest, which almost reaches into your cockpit. One of the most desirable stern-to anchorages can be found along the foreshore of a wooded islet lying between the 2 coves. Early arrival is advised if you plan to claim this spot.

Because there are no major trails through the park, it's fun to explore the scattered islets at LW by foot. An easy climb to the top of "Pinnacle Rock" (named by us) rewards you with an excellent view over the islands, while the smooth, sloping boulders below are great for sunbathing and swimming. The 2 larger islands are private and fires are prohibited.

CHARTS 3537. 3312, page 21.

APPROACH

From the N out of Bodega Anchorage via a narrow passage W of the Octopus Islands. The centre channel of this passage is free of dangers, but numerous rocks fringe the passage and entrances to the anchorages. Dead-slow speed and a bow lookout are recommended.

ANCHOR

There is good shelter from the prevailing westerly and northwesterly summer winds. Stern lines ashore are recommended because swinging room is often limited. Depths of 2 - 4 m (6.5 - 13 ft), holding good over mud.

Note: For alternative southern approaches, see 11.5 (page 146).

Boats tuck into every nook and cranny.

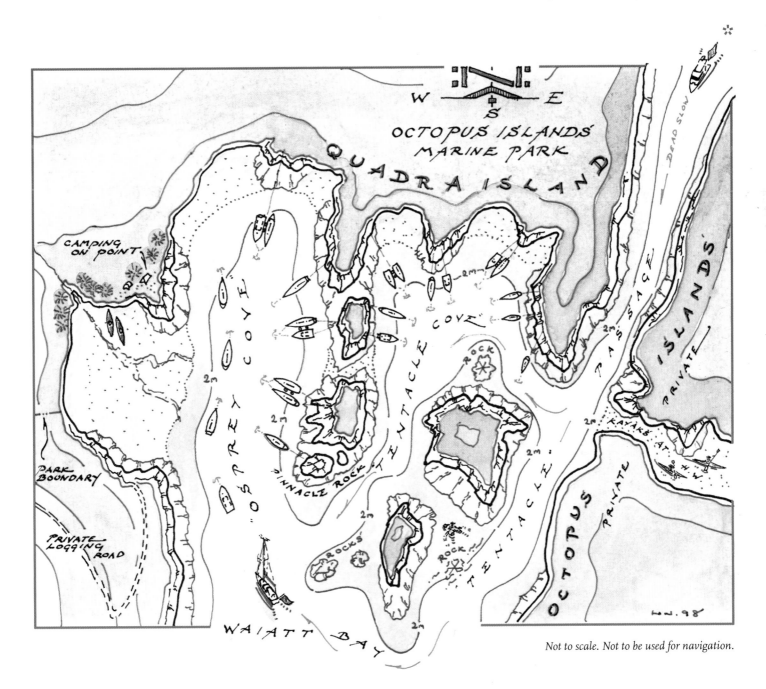

Not to scale. Not to be used for navigation.

11.8   HOLE IN THE WALL, UPPER RAPIDS & OWEN BAY

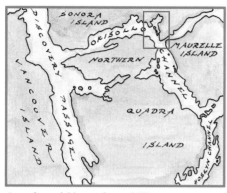

❋ 50° 17.5' N   125° 12.9' W

Approaching Hole in the Wall.

CHARTS 3537, 3312, page 21

APPROACH OWEN BAY

From the SW, favouring Grant Island's western shoreline to avoid being swept by the currents onto the rocks off Walters Point.

ANCHOR

Sheltered anchorage is available throughout Owen Bay. Depths vary, but the holding is good in mud.

Snug in the N.W. corner of Owen Bay.

HOLE IN THE WALL

Hole in the Wall is literally that! A narrow passage, complete with rapids at the western end, links Okisollo to Calm Channel (Chapter 8). The secondary current station lies centre channel off Hole in the Wall western light, recording 12 knots flood and 10 knots ebb. Hole in the Wall should only be navigated at or near slack water. Duration of slack is less than 5 minutes.

Reference current station: Hole in the Wall
Direction of flood: NE
Times of slack water as follows:
• turn to flood minus (–) 55 minutes (on Seymour Narrows)
• turn to ebb minus (–) 50 minutes (on Seymour Narrows)

Note: Don't forget to add 1 hour in periods of daylight-savings time. The eastern entrance experiences a tidal stream of up to 2 knots.

UPPER RAPIDS

The Upper Rapids lie E of Cooper Point and W of the numerous islands that shelter Owen Bay on Sonora Island. The secondary current station lies NW of Bentley Rock, which dries 1.0 m (3.3 ft) and is unmarked. Currents at both flood and ebb are recorded at 11 knots. The overfalls and eddies are extremely dangerous, and the rapids should only be navigated at or near slack water.

Reference current station: Seymour Narrows
Direction of flood: SE
Times of slack water as follows:
• turn to flood minus (–) 55 minutes (on Seymour Narrows)
• turn to ebb minus (–) 55 minutes (on Seymour Narrows)

OWEN BAY

Owen Bay offers a quiet retreat with ample anchorage and sheltered nooks and crannies to explore by dinghy or kayak. Legend has it that the spectacular sheer cliff on the NW shore was created by a wayward meteorite. The public wharf is usually filled with local boats although good anchorage is possible off the wharf.

Local residents welcome visitors to their quiet retreat although they do request that due respect be paid to private property – as even the most tumble-down building has an owner!

Note: Beware of two unmarked rocks that dry NW of Francisco Island, S of Etta Point Okisollo Channel.

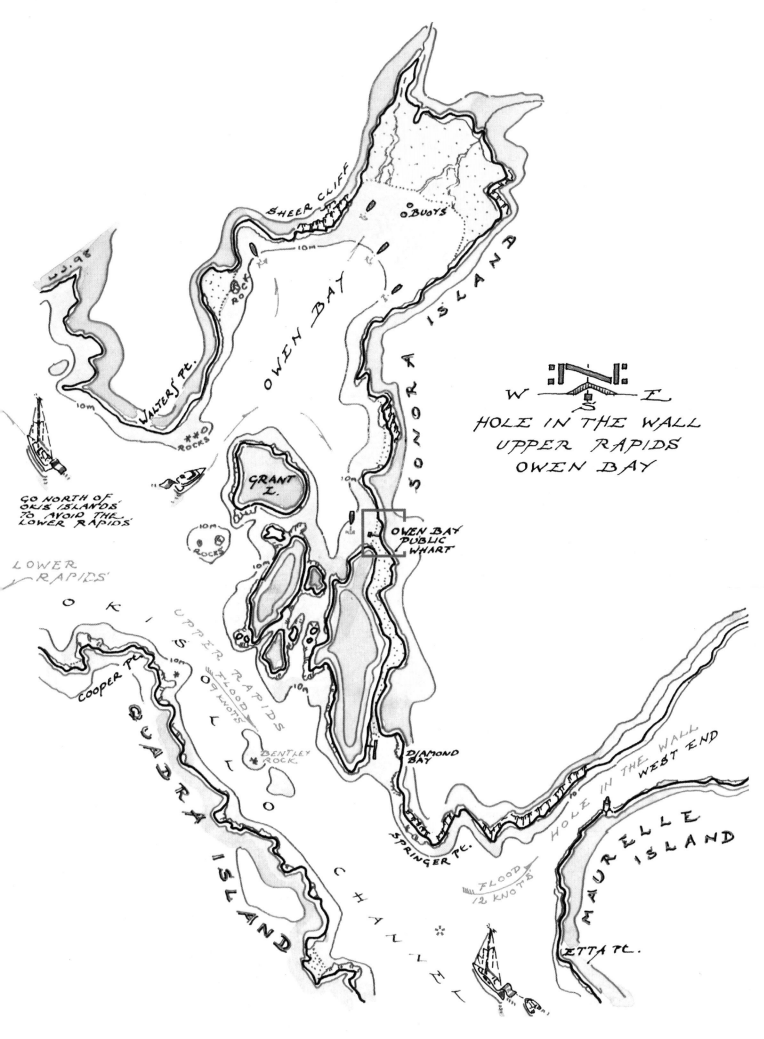

GO NORTH OF
OKIS ISLANDS
TO AVOID THE
LOWER RAPIDS

LOWER RAPIDS

WALTERS PT.

SHEER CLIFF

ROCK

**ROCKS

OWEN BAY

o BUOYS

10M

SONORA ISLAND

GRANT I.

ROCKS

10M

OWEN BAY
PUBLIC
WHARF

W   E
N
S
HOLE IN THE WALL
UPPER RAPIDS
OWEN BAY

O K I S I S L O

COOPER PT.

UPPER RAPIDS

FLOOD
6 KNOTS

10M

BENTLEY
ROCK

DIAMOND
BAY

QUADRA ISLAND

C H A N N E L

SPRINGER PT.

HOLE IN THE WALL

WEST END

FLOOD
12 KNOTS

MAURELLE
ISLAND

ETTA PT.

Not to scale. Not to be used for navigation.

11.9 Owen Bay Public Wharf, Sonora Island

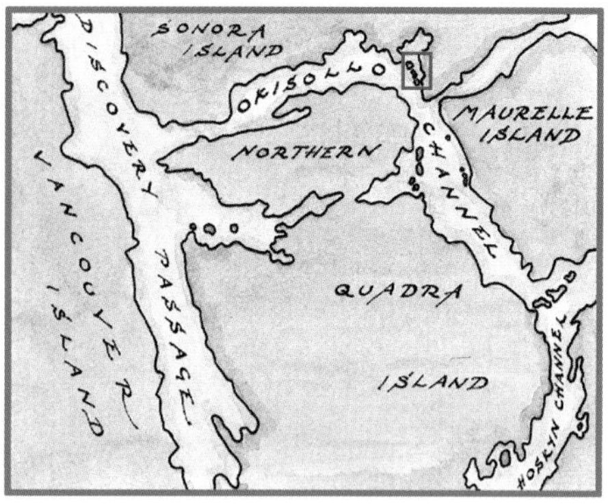

50° 18.7' N 125° 13.5' W

APPROACH

The Owen Bay public wharf lies in the SE corner of the bay.

ANCHOR

Good all-weather anchorage can be found NW of the public wharf. Depths of 4 - 8 m (13 - 26 ft), holding good in mud. Legend has it that the spectacular sheer cliff on the NW shore was created by a wayward meteorite.

PUBLIC WHARF

A small facility, with moorage usually taken up by local craft.

Note: Exploration of the channels between the islands S of the public wharf by dinghy or kayak isn't recommended because the tidal currents rush between them at a remarkable speed.

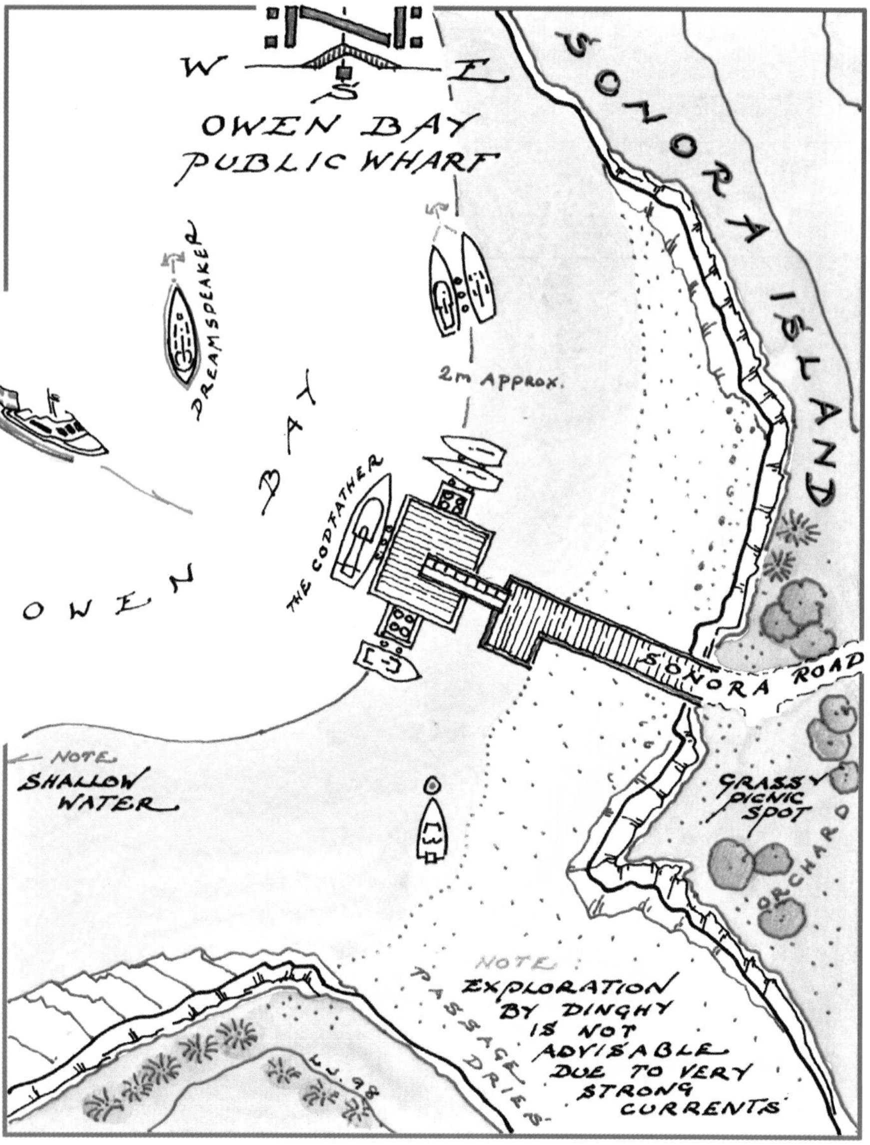

Not to scale. Not to be used for navigation.

Once home to a bustling community, Owen Bay was practically deserted by the early 1950s. A new generation of pioneers has now settled on the island, attracted by its peaceful lifestyle, beautiful surroundings and convenient location.

Although the Owen Bay public wharf needs repairs, it has a low-key charm and is usually filled with local boats. Good anchorage is possible off the wharf in a spot that holds the light well into the evening. The lovely wild apple orchard above the dock produces tasty fruit and leads to a trail that joins the main Sonora Road. An inviting, grassy picnic spot below the orchard is often the gathering place for islanders and their families.

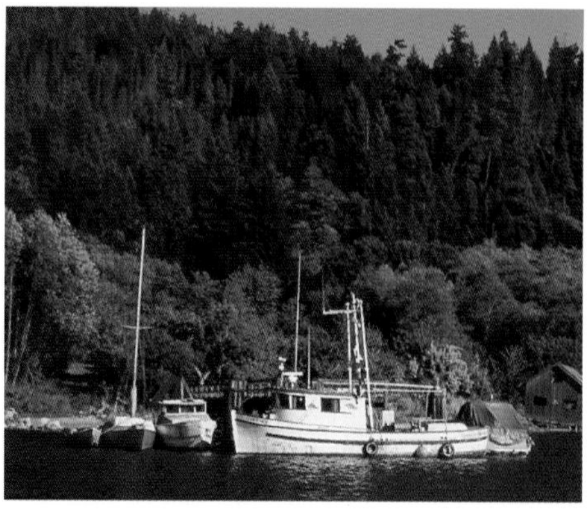

Owen Bay public wharf.

CHARTS 3537. 3312, page 21.

APPROACH

From the SE. out of Okisollo Channel the Islets appear as a small oasis against the more rugged Maurelle Island shoreline.

ANCHOR

Temporary anchorage is possible in the bight between the southern islet and Maurelle Island. A stern line ashore is advisable. Depths of 2 - 4 m (6.5 - 13 ft), holding good in mud and shell.

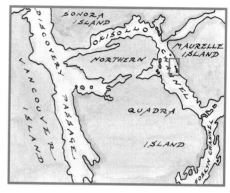

✣ 50° 16.3' N   125° 11.6' W

Named by us, these enchanting islets invite you to stay for a while and enjoy their tranquillity. The tiny cove provides quiet, temporary anchorage and makes a perfect 1-boat picnic stop. There are plenty of nooks and crannies to explore, and at LW it's fun to poke around the rocky pools formed between the 3 islets.

You can take a stern line back to one of the trees on big "Diamond Islet." Its rocky shoreline offers smooth sun-basking boulders that gently slope down into the cool, clear water, and a short climb will take you up to the flat, mossy viewpoint that looks over Okisollo Channel to Waiatt Bay and the popular Octopus Islands.

Anne, Tink and Dreamspeaker bask in the filtered light.

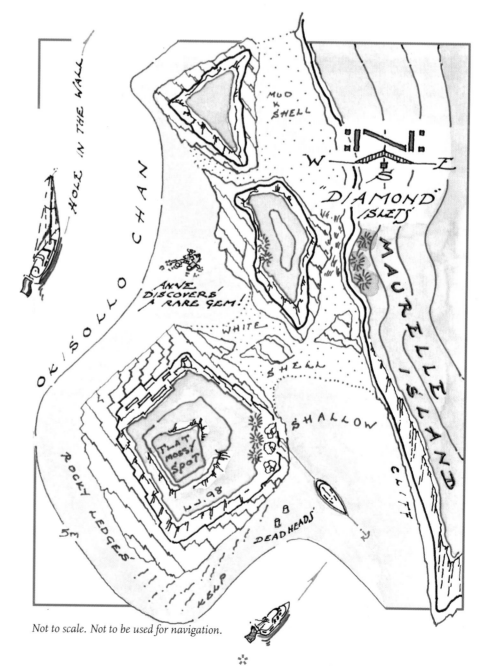

Not to scale. Not to be used for navigation.

11.11 KANISH BAY, QUADRA ISLAND

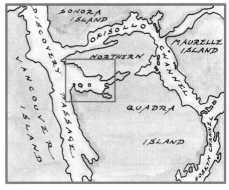

✳ 50° 15.6' N   125° 22.3' W

CHARTS 3539. 3312, page 23.

APPROACH

From the W out of Discovery Passage. The passage between Bodega Point and the Chained Islands is fringed by rocks and best navigated at LW, when the reef and rocks are clearly visible. The passage N of the Chained Islands is deep all the way into Kanish Bay and free of natural obstructions, but fish farms take up large portions of the bay.

ANCHOR

There are numerous temporary anchorages within the bay. The tail end of the westerly wind within Johnstone Strait often penetrates deep into the bay. Depth, holding and bottom condition vary.

Although this large bay is open to the W and is occupied by a number of commercial fish farms, it offers shelter in several temporary anchorages, which are well worth investigating. "Canoe Rock" (named by us), en route to Granite Bay, is worth a stop at LW because a white-shell beach is suddenly revealed. Numerous First Nations villages once occupied the head of Kanish Bay, and ancient kitchen middens can be found in the area.

Not to scale. Not to be used for navigation.

ANCHOR

Temporary picnic stop off the shell and mud beach. Depths of 6 - 8 m (19.5 - 26 ft), holding moderate in mud, rock and shell.

Tucked into the NE corner of Kanish Bay, "Orchard Point" (named by us) offers an idyllic picnic spot steeped in history. Once the site of a prosperous First Nations village, the ancient midden is now covered by an overgrown meadow and wild orchard, reminiscent of our more recent history. The plum and apple trees are laden with fruit in season, and a small creek brings fresh water down to the shell and pebble beach, abundant with squirting clams at LW.

Not to scale. Not to be used for navigation.

"Canoe Rock" at LW.

BODEGA POINT, KANISH BAY   11.13

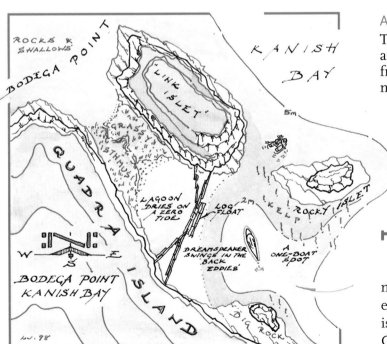

Not to scale. Not to be used for navigation.

ANCHOR

To the E of the lagoon with a log mooring float. This is an anchorage for 1 or 2 boats and offers fair protection from westerlies. Depths of 2 - 4 m (6.5 - 13 ft), holding moderate over rock and mud.

The anchorage behind Bodega Point, SE of "Link Islet" (named by us), provides a delightful temporary anchorage. Protected from westerly and northwesterly winds, you can relax and swing in the back eddies, pick fresh sea asparagus or walk along the grassy isthmus to enjoy an undisturbed view across Discovery Channel.

11.14 GRANITE BAY, QUADRA ISLAND

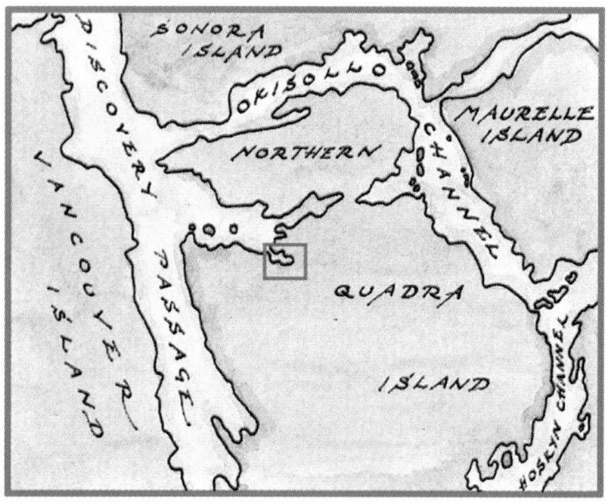

✲ 50° 14.6' N 125° 19.2' W

CHARTS 3539. 3312, page 23.

APPROACH

Granite Bay lies in the SE corner of Kanish Bay. A rock with less than 2 m (6 ft) of water over it lies N of the outer entrance. Stay in the centre channel of the passage because it is free of hazards.

ANCHOR

The anchorage is protected from the chop that sometimes forms in Kanish Bay. At times, though, the westerly winds responsible for the chop funnel into Granite Bay at knot speeds equal to those reported at Chatham Light. Depths of 4 - 8 m (13 - 26 ft), holding moderate in sticky, loose mud.

Note: The community floats are used primarily by local, small sport-fishing boats.

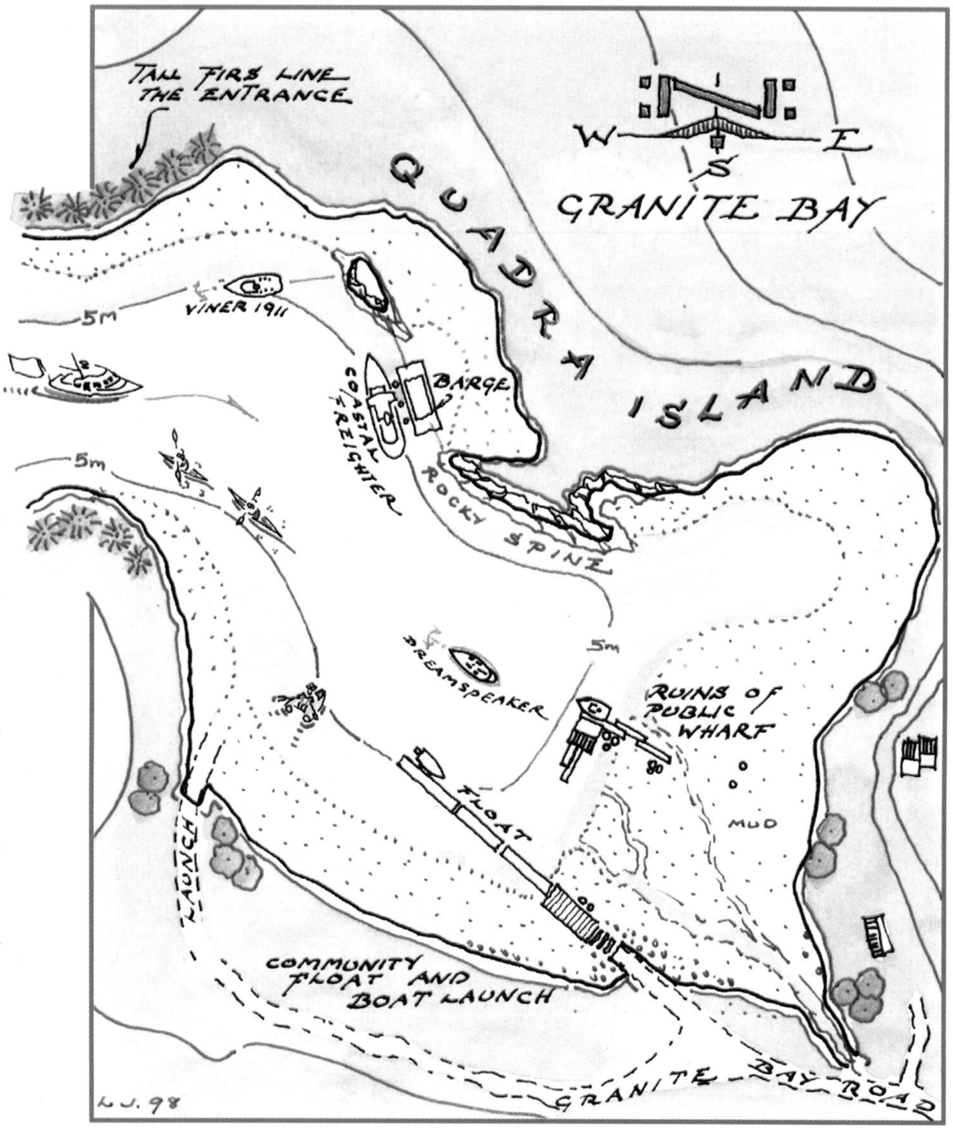

Not to scale. Not to be used for navigation.

As you enter the sheltered waters of Granite Bay, you may find it hard to imagine it as a thriving community of over 500 people in the early 1900s. Neglected remains of an old public wharf give the bay a feeling of desolation, but the friendly locals, who own many of the rustic summer cabins, enjoy its peace and solitude.

There is a kayak and small-boat launch at the end of the road that links Granite Bay with Southern Quadra Island and the community float has been extended in a makeshift fashion, giving public access to the road. Overnight anchorage can be found in the centre of the bay, although the holding is reported to be "somewhat dubious" in loose mud.

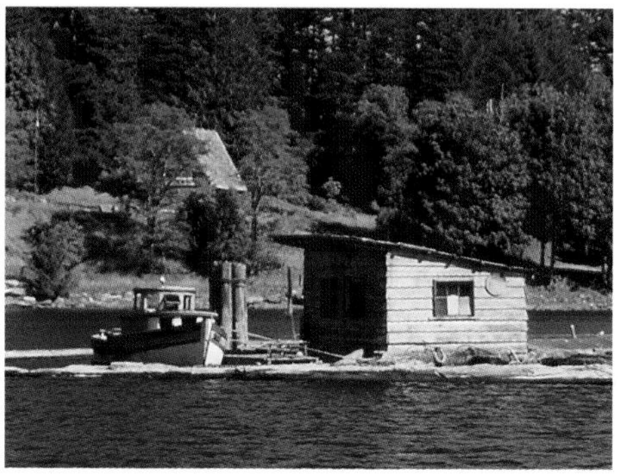

Ruins of the public wharf in Granite Bay.

SMALL INLET, QUADRA ISLAND

CHARTS 3539. 3312, page 23.

APPROACH

The narrow entrance to Small Inlet lies in the NE portion of Kanish Bay and has a minimum depth of 4 m (8 ft). Kelp lines the entrance passage on either side, and although it appears to block the channel in places, safe entry is possible with careful navigation in the centre of the channel.

ANCHOR

Good all-weather protection can be found throughout the inlet. Depths vary, and holding is good in mud and shingle. Entrance to the inner basin is best attempted at LW, when the rocks are visible.

Note: Small Inlet and a portion of the N and S shoreline are part of the provincial parks protected area.

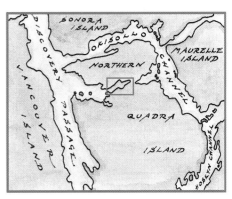

❋ 50° 15.2' N   125° 19.0' W

Once you have successfully navigated Small Inlet's restricted channel, the bay opens up to reveal the tranquil waters of a sizeable all-weather anchorage. Surrounded by lush forest and abundant with wildlife, it is ideal territory to explore by kayak or dinghy. An early First Nations portage trail, found at the head of the inlet, takes you through dappled second-growth forest and past ancient middens to a lovely pebble beach in Waiatt Bay (see page 146). The handcarved driftwood sign also leads you to Newton Lake, a pleasant 1.6 km (1 mi) hike and the possibility of a refreshing warmwater swim. Granite Bay is a more energetic 5 km (3 mi) trip but well worth the effort if you've been boat-bound for a few days (see page 156).

View to Waiatt Bay, end of Portage Trail.

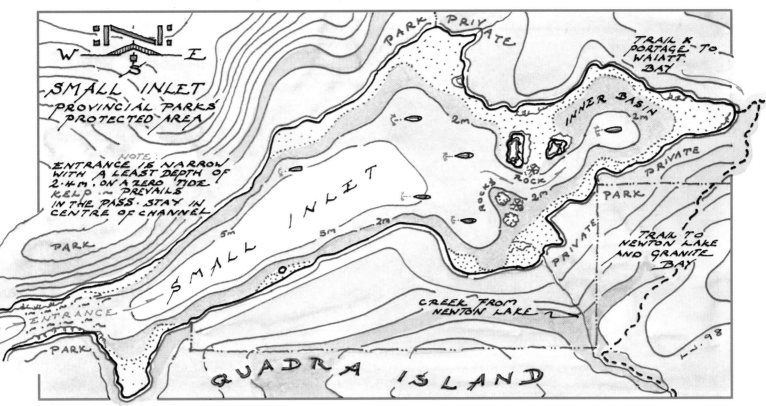

Not to scale. Not to be used for navigation.

11.16   OTTER COVE, CHATHAM POINT

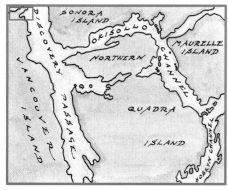

✽ 50° 19.5' N   125° 26.4' W

CHARTS 3539. 3312, page 24.

APPROACH

Otter Cove anchorage from the E, out of Discovery Passage, N of Limestone Island.

ANCHOR

At the head of the cove. Good shelter from the westerlies that rocket down Johnstone Strait and the currents that prevail in Discovery Passage. Depths of 4 - 10 m (13 - 33 ft), holding good in mud, sand and shell.

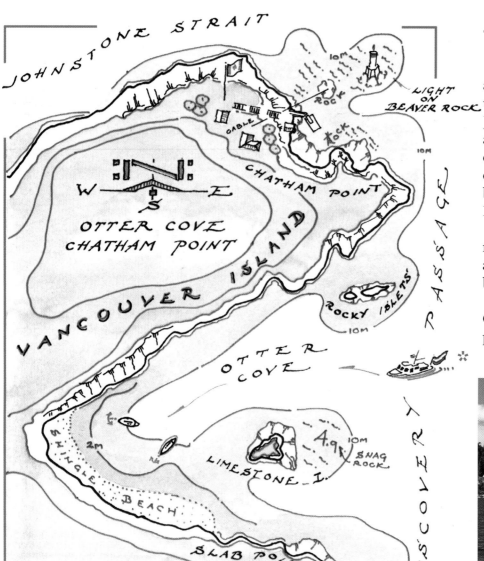

Well protected from westerly winds, Otter Cove provides a convenient spot to stop and relax while waiting for the turn of the tide or calmer wind conditions in Johnstone Strait. The anchorage is apparently unaffected by the strong currents and tidal turmoil outside its entrance, which is best navigated between Rocky Islets and Limestone Island.

Although an extended visit here may not be part of your itinerary, it's a pleasant spot to wait and take stock before continuing on your trip.

Although the land surrounding Otter Cove is private, the cove itself is part of Rock Bay Marine Park.

Looking North up Johnstone Strait.

Not to scale. Not to be used for navigation.

Chapter 12
SEYMOUR NARROWS

Seymour Narrows looking North from Maud Island.

Chapter 12
SEYMOUR NARROWS

TIDES

Canadian Tide and Current Tables, Volume 6
Reference Port: Owen Bay
Secondary Ports: Bloedel, Seymour Narrows, Brown Bay

CURRENTS

Reference Station: Seymour Narrows

WEATHER

Area: Johnstone Strait

Reporting Stations: Chatham Point, Campbell River, Cape Mudge

Note: The strong westerly winds in Johnstone Strait penetrate S into Seymour Narrows. Strong southeasterlies in the summer are less common, but if forecast these winds intensify in strength within the confines of the narrows. Fog, although rare in summer, may drift down from Johnstone Strait and blanket the narrows in the morning hours.

Maud Island anchorage.

CAUTIONARY NOTES

If you've miscalculated slack and the flood is literally taking you S, try to steer the boat between what's left of Ripple Rock and the Maud Island shore, where less turbulent water can be found.

When trying to power against a counter-current, boaters run the risk of overheating their engines.

Seymour Narrows lies midway between Cape Mudge and Chatham Point in Discovery Passage, the primary route to the northern coastal waters of British Columbia and Alaska. The narrows create a tidal pass where slack water is a timekeeper for even the largest commercial vessels.

Since the removal of Ripple Rock (see page 162), Seymour Narrows is now relatively deep and without obstructions. However, perpetual tidal currents, dangerous whirlpools, overfalls and turbulent waters still exist. With up to 16 knots of current on the flood and 14 knots on the ebb (flooding S and ebbing N), it still ranks as one of the most dangerous tidal passes in the world.

Recreational boaters are advised to be wise as commercial skippers to the time of slack water in Seymour Narrows. Keep in mind that cruise liner captains time their passage N from Vancouver and S from Alaska on slack water at the narrows.

SLACK WATER

The reference current station is mid-channel between Maud Island and Wilfred Point, under the hydro lines. This is the narrows proper, where you should be at slack water if the tide is turning in your favour. Slack water lasts for only 12 - 15 minutes, and the narrows are eight nautical miles north from the Campbell River Public Wharf and eight nautical miles south from the entrance to Kanish Bay. (At five knots, your journey will take 12 minutes for a mile, at six knots, it takes 10 minutes, so timing your arrival at slack water is everything!)

Missing the slack and trying to power against the current creates one of the real hazards of this pass, because it accommodates a heavy flow of commercial traffic, and it is common to see vessels come to a standstill. If you are attempting a northbound transit and have missed slack at the pass, convenient anchorage at Maud Island is a good spot to wait out the tide. This is also the dive site of the HMCS Columbia. The marina at Brown Bay (see 12.1, page 164) presents a similar opportunity for southbound boaters. Moor at one of the new floats and then enjoy a meal at the floating restaurant and a peaceful night before tackling the famous Seymour Narrows.

FEATURED DESTINATIONS

NORTHBOUND

It is advisable to stay overnight in the Campbell River vicinity, where good moorage and anchorage can be found (see 13.1, page 168). Proceed on the last hour of the flood so that you arrive at the narrows at slack water, with the turn to the ebb helping your journey north. If you are taking the last of the ebb north, time slack water at Brown Bay and you should get past Separation Head before the flood has time to build.

SOUTHBOUND

Good overnight anchorage can be found in Small Inlet, Kanish Bay (see 11.15, page xx). It's best to proceed during the last hour of the ebb so that you arrive at the narrows at slack water, with the turn to the flood helping your journey south. If you are taking the last of the flood south, time slack water at Race Point and you should get to a safe moorage or anchorage in the Campbell River vicinity before the ebb has time to build.

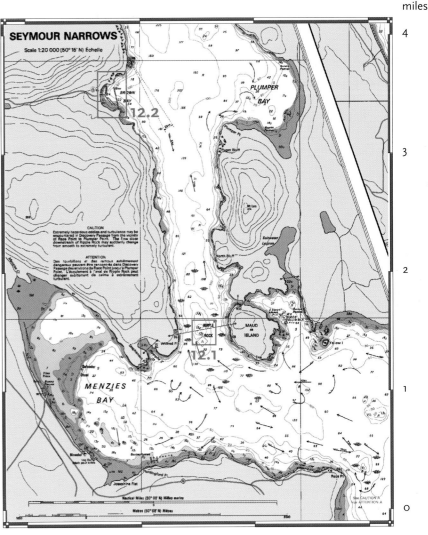

Not to be used for navigation.

12.1 RIPPLE ROCK - THE HISTORY

9:31 a.m., April 5, 1958. Photographs courtesy of the Canadian Hydrographic Service.

Ripple Rock, before and after demolition.
Courtesy of the Canadian Hydrographic Service.

Ripple Rock, which, prior to 1958, lay just nine feet below chart datum, was once the scourge of Seymour Narrows. Together with ferocious currents, overfalls and boat-swallowing whirlpools on all sides, it has claimed 114 lives and sunk or badly damaged over 100 small craft and 14 large ships, many of them American vessels.

Determined to remove this costly shipping hazard and encouraged by the U.S. government, the Canadian government began extensive research, and several plans for removal were considered over the years. Unfortunately the first attempt, in 1942, ended in tragedy when a work boat anchored over the rock was sucked into a whirlpool and all nine men aboard drowned.

Finally, in 1953, a proposal previously shelved due to expense was renewed. The twin heads of Ripple Rock had to be removed forever. Canada's Department of Public Works, together with a team of CHS surveyors, set out to build a tunnel from Maud Island, under the narrows, to the dangerous rock. Five years later, Seymour Narrows made international news: at 9:31 a.m. on April 5, 1958, the world's largest non-nuclear explosion, using 1,500 tons of cordite, blasted 11 m (35 ft) of rock over 91 m (300 ft) into the air and briefly emptied nearby Menzies Bay of most of its water. Spectators included curious scientists from around the world and apprehensive local residents who feared that an aftermath of tidal waves and earthquakes would destroy their homes, but their fears were never realized. The "big blast" was over in minutes, wave action and rubble settled, the air cleared and a charted depth of 13 m (45 ft) replaced menacing Ripple Rock.

Schematic drawing showing the mining of Ripple Rock.
Courtesy of the Canadian Hydrographic Service.

The "big blast" at Ripple Rock in 1958 was the largest non-nuclear human-made explosion in history.

⟶

CHARTS 3539 (inset). 3312, page 23.

APPROACH

From the E. A floating breakwater of former oil barrels protects the marina. Enter N of the breakwater.

MARINA

Brown Bay Marina, 250-286-3135, has extensive visitor moorage and monitors VHF 69-71.

FUEL

Fuel barge at the marina.

BOAT LAUNCH

Private, at the marina.

Note: When approaching the fuel barge or a designated moorage, exercise caution because strong tidal currents sweep through the bay.

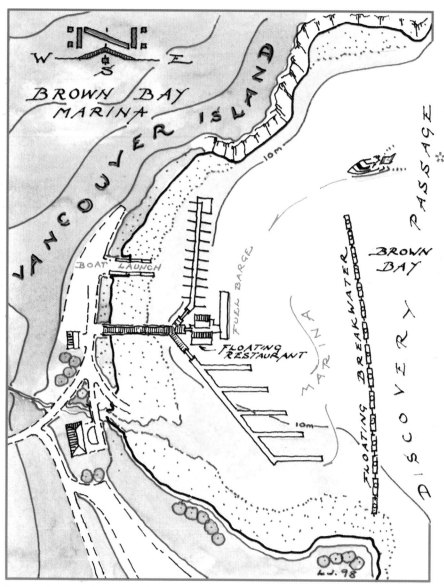

Not to scale. Not to be used for navigation.

Entrance to marina from Discovery Passage.

Located just N of Seymour Narrows in sheltered Brown Bay, the efficiently run BROWN BAY MARINA is conveniently situated for boaters transiting Discovery Passage or waiting for slack water in Seymour Narrows. The marina offers comfortable moorage for boats of all sizes and includes a floating bed-and-breakfast. Shower and laundry facilities are available and the small grocery store keeps basic provisions and a tackle shop sells live bait and fishing licenses. If you have time, take a break from the galley and enjoy fresh fish & chips (helpings large enough for two) in the floating restaurant overlooking Discovery Passage.

Chapter 13

CAMPBELL RIVER & SOUTHERN QUADRA ISLAND

*Boats anchoring at the tip of Rebecca Spit with
the* Cortes Queen *steaming to Whaletown.*

Chapter 13
CAMPBELL RIVER
& SOUTHERN QUADRA ISLAND

TIDES

Canadian Tide and Current Tables, Volume 6
Reference Port: Campbell River
Secondary Ports: Quathiaski Cove, Gowlland Harbour

CURRENTS

Reference Station: Seymour Narrows

Note: Currents in Discovery Passage, S of Seymour Narrows, reach 6 - 7 knots off Campbell River and 7 - 9 knots off Cape Mudge. The flood tidal stream sets S and the ebb N through Discovery Channel.

WEATHER

AREA: Johnstone Strait, Northern Strait of Georgia

REPORTING STATIONS: Chatham Point, Campbell River, Cape Mudge

Note: The strong westerly winds in Johnstone Strait penetrate S into Discovery Passage. Strong southeasterlies (less common in summer) intensify within the confines of Discovery Passage. Fog, although rare in summer, usually blankets Discovery Passage in the morning but dissipates by early afternoon.

Rebecca Spit Marine Park (13.8)

CAUTIONARY NOTES

Cape Mudge should be approached with caution because Wilby Shoals extends a considerable distance S from Quadra Island. Even in light southeasterly winds and against a flooding current, dangerous seas can be generated over the shoals and right across the entrance to Discovery Passage. These conditions present an extreme hazard to all craft.

Conveniently located and well serviced by land, sea and air, Campbell River has fast become a major rendezvous and provisioning stop for cruising boaters and yacht-charter companies that view it as a gateway to the Discovery Islands and Desolation Sound.

Quadra Island, the largest of the Discovery Islands, lies at the northwestern end of the Strait of Georgia. Cape Mudge Lighthouse, perched above the 61 metre (200 foot) cliffs on the island's southern tip, affords stunning vistas and has witnessed the sinking of numerous ships off Wilby Shoals.

The hazards of Cape Mudge aside, the shoreline of Southern Quadra Island is a delight to explore, enticing the cruising boater with a selection of excellent marinas, provisioning stops and anchorages, with magical Rebecca Spit Marine Park providing the jewel in the crown. To best enjoy all that this friendly island has to offer, go all-out and rent a bike, join a sunset kayaking expedition or pick up a map and hike the many scenic trails that crisscross the island from Cape Mudge Lighthouse in the south to Newton Lake in the north.

On the island's western shoreline, peaceful Gowlland Harbour offers sheltered anchorage, pockets of wilderness and a quiet moment to enjoy the fascinating seal population. Comfortable overnight moorage, numerous lodge amenities and fine dining are available at the renowned APRIL POINT RESORT AND MARINA, and Quathiaski Cove, a short ferry ride from Campbell River, provides a charming provisioning stop with all the amenities, including an excellent bakery, supermarket and colourful farmers' market in the summer months. The HERIOT BAY INN AND MARINA, on Quadra's eastern shore, has a charm all its own and is a favourite rendezvous for locals and ferry passengers en route to Cortes Island. Juicy blackberries in season and free delivery to your boat are included when provisioning at the nearby QUADRA ISLAND MARKET.

Rebecca Spit Marine Park, celebrated as one of our oldest and most loved marine parks, entices the cruising boater year after year to its sheltered waters, picnic meadows, sandy beaches and well-maintained trails. From here you can pop over to Open Bay for some warm-water swimming or to Moulds Bay for a peaceful picnic. With Heriot Bay and its amenities close by, this is the perfect spot to begin or end a voyage while cruising the Discovery Islands and Desolation Sound.

FEATURED DESTINATIONS

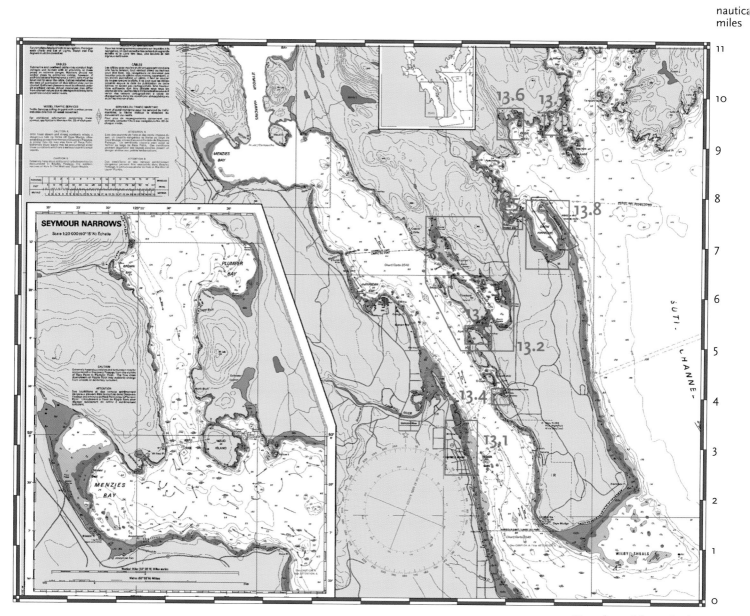

Not to be used for navigation.

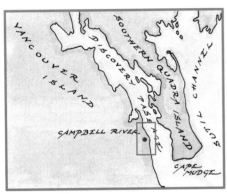

✳ 50° 1.3' N   125° 13.9' W

CHARTS 3540. 3312, page 18.

APPROACH

At or near slack water for all the downtown marine facilities. At any other time, allow ample sea room to counter the S-flowing flood or N-flowing ebb tide.

Note: Ensure that moorage is available prior to approaching any of the following facilities, because marinas fill up quickly in the busy summer months. Moorage can be reserved at both Coast Marina and Discovery Harbour Marina.

PUBLIC WHARF

The phone number for the wharf manager is 250-287-7931. Enter close to the tip of the breakwater. If the fishing fleet is out, there's usually ample moorage; if not, rafting up on the southern inner floats is the norm. Washrooms and showers are available at the Wharf Manager's office.

Downtown Campbell River from the South.

Although Campbell River built its reputation over the years as a centre for excellent sport fishing, it is now recognized as a gateway to the popular Discovery Islands and Desolation Sound. Known locally as "The River," Campbell River, easily accessible by land, sea and air, provides excellent provisioning facilities and offers 3 diverse marinas to choose from – one being the often crowded public wharf, just S of the downtown core. Pleasure boaters can still find room here with a little perseverance, although priority is given to commercial vessels. Sheltered by a substantial breakwater and the longest fishing pier in Canada, the wharf provides basic washroom and shower facilities and the opportunity to gossip with local fishers. A visit to the nearby CAMPBELL RIVER MUSEUM, 250-287-3103, which has an excellent display of handcarved First Nations masks, is certainly worthwhile. It offers special summer events and guided historical and nature tours.

As a guest at the COAST MARINA, 250-287-7455, you can enjoy the fitness facilities at the COAST DISCOVERY INN at no extra charge. The marina offers full facilities and is conveniently situated adjacent to the Quadra Island Ferry Terminal and to Foreshore Park. Shower and laundry facilities, ice, fuel and sewage pump-out are available at the end of C Dock on the Chevron Float, and the floating café, offers an endless variety of ice cream flavours.

Just across the road is the TYEE PLAZA & SHOPPERS ROW. Here you'll find a variety of bookstores, shops and cafés, including a large supermarket, pharmacy, post office, laundromat, and 2 cold-beer-and-wine stores. THE VISITOR INFOCENTRE, PUBLIC ART GALLERY and historic TIDEMARK THEATRE are also located here. All community buses service the plaza, including a seasonal shuttle to the renowned PAINTERS LODGE RESORT AND RESTAURANT. 250-286-1102.

The large DISCOVERY HARBOUR MARINA, 250-287-2614, with full facilities, is backed by the HARBOUR CENTRE, a vast shopping complex complete with waterfront restaurants, gift stores and banks. The complex includes THE GREAT CANADIAN SUPERSTORE, CANADIAN TIRE and a well-stocked B.C. LIQUOR STORE. The marina, developed by the Campbell River Indian Band, is busiest in July and August, especially on weekends. Shower and laundry facilities are provided at the RIPTIDE MARINE PUB, just up from the docks. OCEAN PACIFIC MARINE SUPPLY will look after all your boating needs.

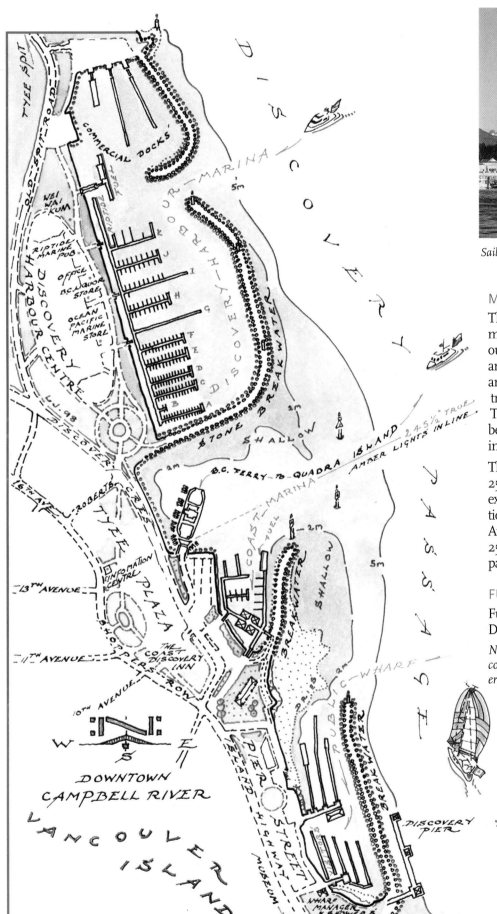

Not to scale. Not to be used for navigation.

Sailboat departing Discovery Harbour marina.

MARINAS

The COAST MARINA 250-287-7455, monitors VHF 73. Keep a careful lookout for the ferry arriving or departing, and don't obstruct its passage. The 2 amber lights that come into line at 245° true are the range lights for the ferry. They are visible day and night and can be used as a navigational aid by cruising boaters.

The DISCOVERY HARBOUR MARINA 250-287-2614, monitors VHF 73. It has extensive visitor moorage, but reservations are recommended during July and August. The RIPTIDE MARINE PUB, 250-830-0044, has a day float for patrons.

FUEL

Fuel floats at both Coast Marina and Discovery Harbour Marina.

Note: An extensive floatplane and helicopter terminus is located just N of Discovery Harbour marina, behind Tyee Spit.

13.2 GOWLLAND HARBOUR, QUADRA ISLAND

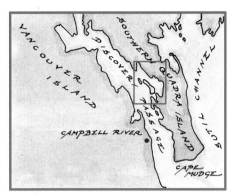

❖ 1) 50° 5.1' N 125° 15.2' W
❖ 2) 50° 3.9' N 125° 14.4' W

CHARTS 3540. 3312, page 18.

APPROACH
From the W, entering N of the Vigilant Islets. Favour the Vigilant Islets side because the shallows off Entrance Rock and Entrance Bank lie to the N.

ANCHOR
Reasonable all-weather anchorage can be found in the harbour. Depths vary, holding good in mud.

MARINA
SEASCAPE WATERFRONT RESORT, 250-285-3450, offers visitor moorage.

Sheltered by Gowlland Island, the peaceful anchorage in Gowlland Harbour offers you refuge and the opportunity to discover 5 delightful islets protected as provincial park reserves. Vigilant, Wren, Crow, Fawn & Mouse Islets are ideal for exploration by kayak, canoe or dinghy, providing visitors with individual pockets of wilderness and a quiet moment to commune with the fascinating seal population.

Boaters can anchor behind Vigilant Islets and between Crow and Fawn Islets or tie up at the SEASCAPE WATERFRONT RESORT, which offers moorage (subject to availability) with both power and water. Shower, laundry and garbage facilities, self-catering chalets and a camping area, kids' park and canoe and kayak rental are also available at this charming family resort.

Less quiet anchorage, but protected from southerly winds, can be found in the southern portion of the harbour. The navigable boat passage nearby is used by small speedboats taking a shortcut to April Point, but it shouldn't be attempted without thorough local knowledge because of the strong tidal currents, mid-channel rocks and shallow depths.

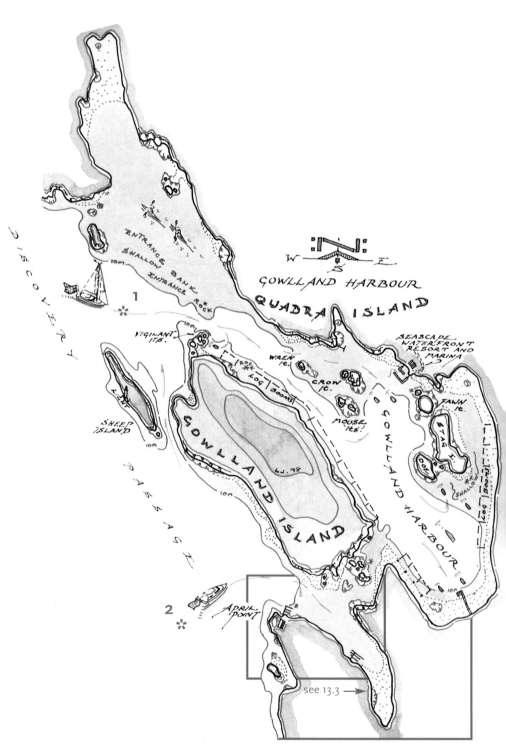

Not to scale. Not to be used for navigation.

CHARTS 3540. 3312, page 18.

APPROACH

From the W, leaving the starboard-hand (red) buoy to the S.

ANCHOR

Good anchorage with fair shelter can be found N of the marina. Depths of 4 - 6 m (13 - 19.5 ft), holding good in mud.

MARINA

The APRIL POINT LODGE & MARINA, 250-285-3621, has extensive visitor moorage and a full-time dock staff. It monitors VHF 10.

Note: There's a shallow sandbar S of the star-board-hand (red) buoy. Floatplane operations are frequent in the busy summer months.

Totem Pole at April Point Lodge.

APRIL POINT LODGE AND MARINA was originally founded by the Peterson Family in 1945. With a magnificent view of Discovery Passage, the lodge and its surrounding cottages offer rustic luxury that includes hot tubs, jacuzzi baths and cosy fireplaces. Although sport fishing is one of the key activities available at the lodge, kayaking, whale watching and ecotours are also offered. The meals are as spectacular as the surroundings and feature favourite classics with a West Coast twist. Lunch and dinner guests can tie up at the visitors' dock adjacent to the main lodge. Call 250-285-2222 for reservations.

The marina, just a short walk from the lodge, is serviced by the resort water taxi and provides on-site shower and laundry facilities. Overnight moorage includes the use of all lodge amenities.

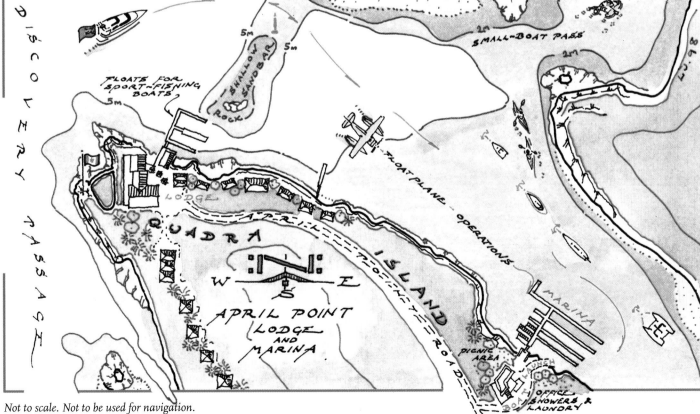

Not to scale. Not to be used for navigation.

13.4 QUATHIASKI COVE, QUADRA ISLAND

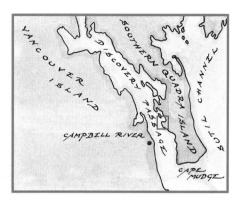

❊ 50° 2.6' N   125° 13.4' W

The public wharf looking North from Whiskey Point.

The ferry comes and goes every hour.

Known locally as "Q. Cove" and only a 15-minute ferry ride from Campbell River, Quathiaski Cove has a charming island plaza that provides a pleasant alternative to shopping in the big city. The island's main road also connects the cove to Heriot Bay and the Cortes Island ferry. Call QUADRA TAXI, 250-285-3598.

Space for local and visiting boats is often possible at the friendly public wharf, (subject to ferry wash) and fuel, ice, garbage drop-off and efficient, friendly service are available at the fuel dock N of the public wharf. DOCKERS EXPRESS, at the ferry landing, specializes in good coffee to go, and THE LANDING PUB offers great food, local beer and a cosy meeting place for visitors and locals waiting for ferry connections. Spic-and-span shower and laundry facilities are located at the WHISKEY POINT RESORT.

THE PLAZA and COVE CENTRE, a short walk up the hill, house a variety of shops, including a post office, a credit union with an ATM and a local tourist information booth, where an excellent Quadra Island visitors' map and trail map are available.

The LOVIN' OVEN II bakes heavenly loaves of bread that stay fresh for days, and its delicious, thick-crust pizza comes with unusual toppings. QUADRA FOODS, open 7 days a week, has a B.C. LIQUOR STORE outlet and carries bulk foods, specialty and organic produce and natural health products, and it offers free delivery to the public wharf. Pop into EXPLORE, a tranquil store that stocks a diverse selection of fine art, books and music and provides photocopy, fax and courier services. ISLAND TREASURES is filled to the brim with unusual gifts, and DISCOVERY ANTIQUES is worth a quiet browse. Enjoy an international blend of coffee at AROMA, "micro roasters of fine world coffees." A colourful outdoor FARMERS' MARKET takes place at the Cove Centre every Saturday between May and September (10 a.m. - 1 p.m.) and offers a selection of local preserves, baking and crafts.

A short walk N will take you to VILLAGE SQUARE, where you can refill your propane tank, explore the well-stocked K.T.'s GENERAL STORE, browse in local gift stores or enjoy a relaxing lunch on the shady deck of the RED-RADISH CAFÉ, which also offers a special kids' menu. Biking around beautiful Quadra Island is a lot of fun, and ISLAND CYCLE specializes in custom tours of the island. Its "cultural excursion" tour stops at local artisan studios and the impressive KWAGIULTH MUSEUM & CULTURAL CENTRE. The "peddle and paddle" tour includes a day of cycling and kayaking and ends with a sunset barbecue. Call 250-285-3627 for more information.

CHARTS 3540. 3312, page 18.

APPROACH

From the W, keeping a sharp lookout for the ferry arriving or departing, because boaters are often taken by surprise when it rounds "Whiskey Point" en route to Campbell River.

ANCHOR

Anchorage is possible in the channel between Grouse Island and Quadra Island, but the holding is only moderate over a rocky bottom and varying depths. Alternative anchorage can be found at the mouth of Unkak Cove N of Quathiaski Cove.

PUBLIC WHARF

This is a well-used island facility, with ample room for visitors if the fishing fleet is out; if it's in, be prepared to raft up.

BOAT LAUNCH

Public, adjacent to the wharf.

FUEL

A fuel float lies N of the public wharf.

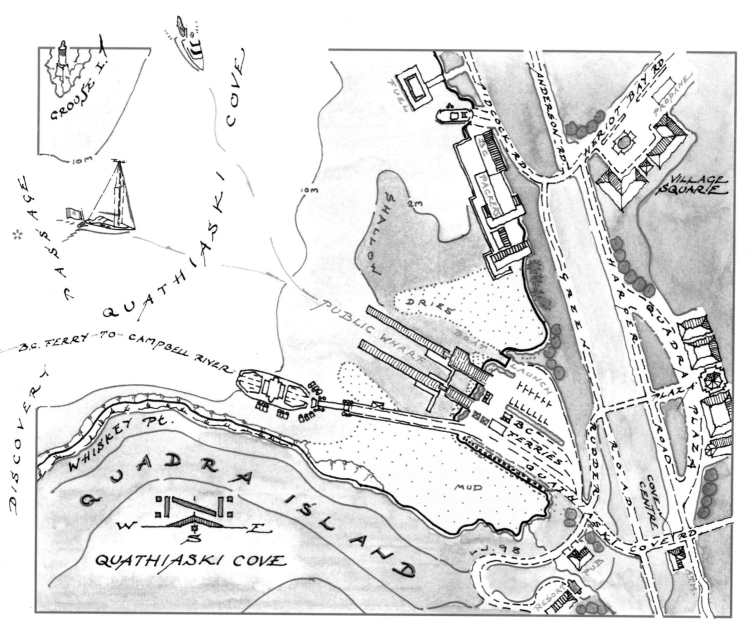

Not to scale. Not to be used for navigation.

13.5 Heriot Bay, Quadra Island

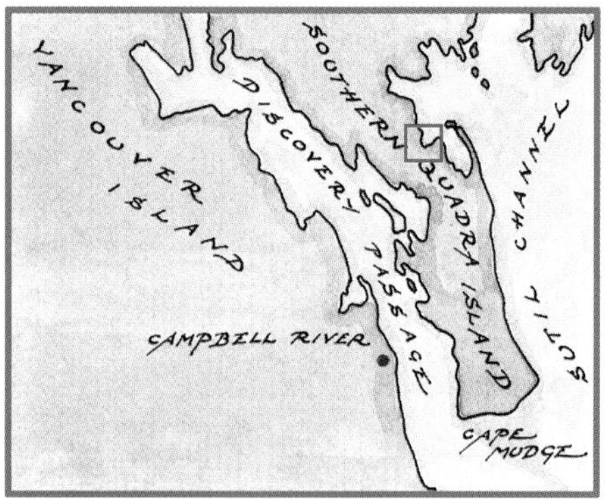

50° 6.5' N 125° 12.5' W

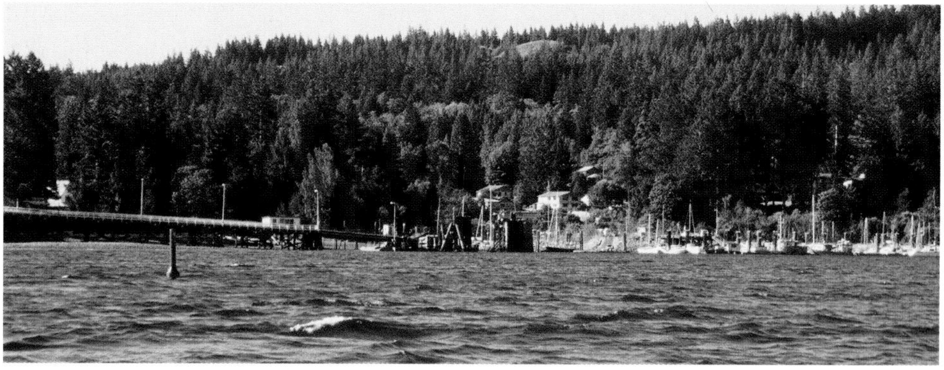

Approach to Heriot Bay from the NE.

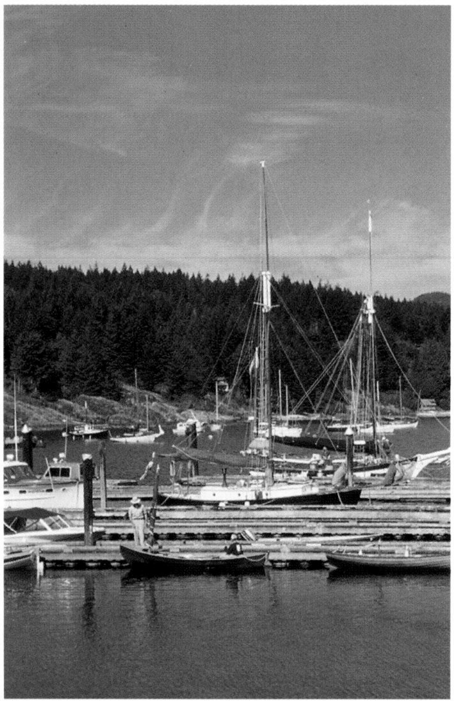

The colourful Heriot Bay Marina.

With a charm all its own, Heriot Bay provides a convenient stop to fuel, provision and get the boat and crew shipshape. The delights of Rebecca Spit Marine Park are just across the bay in Drew Harbour, and the Cortes Island ferry makes scheduled departures to Whaletown on Cortes Island from here. A short taxi ride will take you to Quathiaski Cove (see 13.4, page 172) to connect with the Campbell River ferry.

The hospitable Heriot Bay Inn & Marina has a fuel dock and ample moorage for visiting boats; it also supplies power and water (for drinking only), showers and spacious laundry facilities. Day moorage, on the outside dock, is $5 if you plan to stay for more than an hour. Garbage drop-off is $1 a bag, and propane is available. Tokens for the vigorous showers can be purchased at the inn store, along with ice, fishing licenses, books and gifts. The Heriot Bay Inn Pub is a popular rendezvous for locals, visitors and ferry passengers, and the inn restaurant serves up fresh seafood specials and scrumptious oyster burgers. Ocean-view cottages and a large RV campground are also part of this diverse complex, and kayaking and fishing packages can be arranged at the inn office.

The public wharf and the surrounding anchorage are often filled with local craft, but this is a friendly spot to tie up or anchor if any space is available. The headquarters for Paradise Bay Fishfarms are also located here. Pick up a list of its various island locations, which will often give impromptu tours.

A short walk up the hill from Heriot Bay Inn will take you to Quadra Island Market, complete with in-house bakery, B.C. Liquor Store outlet and post office. The market carries a good selection of basic provisions, fresh produce and frozen foods, and it offers a complimentary delivery service to the marina. Fools Gallery and Quadra Crafts specialize in excellent local art, pottery and unique gifts. Pick up a visitors' map of Quadra Island at the Consignment Shop across the way. They carry marine supplies and a fascinating variety of new and used paraphernalia which will keep you amused for hours. Take a break at the Ice Cream Bar and sample a selection of the 16 tempting flavours.

Kayaking around Southern Quadra Island or through the peaceful Main Lakes Chain is a wonderful way to enjoy the island's tranquil charm. For day trips, custom packages and sunset tours, call Spirit of the West Adventurers, 250-285-2121, Coast Mountain Expeditions, 250-287-0635, and Coastal Spirits Wilderness Expeditions, 250-285-2895.

CHARTS 3539. 3312, pages 18 & 19.

APPROACH

From the NE, leaving the porthand (green) buoy to the S. The ferry terminal, marina and public wharf are all close to one another.

ANCHOR

Moderately sheltered anchorage can be found among the local boats at anchor and on mooring buoys. Less congested and better protected anchorage is possible in the NW corner of the bay, in the lee of Heriot Island. Depths, holding and bottom condition unrecorded.

PUBLIC WHARF

Well used by local island craft, with limited visitor moorage.

MARINA

The HERIOT BAY INN & MARINA, 250-285-3322, has extensive visitor moorage. It monitors VHF 73.

BOAT LAUNCH

Public, adjacent to the public wharf.

FUEL

At the marina.

Note: Watch for the ferry manoeuvring adjacent to the marina. The afternoon northwesterly wind causes quite a chop in the bay, making moorage on the outside of the marina and public wharf rather bumpy.

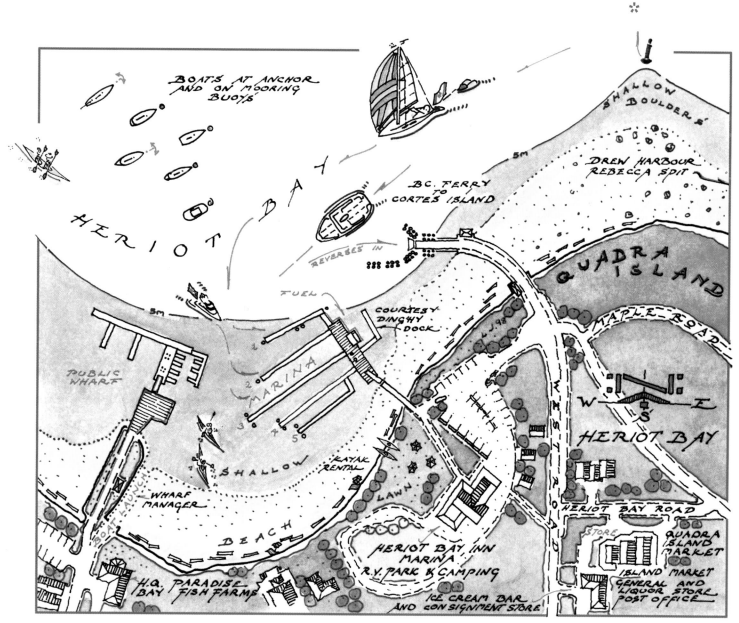

Not to scale. Not to be used for navigation.

13.6   OPEN BAY, QUADRA ISLAND

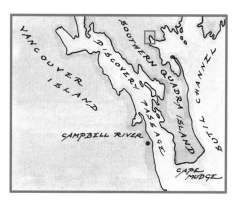

✣ 50° 8.0' N   125° 12.6' W

CHARTS 3539. 3312, page 19.

APPROACH
From the SE.

ANCHOR
Temporary anchorage, although well sheltered from the W and NW, is totally exposed to the S. Depths of 4 - 8 m (13 - 26 ft), holding good over a sand and gravel bottom.

Note: Rather idyllic on a fine summer day but treacherous if the wind switches to the SE.

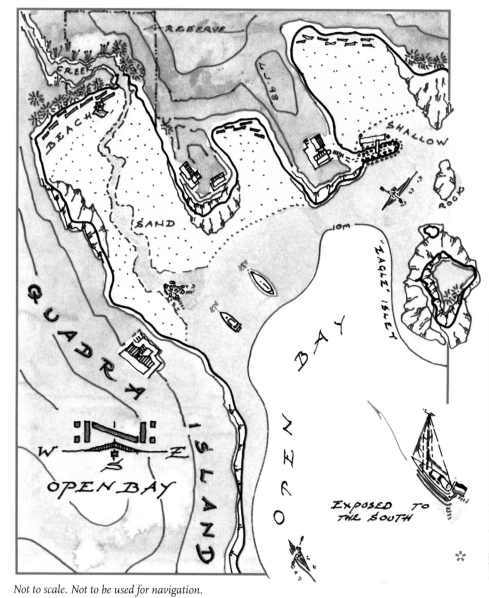

Not to scale. Not to be used for navigation.

On a sunny day when the tide begins to cover the exposed stretch of sand, Open Bay offers fine warm-water swimming. It is a glorious picnic stop for boaters and kayakers, with a freshwater estuary sheltering plants and wildlife and a stream flowing down onto the beach. At low tide, it's fun to explore the pools teeming with small fish, crabs and other fascinating sea life. There are rocks for climbing and weathered logs to laze on, and "Eagle Islet" (named by us) is great to explore by dinghy, but don't forget your binoculars.

The creek North of Open Bay beach.

MOULDS BAY, QUADRA ISLAND 13.7

CHARTS 3539. 3312, page 19.

APPROACH

From the S, W of the Breton Islands. The passage to Hoskyn Channel has a minimum depth of 7.9 m (26 ft) mid-channel.

ANCHOR

Temporary anchorage, sheltered from all quarters except the S. Depths of 6 - 12 m (19.5 - 39 ft), holding moderate over a rock and shingle bottom.

Note: Although the Breton Islands provide some protection from southeasterly winds, chop still enters the bay.

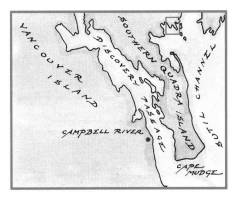

✳ 50° 8.0' N 125° 11.4' W

A small, perfectly serene tea or lunch stop awaits you in Moulds Bay, and the most wonderful rock formations criss-crossed with colourful fissures can be found while you explore the NE corner by dinghy or kayak. A log-strewn pebble beach is backed by private property, with a blue-roofed cabin tucked away in the tall trees. Kayakers exploring the nearby Breton Islands and boaters looking for a peaceful spot often pop into this quiet, unassuming bay. Private boundaries should be respected.

Kayaks transit Moulds Bay.

Not to scale. Not to be used for navigation.

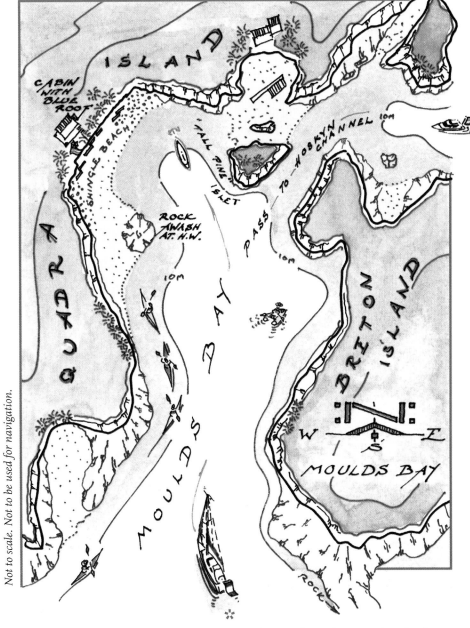

13.8 REBECCA SPIT MARINE PARK, DREW HARBOUR, QUADRA ISLAND

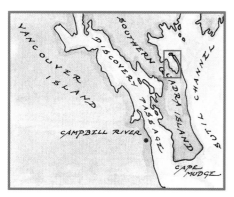

✴ 50° 6.6' N   125° 12.0' W

CHARTS 3539. 3312, pages 18 & 19.

APPROACH

From the NE out of Sutil Channel, giving the tip of the spit (especially at HW) a wide berth. Maintain a wake-free speed after clearing the tip.

ANCHOR

The spit offers well-sheltered anchorage along its western side. The harbour affords ample swinging room for larger craft in the S.

MARINA

The TAKU RESORT, 250-285-3031, has limited moorage by prior arrangement. Dinghies are welcome to tie up when visiting the resort or BAY CAFÉ.

BOAT LAUNCH

Public in the marine park. Private at Taku Resort.

Note: In a strong northwesterly wind, a chop will often build W of Rebecca Spit's tip, but this chop doesn't normally penetrate deep into Drew Harbour.

A log-strewn beachcombing paradise.

Magical Rebecca Spit creates a natural breakwater on Drew Harbour's eastern side and is celebrated as one of British Columbia's oldest and most loved marine parks. Year after year, it continues to entice the cruising boater to its sheltered waters, picnic meadows, shaded trails and gently sloping beaches. With Heriot Bay and its amenities close at hand (see 13.5, page 174), this is the perfect spot to begin or end a voyage while cruising the Discovery Islands and Desolation Sound.

Well used and respected by all Quadra Island residents, the park also provides well-maintained trails for running, cycling, walking the dog or just taking a leisurely stroll, and suitably placed benches welcome you to relax and enjoy the breathtaking view. The sand and shingle beaches on either side of the spit are wonderful to explore, and they offer safe warm-water swimming on the inside and a log-strewn beachcombing paradise on the outside.

Its history as a First Nations fortress between the 16th and 18th centuries and its survival, after an earthquake in the 1940s, make Rebecca Spit an intriguing though fragile landmark. To protect the spit from additional erosion today, the park has been designed for day use only. Picnic tables and fire pits are provided for comfortable family get-togethers, pit toilets are placed at convenient intervals and water is available from a hand pump located near the parks information shelter.

The park has also become a popular kayaking destination, and excellent overnight camping facilities are available at the nearby WE WAI KAI CAMPSITE, which is owned and operated by the Cape Mudge Indian Band. Shower and laundry facilities are provided, and a small convenience store sells ice, pop and snacks. Early reservations are recommended; call 250-285-3111.

The well-maintained TAKU RESORT on Drew Harbour's western shoreline provides tenting sites for kayakers, moorage for boaters by prior arrangement, self-catering cottages and shower and laundry facilities. The charming stone beach house can be reserved as a base camp for kayaking tours and is available for group barbecues, call 250-285-3031.

To enjoy one of the best spots in Drew Harbour, tuck into the NW tip of the spit, take a line ashore, adjust your watch to "island time" and then sit back and enjoy a glorious view out to the islands and beyond.

A sunset stroll on the spit.

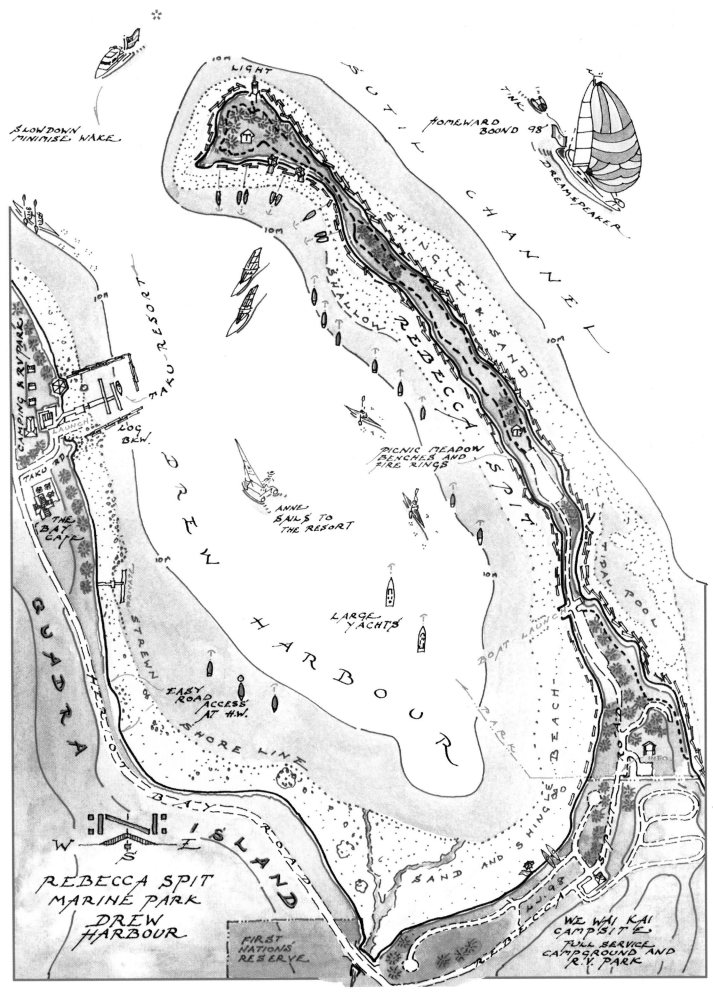

SLOWDOWN
MINIMISE WAKE

LIGHT

SOYIL CHANNEL

HOMEWARD BOUND '98

TINK

DREAMSPEAKER

10M

10M

SHINGLE & SAND

10M

CAMPING & R.V PARK

TAKU RD

TAKU RESORT

LOG BKW.

LAUNCH

THE BAY CAFE

DREW HARBOUR

REBECCA

SPIT

PICNIC MEADOW
BENCHES AND
FIRE RINGS

ANNE SAILS TO
THE RESORT

10M

LARGE
YACHTS

10M

PRIVATE

STREWN

SHORE LINE

EASY
ROAD
ACCESS
AT H.W.

10M

BOAT LAUNCH

TIDAL POOL

SAND AND SHINGLE BEACH

REBECCA RD

INFO

QUADRA ISLAND

W   E
S

ROAD

FIRST
NATIONS'
RESERVE

SAND AND SHINGLE

REBECCA SPIT '98

WE WAI KAI
CAMPSITE
FULL SERVICE
CAMPGROUND AND
R.V. PARK

REBECCA SPIT
MARINE PARK
DREW
HARBOUR

Not to scale. Not to be used for navigation.

SELECTED READING

Baron, Nancy, and John Acorn. *Birds of Coastal British Columbia*. Edmonton: Lone Pine Publishing, 1997.

B.C. Marine Parks Guide. Vancouver : OP Publishing and *Pacific Yachting*, 1999.

B.C. Parks Visitor Pamphlets *(Campground Critters; Principal Berries; Principal Trees; Life at the Edge; Things to Do Outdoors)*. Call 250-387-5002.

Blanchet, M. Wylie. *The Curve of Time*. Sidney, BC: Gray's Publishing, 1968.

Chettleburgh, Peter. *An Explorer's Guide to the Marine Parks of British Columbia*. Vancouver: Special Interest Publications, 1985.

Christie, Jack. *Inside Out British Columbia*: A Best Places Guide to the Outdoors. Vancouver: Raincoast Books, 1998.

Clark, Lewis J. *Wild Flowers of British Columbia*. Madeiro Park, BC: Harbour Publishing, 1998.

Cummings, Al, and Jo Bailey Cummings. *Gunkholing in Desolation Sound and Princess Louisa*. Edmonds, WA: Nor'westing, 1986.

Douglass, Don, and Reanne Hemingway-Douglass. *Exploring the South Coast of British Columbia: Gulf Islands and Desolation Sound to Port Hardy and Blunden Harbour*. Bishop, CA: Fine Edge Productions, 1996.

Hale, Robert, ed. *Waggoner Cruising Guide*. Bellevue, WA: Weatherly Press, 1994 to present. Updated and published annually.

Hill, Beth. *Guide to Indian Rock Carvings of the Pacific Northwest Coast*. Surrey, BC: Hancock House Publishers, 1984.

---. *Upcoast Summers*. Ganges, BC: Horsdal and Schubart, 1985.

Jones, Elaine. *The Northern Gulf Islands Explorer: The Outdoor Guide*. Vancouver: Whitecap Books, 1994.

Kennedy, Liv. *Coastal Villages*. Madeira Park, BC: Harbour Publishing, 1991.

Maude, Emery. *Seagull's Cry*. Surrey, B.C.: Nunaga Publishing, 1975.

Lillard, Charles, ed. *The Call of the Coast*. Victoria: Horsdal and Schubart Publishers, 1992.

McIntosh, Barbara-jo. *Tin Fish Gourmet: Great Seafood from Cupboard to Table*. Vancouver: Raincoast Books, 1998.

McKervill, Hugh. *The Salmon People*. Sidney, BC: Gray's Publishing, 1967.

The Museum at Campbell River. *The Raincoast Kitchen: Coastal Cuisine with a Dash of History*. Madeira Park, BC: Harbour Publishing, 1996.

Obee, Bruce. *Coastal Wildlife of British Columbia*. Vancouver: Whitecap Books, 1991.

Pacific Yachting's Marina Guide and Boaters Blue Pages: The Complete Guide to B.C. Marinas and Marine Services. Magazine supplement (January issue), updated and published annually by *Pacific Yachting*.

Pinkerton, Kathrene. *Three's a Crew*. Ganges, BC: Horsdal and Schubart, 1940.

Pojar, Jim, and Andy MacKinnon, eds. *Plants of Coastal British Columbia, Including Washington, Oregon and Alaska*. Vancouver: Lone Pine Publishing, 1994.

Sass, Lorna J. *Cooking Under Pressure*. New York: William Morrow, 1989.

Snively, Gloria. *Exploring the Seashore in British Columbia, Washington, and Oregon: A Guide to Shorebirds and Intertidal Plants and Animals*. Vancouver: Gordon Soules Book Publishers, 1978.

Spalding, David, Andrea Spalding, and Lawrence Pitt. *B.C. Ferries and the Canadian West Coast: An Altitude SuperGuide*. Canmore, AB: Altitude Publishing Canada, 1996.

Stewart, Hilary. *Looking at Indian Art of the Northwest Coast*. Vancouver: Douglas and McIntyre, 1979.

---. *On Island Time*. Vancouver: Douglas and McIntyre, 1998.

Turner, Nancy J. *Food Plants of Coastal First Peoples*. Vancouver: UBC Press, 1995.

Vassilopoulos, Peter. *Anchorages and Marine Parks*. Vancouver: Seagraphic Publications, 1998.

---. *Docks and Destinations: Coastal Marinas and Moorage*. West Coast Cruising Dock-to-Dock Destinations Guides. Vancouver: Seagraphic Publications, 1996.

White, Howard, and Jim Spilsbury. *The Accidental Airline: Spilsbury's QCA*. Madeira Park, BC: Harbour Publishing, 1988.

---. *Spilsbury's Coast*. Madeira Park, BC: Harbour Publishing, 1988.

Wolferstan, Bill. *Desolation Sound and the Discovery Islands: Cruising Guide to British Columbia, Vol. 2*. Vancouver: Whitecap Books, 1987.

Wood, Charles E. *Charlie's Charts: North to Alaska (Victoria, B.C., to Glacier Bay, Alaska)*. Surrey, BC: Division of Polymath Energy Consultants, 1986.

CHS Chart Dealers

The following are Canadian Hydrographic Service (CHS) authorized chart dealers in the Desolation Sound & Discovery Islands area:

LOCATION:	NAME & ADDRESS:	TELEPHONE:
BLACK CREEK	PACIFIC PLAYGROUNDS LIMITED, 9082 CLARKSON DRIVE, V9J 1B3	(250)337-5600
BLIND CHANNEL	BLIND CHANNEL RESORT, V0P 1B0	(250)830-8620
CAMPBELL RIVER	OCEAN PACIFIC MARINE SUPPLY LTD., UNIT 100, 1334 ISLAND HIGHWAY, V9W 8C9	(250)286-9600
	OCEAN PACIFIC MARINE SUPPLY LTD., 871A ISLAND HIGHWAY, V9W 2C2	(250)286-1011
		1-800-663-2294
	RIVER SPORTSMAN LTD., 2115 ISLAND HIGHWAY, V9W 2G6	(250)286-1017
	SPINNERS SPORTS, DISCOVERY HARBOUR, 1436 ISLAND HIGHWAY, V9W 8C9	(250)286-6166
		1-888-306-4444
	TYEE MARINE, FISHING & HUNTING SUPPLIES LTD., 880 ISLAND HIGHWAY, V9W 2C3	(250)287-2641
COMOX	THE CROW'S NEST, #204 - 1797 COMOX AVENUE, V9N 4A1	(250)339-3676
	TED'S TROLLING & MARINE SUPPLIES LTD., 151 PORT AUGUSTA V9N 5H3	(250) 339-4942
COURTENAY	COMOX VALLEY KAYAKING LTD., 2020 CLIFFE AVENUE, V9N 2L3	(250)334-2628
	HAPPY'S SOURCE FOR SPORTS, 256 - 6TH STREET, V9N 1M1	(250)334-4143
	PETER'S SPORT SHOP, 505 DUNCAN AVENUE, V9M 2M6	(250)334-2942
	ROY PARKER MARINE LTD., 1605 COMOX ROAD, V9N 3P7	(250)334-4808
HERIOT BAY	HERIOT BAY INN & MARINA, HOTEL ROAD, P.O. BOX 100, V0P 1H0	(250)285-3322
HORNBY ISLAND	HORNBY ISLAND COOPERATIVE, 5875 CENTRAL ROAD, RR#1, V0R 1Z0	(250)335-1121
LUND	HOEGER YACHTING LTD., PO BOX 73, V0N 2G0	(604)483-9002
POWELL RIVER	MARINE TRADERS (1983) LTD., 6791 WHARF STREET, V8A 1T9	(604)485-4624
	SUNSET COAST MARINE LTD., 7124 THUNDER BAY STREET, V8A 1E6	(604)485-4727
STUART ISLAND	BIG BAY MARINA LTD., V0P 1V0	(250)286-8107

Index to Charts as Referenced in Vol. II

NUMBER	TITLE	SCALE	NUMBER	TITLE	SCALE
3311	SUNSHINE COAST, VANCOUVER HARBOUR TO DESOLATION SOUND	40,000	3542	BUTE INLET	40,000
			3543	CORDERO CHANNEL	40,000
3312	JERVIS INLET TO DESOLATION SOUND	VARIOUS	3543	GREENE POINT RAPIDS	20,000
3536	PLANS – STRAIT OF GEORGIA		3543	DENT AND YACULTA RAPIDS	20,000
3536	FALSE BAY	12,000	3555	PLANS – VICINITY OF REDONDA ISLANDS AND LOUGHBROUGH INLET	
3536	POWELL RIVER AND WESTVIEW	10,000			
3536	STURT BAY AND VAN ANDA COVE	8,000	3555	REFUGE COVE	12,000
3537	OKISOLLO CHANNEL	20,000	3555	SQUIRREL COVE	12,000
3537	WHITEROCK CHANNEL	10,000	3555	REDONDA BAY	12,000
3538	DESOLATION SOUND AND SUTIL CHANNEL	40,000	3555	BEAVER INLET	18,000
3539	DISCOVERY PASSAGE	40,000	3555	PRIDEAUX HAVEN	6,000
3539	SEYMOUR NARROWS	20,000	3559	MALASPINA INLET, OKEOVER INLET AND LANCELOT INLET	18,000
3540	APPROACHES TO CAMPBELL RIVER	10,000			
3541	APPROACHES TO TOBA INLET	40,000			

To obtain a list of local chart dealers or to order navigational charts and publications directly from the Canadian Hydrographic Service, contact:

Sales and Distribution Office
Canadian Hydrographic Service
Department of Fisheries and Oceans

Institute of Ocean Sciences, Patricia Bay
P.O. Box 6000, 9860 West Saanich Rd.
Sidney, B.C., V8L 4B2
tel: (250) 363-6358 fax: (250) 363-6841
E-mail: chartsales@pac.dfo-mpo.gc.ca
Web site: http://www.ios.bc.ca/ios/chs

For dealers outside of the area covered by this cruising guide, refer to the *Catalogue of Nautical Charts and Related Publications: Pacific Coast 2* (published by CHS) or contact the CHS Chart Sales and Distribution Office directly (contact information above).

NOTES ON THE PHOTOGRAPHY

All of the photographs, except the three by Lynn Ove Mortensen, were taken by the author, Laurence Yeadon-Jones. The majority of these pictures were taken from the deck of Dreamspeaker, *a challenge at the best of times as the boat was always moving. To help overcome the movement, Laurence used a Canon EOS A2E with Ultrasonic Image Stabilizer Lenses 28-135 and 75-300. The use of this camera and the use of 35mm Kodak Ektachrome E200 professional slide film yielded exceptional results.*

Errata

Due to an unforseen technical error in the production of this edition of *Desolation Sound and the Discovery Islands*, Raincoast Books has provided the following replacement maps for reference when consulting this book. We apologize for any inconvenience this may have caused the reader.

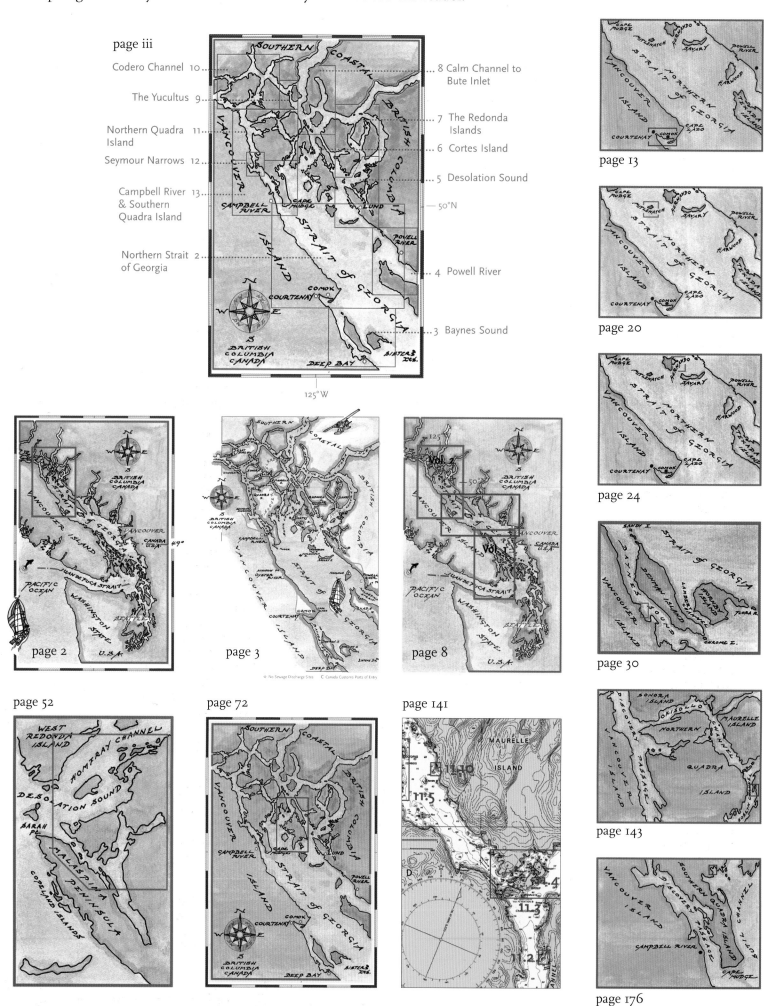

page iii

Codero Channel 10...

The Yucultus 9...

Northern Quadra 11... Island

Seymour Narrows 12...

Campbell River 13... & Southern Quadra Island

Northern Strait 2... of Georgia

...8 Calm Channel to Bute Inlet

...7 The Redonda Islands

...6 Cortes Island

...5 Desolation Sound

— 50°N

...4 Powell River

...3 Baynes Sound

125°W

page 13

page 20

page 24

page 30

page 2

page 3

page 8

page 143

page 52

page 72

page 141

page 176

☆ No Sewage Discharge Sites   C Canada Customs Ports of Entry